IN THROUGH THE REEF

A voyage around the world on Little Coconut

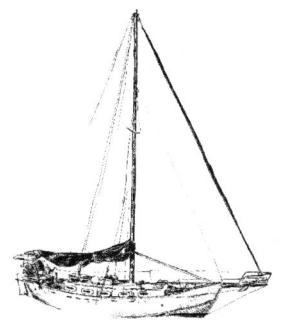

HUGH BONN

Rock Pipit Publishing

Rock Pipit

Contents

Preface VI

Maps VIII

Maps IX

Maps X

Maps XI

1. Making Straight the Way 1

2. A Shell Made Ready 8

3. Sea Air 16

4. Running North 21

5. Ballard Of Mary Bryant 26

6. Ducking into Darwin 36

7. Ocean Waves and Coral Sand 45

8. Small Island, Big Hill 55

9. A Cove in the Current 73

10. Slow Water off Madagascar 83

11. The Cape of Good Hope 91

12. Dunes of Sand 99

13. St Helena 107

14. Golf In Ascension 115

15. A Short Stay in Brazil 125

16. Caribbean Punch 131

17. Homeward Bound in the North Atlantic 141

18. Grandma and the Sea 149

19. Spire above the Grass 158

20. Gold Rush 166

Photos 176

Photos 177

Photos 178

Photos 179

21. Bay of Biscay 180

22. South with the Sun 188

23. Offshore At Last 199

24. To Be or Not to Be 219

25. The Panama Canal and Ecuador 230

26. Marquesas Crossing   245

27. Blossom in the Blue   250

28. Treasure Island   260

29. A New Dawn   266

The Bear Tune   276

Endnotes   278

Preface

Harder than crossing the sea, writing the book. She's a finished, overcooked no doubt, like Granddad's fried eggs, long overdue, like a sun set on a Scottish beach, but the book has landed, words lost to the wind, laid back down on the page, with the hope you find them and they find you. To kick things off, on this laymen's journey around the world, a poem from brother Ed, our family's literary weatherman.

"The ink runs its furrow across a white expanse. Searching for an unseen landfall, a harbour of words on the vast page.

Past journeys in other vessels overlay its track, just as fragile and feather light when set against storm blasts, sunken reefs and time's slow march.

And their countless human agents, absorbed in wandering. Restless, pining for new worlds within the compass of this spinning globe. Amongst this immense and varied horde – of traders, navigators, story-makers, sailed another ship. Its captain, fiery and writ large in life, its engineer, a fixer and a shaper, their Dad a deckhand, a skilled hand to catch countless moments in careful brushstrokes.

Their voyage another thread in a vast tapestry, from carved long ships set for plunder, deer-hide coracles questing to find solitude on remote isles, eiders nesting under the alter, tall ships scouring horizons, bound for spice islands, furred crews following whale fins in the deep blue.

And carrying all, moving all, destroying all, re-making all, the rushing winds and the roar of crashing water."

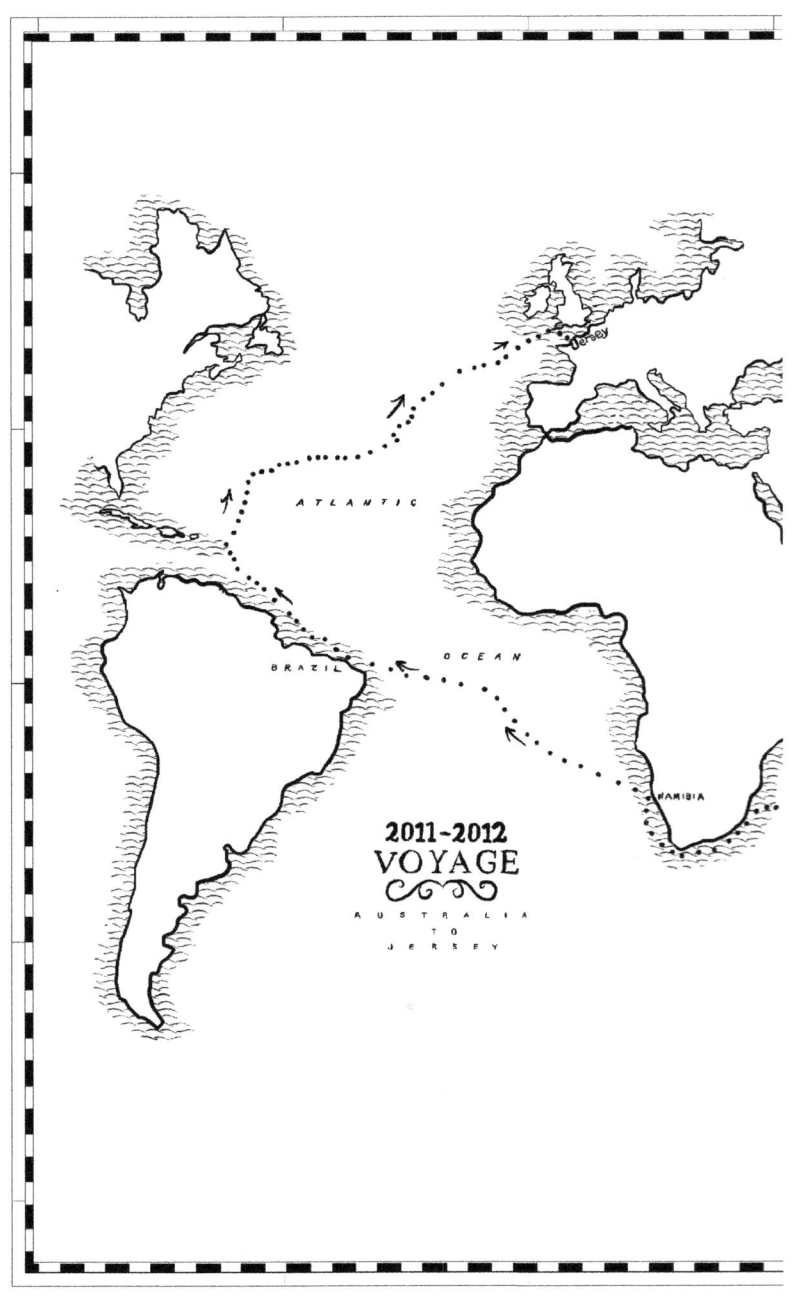

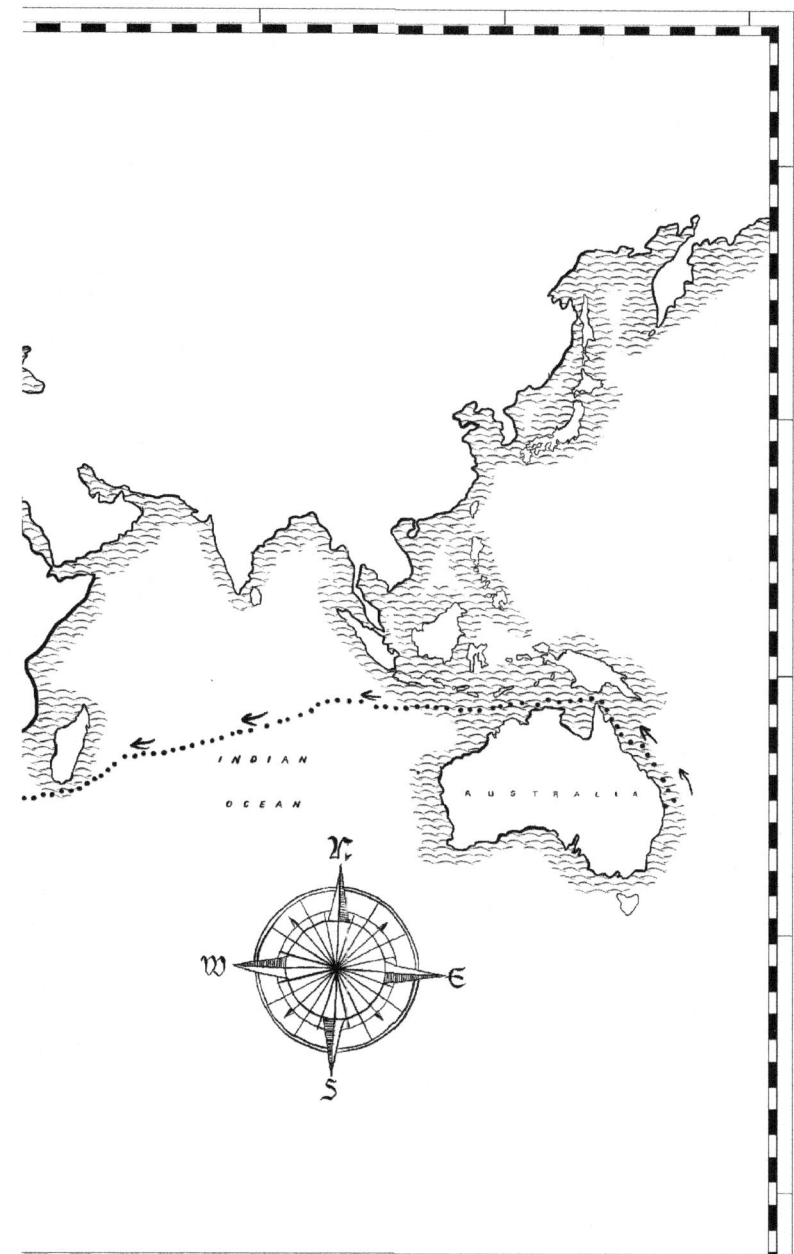

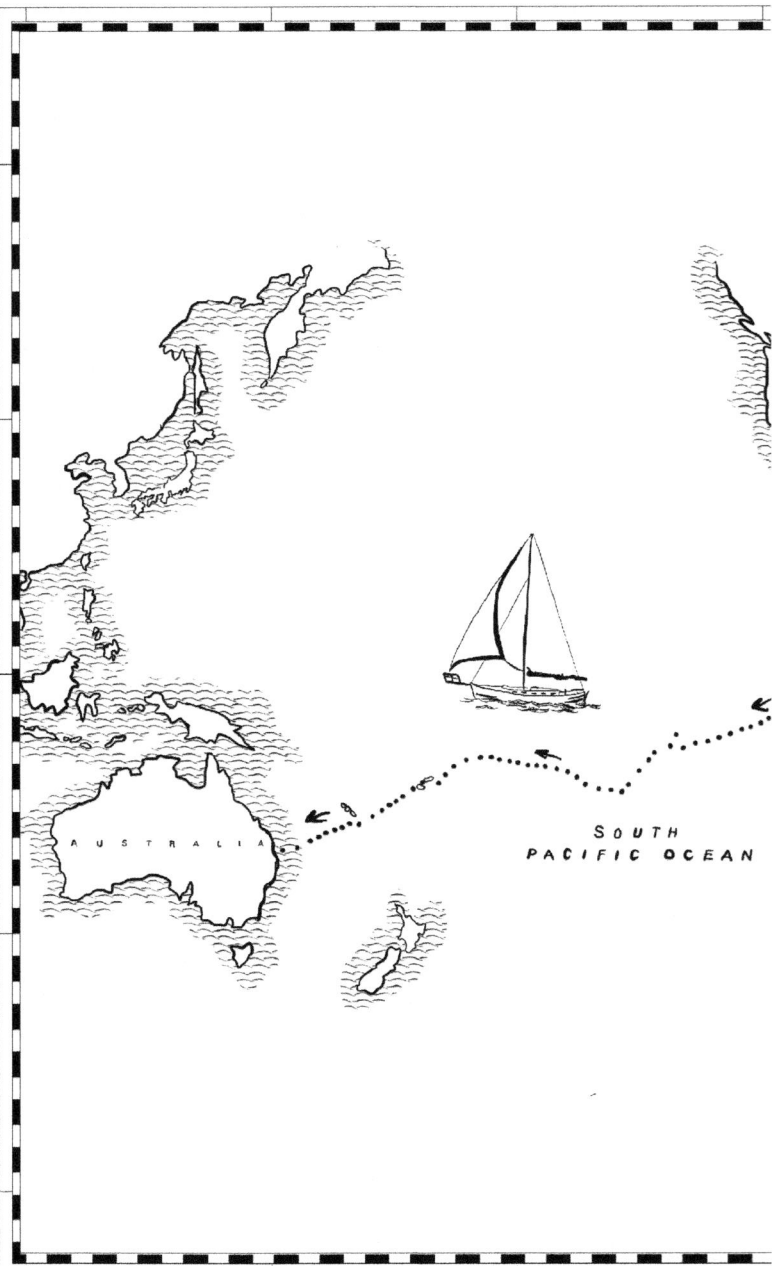

AUSTRALIA

SOUTH
PACIFIC OCEAN

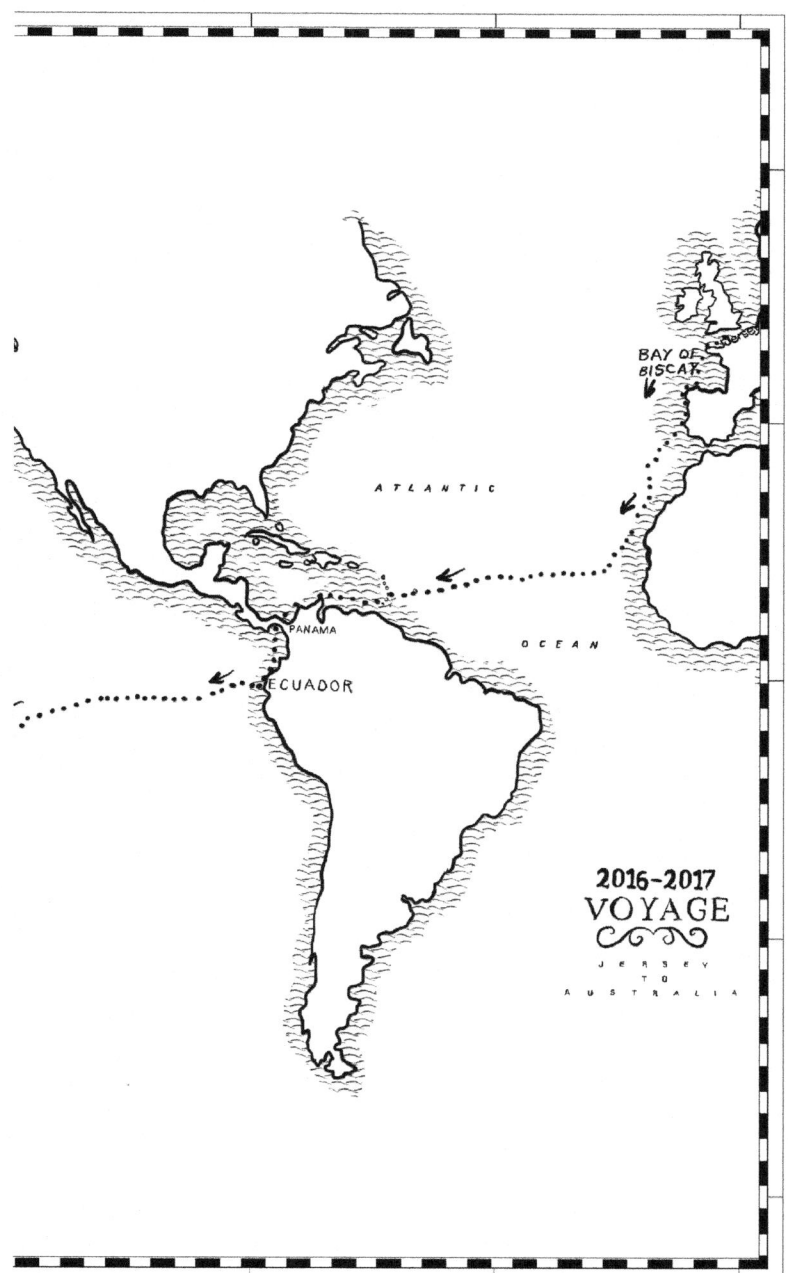

Making Straight the Way

Introduction

Helplessness on the hill. Even brother Ed, blind as a mole, caught those dark clouds clean, as he danced in a flustered trot across the wet banks of a peat black stream. We were too close to the car doors to call it an adventure, that said, my first experience, of wilderness wandering, came in with a cloud of midges. I can picture it to this day, running alongside my old man and brothers, trying desperately to escape across a plane of what we called 'moon grass.' Laughing hard and laughing cruel when a party member lost their footing and tripped. 'Maintain your balance,' the cry, a double-barrelled punchline, second shot of laughter to drop when the next victim took their fast-approaching fall. It was midday when the wind stopped blowing and our buckets were still empty of fish. Out from the reeds rose thousands of ravenous mouths. The glen was alive, and we were on the lunch menu, cursing and thrashing erratic tracks back down the valley and up the hill to our car. It was with wet feet and empty bellies we bid our retreat, skin itching and heads down, felled by the mighty midge.

'You broke your fishing rod,' said the first brother smiling cruelly.

'You left our picnic on the riverbank,' replied the second.

'And none of us caught a fish,' added the third, as all eyes looked desperately to Dad, who was padding his hollow pockets in the ongoing search for car keys.

The wilderness is a place where humanity gets tested. There is a deep silence to history's most jaw-dropping walks, no murmurs of discussion, no opinions, no shouts of pride, no boasts and no slander, our voices hushed, so fragile the breath of life in such a place we stop and listen. Thankfully the midge story will do, we don't all have to become characters in Touching the Void, or punters on Ernest's trip south, we shan't be joining Captain Bligh across the South Pacific, or escape imprisonment and sail up an uncharted coast with convict Mary Bryant. In a strange way these awesome endeavours have given us a glimpse of something much bigger. Their pages have ploughed pathways across the far reaches of our planet, not for us to travel down necessarily, but so that light can run in and hit home soil. We can part the curtains, open the door, take out a pot of steaming coffee and witness the miraculous beneath our very nose, flowers blooming and life growing, right up through the cracks in our garden paving.

There was a man called John the Baptist whose life in the wilderness sums up what I'm trying to say. No doubt everyone has heard of him, the man who baptized Jesus. John understood the nature of light, the need of a straight line for it to travel far, he also understood the Fall, and his place on Earth connecting what lay beyond it to the villages within its walls. His life was a corridor for light. With this in mind, I attempt to write this book, not as one of those ground-breaking adventurers and not as someone who went out so that light could come back in, but simply as a witness to the gift that was my voyage around the world on a small budget cruising yacht called the Little Coconut.

Upon a bed of broken shells, the hermit crabs find their shelter, part opportunist, part beggar, one claw to barter and one to borrow, arms like merchants, legs like thieves! The crabs congregate, in small gatherings, in quiet huddles, heads all turned in from the happenings of the beach. Small islands in the sand, islands unto themselves. They meet to find a better fit, the shell to a hermit crab is the cornerstone of a happy life on the seashore.

These shells come not from the crab of course, but instead from the mollusc, an inhabitant long dead, who out of invisible elements in the sea somehow produce their bricks and mortar, who whilst chilling on the seabed, build a house. No blue language bouncing off the rocks down there, no pointed fingers, no heavy machinery, no rowdy gangs of block layers and no project managers shouting down the phone, they simply breathe and construction begins. This house blends in perfectly with the natural environment, it is light and strong, the curves are flawless, the internal walls finished with mother of pearl, they can withstand punishing waves and long stretches of water, they wash up years after the mollusc has gone, providing new shelter for a totally different inhabitant. With intricate patterns, with fans and spires, with colour and precision, the shell is formed, a truly awesome creation.

Our journey began with a scuttle across the sand. We were naked and in search of shelter. We were of the crab of course, and not of the mollusc. Twelve tons of steel floating effortlessly on the drink like a duck's feather, we knew nothing about the boat, we did not arrive by way of water. All Walt, my Cornish friend, could do was kick the hull and cry 'Solid boat.' All Brother H and I did in reply was nod our heads and climb aboard. Looking back into the life of John Hanna, the man who designed the blue print for Little Coconut, I see a different breed of sailor, a true sailor, one who took no short cuts, who had life tough, who meditated on laws both unseen and seen. A man who lived for much of his life beneath the waves. Struck down by a torrent of scarlet fever as a child he just survived, rising from that bed of sickness deaf as a post, to be felled not long after by a passing trolley in Galveston Texas, his right foot, severed at the ankle. Nothing could stop John Hanna, everything handed down fed into his passion for design, even the bad times and the hard times helped forge his legacy of seaworthy boats. His life was a testament to that unstoppable formula of character first and talent second. A combination you can feed with heavy rocks of suffering and get in return unsinkable hulls, hulls that sail off in distant winds, through the fog of time, into the depths of generations not yet born.

If we'd been born back then, in around 1900, if we had lived down by the sea in Dunedin Florida, we'd have witnessed John Hanna at work, making straight our paths across the water. It was a time when small boat cruising had only just become possible. By cruising I mean passage-making for pleasure, which I realize seems a slightly extravagant word for what is essentially getting rolled round in a can for some weeks. The cruising community had begun its assembly, lining up in various harbours around the world. Back then boat building in the leisure sector wasn't the mountainous landscape it is today, full of tall trees and thick shadow, it was a flattish plane of many shy hills, even the moles were making a difference. Every harbour had a tradesman capable of knocking something together and every town had a designer hoisting high a set of plans in the hope of attracting a would-be adventurer. The doors were open, so to speak; Tahiti and back again was a reality, not just for the merchants and the whalers with their crews of hardened vagabonds, but this time for the amateur adventurer. It was in this rich vein of discovery and optimism, a vein bound so closely to those unbreakable laws etched beneath the seams of this world, that gave the direction required to put any old Tom, Dick and Harry on the water, and get them in, 9 times out of 10, on the other side. Designers like John Hanna, they blew out boats like bubbles, catching the light, prompting a new generation of Noahs to make true their arks, grab the wife and kids, round up the family cat, throw in a sack of potatoes and head off into the flood.

Beneath a blanket of stars and stripes, the Tahitian ketch broke surface. America at that time was isolationist, she sat off to one side of the word stage, bolstered by a constant flow of migrants flooding in. With regard to boat design, Europe's old apple cores got a new lease of life. John took the lines of a Greek sponge fishing boat, a hull from the Mediterranean of all places, with that rich history of boat building spanning back thousands of years, modifying certain characteristics for offshore use. The blueprint for his Tahitian ketch sat dormant for a decade or so, it took a pretty major shakeup for America's boating population to take notice. The great depression threw out its fists of winter in 1930. A few years later when the hardship subsided his ketch started to attract some attention. With a name like Tahiti, she had that exotic lure. Hanna was calling on a Polynesian paradise when he used that name, Mutiny on the Bounty all over again, minus the bloodshed and plus the chance of making it back. By 1935 the blueprint was selling at last. Designed at 30 feet, this was a boat tailored for everyday adventurers, not for big budget professional endeavours but for flash in the pan hacks.[1]

John Hanna managed something pretty momentous when he published those plans. One hundred years on and his boats are still doing laps of the planet. In November 2017 aboard Little Coconut, Miranda my wife and I made it in to Australia, seven years after I left with Brother H. At the finish line we were greeted like true hermits, no red carpet or Hollywood smile. The woman at the marina we had entered looked like she'd spent the duration of my circumnavigation sucking on a lemon. 'Bum's Bay is around the corner, you have no insurance, please leave our pontoon as soon as you've cleared in.' That was our greeting, Miranda was refused a shower, after crossing the Pacific Ocean without running water, a working toilet or a fridge, washing in one bucket, answering nature's call in another, for over a year, you couldn't write it, but that was the purpose of Hanna's design, our trip was a testimony to its success. If boats ever needed bumper stickers, Little Coconut's would read, 'Carrying bums around the world since 1923.' The thorny reception we got in that flash marina crowned our trip, it crowned the tale of this remarkable little cruising boat and its ability to take sailors with little experience across the sea and back again.

2

A Shell Made Ready

The beginning, that wake-up call, it wasn't quite the same as those seafarers of old. I wasn't clubbed on the back of the head and dragged off to sea, waking to the smell of salt and the bosun's angry whistle. The stream that carried us down had a much kinder hand. Like all salt-worthy sailors one must accept the reality of becoming a leaf, cut from the tree and blown into the river, taken down to the sea. Our journey to the water's edge was different in that it was privileged, there were no rocks or rapids, no whirlpools, no snapping turtles or hungry fish, we made it into Little Coconut with fat bellies and soft hands.

Thankfully I wasn't alone, Brother H heard the call of the wild too, putting a mule's hoof on his job, all in the space of a few months. By June 2011 Harry aged 24 was free from his employment in Hong Kong working on a rail tunnel, and I aged 26 had escaped the mines. It was a side scuttle across the sand for H and I, finding adventure in a washed-up boat called Little Coconut. In the meeting of these three streams new life began, just before the sand soaked away our dash, just before the boat hit that scrapyard back eddy, the timing was perfect, we joined paths to make that last push together, trickling out quietly into the crashing waves.

The day we found Little Coconut stands in front of all the other days spent working underground in Australia, hundreds of twelve-hour shifts sit behind, indistinguishable like drops of rain in a grey cloud. I felt guilty driving past the construction sites in the middle of the week, I'd somehow been released, it was all suddenly outside Walt's car window, flashing by on the roadside, slowly dropping away into the wing mirror, a blur of dust and high vis jackets. We crossed the Gateway bridge heading for the first harbour available, pangs of guilt gave way to a burst of excitement, out in the distance a sea of blue awaited, an oblivion of sparkling water.

The harbour we found ourselves walking along was Manly in Queensland, just outside Brisbane, a quiet village at the bottom of a shy hill, peaking out across a sheltered bay from between the mangroves. Manly's yacht basin manmade, the shallow mud banks dug away, a channel dredged and walls dropped in, home to an armada of leisure, cruising yachts and private fishing vessels, house boats and racers, day sailors and dinghies. Brisbane the city over the hill, Manly, a quiet retreat, a place where sailors spring out from at the end of their working week.

It was an abstract image of adventure which brought us to Manly, a cloudy vision more than anything else, so void of definition and so full of colour, one couldn't see the break between land and sea. Harry was across the water in Hong Kong finishing up work, it was my job to find us a boat. Our brief, something to sail home on, the money, five grand English a piece. Pretty clear instructions on the computer screen, a tad hard to get one's head around in reality. It was with glazed eyes our trip wallowed, unidentifiable like an amphibian in the mud. Walt and I rocked down to the harbour as one might to a Saturday morning car boot sale, there was no effort required, we bought coffee, we walked the sidewalk, and we shot the breeze. A telephone conversation about a possible boat in Manly had fallen through, we drove down anyway, it was all theoretical at this point, a flat featureless plane. Walt stopped at a sidewalk billboard; the advert read 'Budget cruiser.' 'No way, that boat is right here,' said Walt, pointing to the words Manly, he then read out 'East Coast marina.' Pausing for a second before adding 'This is East Coast marina.' I looked up, the sidewalk had vanished, it had given way to a marina carpark, we'd walked right into the lion's mouth.

Sitting on Little Coconut was as good as coming to, the salesman didn't have to say anything and I didn't have to ask anything, I didn't need the specs, or the dims, or the boat history, it was all laid bare before us. If you imagine an infant, an infant without yet the words to speak, who sits there in the sun and cries out for an apple, cursing with splutters and shouting in babble. It is of that moment, when the child's thirst is quenched, I speak. When the vision suddenly gains focus and the taste of an orchard is delivered to the lips. That was what it felt like sitting on Little Coconut. One man's junk is another man's treasure. The sun was falling hard and hot, my T-shirt damp with sweat, Walt had his head back and feet up by the wheel, a Cornishman whose only link to boats being his Dad, who once worked on a trawler out of Newlyn. 'This is it,' Walt said, 'You boys are off! H is going to love it.' And with that, in a simple twist of fate our journey began.

To layout a picture of Little Coconut she is about 30-foot-long with an extra four-foot bowsprit. Her cockpit non-existent, instead she had a high-sitting flush deck, her wheel was bolted straight on and set up with a lock and pinion steering device. Her stern was shaped like a canoe with a heavy-set cast-iron rudder hung on three fist-sized hinges. She had a full keel, a cutter rig and a huge genoa, her mast thick like a tree trunk. There was no furler up front, the sails all hanked with free running halyards cleated to the mast. The rigging was high quality with strong fixings to the deck. Below she had a cave for a cabin, walls of bare steel accompanied by primitive carpentry. Each bunk distinct in appearance, each bunk displaying a different epoch of human development, from prehistoric lashing to rusty iron nails clubbed down into splintered planks. The wood part foraged between the tides, part begged for at the scrap heap and part no doubt borrowed from various building sites around the globe, an eclectic mix of varied hues. My favourite piece, which represented the best of Little Coconut's seven wonders, the engine box, a complex entanglement of different wood types, a jigsaw of many parts, each differing in length, breadth and thickness. The structure, having scaled all three of the physical dimensions reached out for a fourth, with a spiritual element definitely present. The practice of engine maintenance, a mini pilgrimage aboard Little Coconut. Having been locked in an awkward pose, having dropped the spanner into the bilges and lost the screws, drenched in sweat and oil, it was the reassembly that had the potential to make you crack. The only way to avoid 'frog in the sock' syndrome was slow meditative breaths and calculated steps.

There was no plumbing on the boat in the conventional sense, no toilet, no water tanks, no shower and no taps. In terms of millennial technology Coconut had resisted all temptation, there was not so much as a chart plotter. The galley no better and arguably even worse, missing the whole concept altogether, Little Coconut had no fridge and no cooker. Her engine definitely represented another boat wonder, how vividly I remember my dad flying over to visit before we left, the gravity of this misunderstood beast was overwhelming. Dad opened the box and peered down, an ink-stained octopus draped in shadow gazed back, sitting in a sewer of black sludge. It was too much to handle, out of his pocket came not the sailor's trusty Leatherman but instead a bottle of Holy water, he doused the engine generously before closing the box for good, checks not necessary and blessing complete.

All the wonders and missing teeth aside, all cladding forgotten and garnishes dropped, Coconut was the real deal, a war horse, a working mule, a sure thing, a good sort. She had integrity, personality, grit and class, she was strong like a bull, she was uncomplicated, forgiving and brave, all the things you want in a boat lost 1,000 miles from anywhere, caught three days into a blinding north Atlantic gale. Dad flying over and blessing the boat was his way of letting go, surrendering his job as an Earthly father to our Heavenly one, it was out of his hands, Holy water on a rusty old tractor engine, what better symbol of human surrender is there under the sun?

Once we got the boat, everything fell into place pretty quickly. In Queensland the best cruising season is June, July and August, the winter months. Our purchase came through around April sometime, which was perfect. I had eight weeks to get her ready. Jamie, a friend from Jersey, was flying over to try his hand at sailing which meant we were a crew of three, our start date early June. During those eight weeks I was working nine days on five days off, a FIFO (fly in and out) gig at Broken hill a small mining town in outback New South Wales. That brief chapter between buying Little Coconut and leaving was pretty crazy. I was flying one thousand miles, dropping down to the bottom of a busy and complex underground mine, then flying back and working on the boat. I'd somehow got myself superglued to a yoyo, I was dunked, in and out of the darkness, up and down from earth to sky. It was mine, clouds, boat, then clouds, mine, clouds, boat, my head was spinning, those dark lonesome tunnels turned and twisted, hundreds of miles worth, spinning in infinity, I was praying for it all to end. I managed to get a chart plotter fitted, I antifouled the bottom and changed the anodes, I organized some new sails, brought an offshore life raft and some life jackets, I repainted the inside and changed the engine filters. We were ready for the off, those old oak doors had creaked open, and with that came the first notes of spring.

There really aren't that many routes around the world under sail, not for us budget cruisers anyway. Some passages may be harder than others to find, some may be wide, and others narrow, certain roads not for the faint-hearted, but there aren't many. It is no wonder we find ourselves walking a path of footsteps, of rounded stones and charred ground. It is no wonder we often retrace our steps to find the right road. Sailors don't make up routes around the world, they follow them, written into the makeup of this planet like a fingerprint.

Planet Earth has an uneven distribution of heat from the sun. If Earth was big George Foreman's punch bag, and if his fists were light, that mid-section of the bag, the area permanently indented like a fat man's couch, that would be the Equator, soaking up all the heat. At either end of the punch bag, above the big guy's straight and below his rib shot, sit the poles, regions where rays of light hit at an angle and reflect back off into the atmosphere. These polar regions are areas of high pressure due to the cold sinking air, that belt round the middle is a band of low pressure where the air gets hot and rises. This is the main engine behind our weather. A pressure gradient is formed, this gradient produces two additional belts in each hemisphere, as the cold air runs off down the latitudes it heats up, rising to form a sub-polar low. In turn, as hot air is drawn away from the Equator it cools, sinking to form the horse latitudes, a sub-tropical high.

This set up is genius for a sailor, you get two directions of travel in each hemisphere, the wind always moves from high to low and it can only move right because of the Earth's spin, sub-polar low to sub-tropical high equals westerlies, Equator to sub-tropical high equals easterlies. Two highways etched into each hemisphere, one road heading out full of dreams and one road heading in full of stories. The planet is unlocked in this way, through a series of corridors. Sitting on the Cornish coast copping a prevailing southwester right on the nut one might think it impossible to reach America under sail; not so, all the boat need do is head south till the butter melts, catch hold of that trade, then head off with the setting sun. Now it gets a little more complicated with the doldrums mixing up life in the middle, tropical storms affecting the trade wind belts and the adverse effect of large land masses. The other area which might shake up one's sailing route, once the physical possibilities of actually making the trip have been addressed, is the whole human aspect. When you rock in after a month at sea, your boat hasn't changed, it is still your home, the water is still water, the weeks have ticked by, all of a sudden you're facing a shoreline 3,000 miles away from where you started, debating what the crack is ashore. Is that crazy one-eyed fisherman trying to rob us or does he just want a bottle of Jack Daniels?

For us, given our levels of inexperience, we thought a trip up the east coast was the way to go, Brisbane to Darwin over the winter months, a great shake down leg. The cyclone season in the Indian Ocean runs from November through to March, so if we left Darwin in August, with a view to getting out of the Mauritius area sometime within the month of October, it made a summer in South Africa possible, Cape Town for New Year. This rough outline was in the back of my mind, but we didn't talk about it much, getting our mini battleship out of a packed harbour was number one priority, by June 1st Little Coconut hadn't yet left Morton Bay.

3

Sea Air

The first leg of any journey across the sea is quite an ordeal, it takes life to draw breath. What has been resting beneath the surface for some time, happily and safely cocooned dockside, drives out alone, landing beyond the harbour with an almighty thud. Aboard Little Coconut it was a moment of acknowledgment, we became ants in a thimble, the windows vanished and the walls fell away. Our reality had changed. Our faces were red and flustered. We trailed a cord of knotted warp, our sails flapped like the panicked legs of a kicking baby, and upon that desolate scape, caught beneath the cloak of nightfall, it was the wind that grabbed us close, whispering in a cruel voice, 'your mother won't be coming,' pointing back in a chuckle of gusts to the bed where she lay, her face not visible, lying in a gown of shadow, her lights blinking out from the darkness in teardrops of crushed glass, scattered helplessly across a shoreline far out of reach.

Our first breath, it came in the dead of night, the wind was dancing some drunken jig around our compass, softly humming one minute and roaring the next, rushing in with flurries of white horses. I was on the foredeck while Jamie held the wheel into wind, I was pointing out to some unobservable destination, 'That way Jim, steer that way.' The light of his head torch was blinding, it shot off a deck of white sails drowning our surroundings in a thick wave of darkness. I'd dropped our big jib and was sporadically trying to tie in some reef lines, sweat was running down my back as spades of salt spray leapt over the rail, cheap plastic waterproofs clung to my skin. We just couldn't balance Little Coconut, nothing was working, even finding some rope thin enough to fit through the reef holes had been a challenge, our sleeping quarters had been turned upside down. Harry, who was meant to be resting below for a later watch, popped his head out every half an hour or so, kind of like a desert meerkat checking his surroundings, saturated with the excitement of life beneath the stars, unable to rest amidst an orchestra of sound which reverberated inside the ribs of Little Coconut. There was the steady chime of water on steel, the whistle of wind through rigging, the shaking sails, there were footsteps up and down the deck, not to mention a rally of voices being thrown from bow to stern, there was the erratic motion of Little Coconut getting swung in and out of the wind, with changes in roll, pitch, direction and speed, on top of this our old diesel tractor engine was coming in and out of the composition, kickstarted into life with angry coughs of smoke only to be cut off minutes later. It was a train wreck, the blood vessels in my head were beating, an ocean indifferent to our inexperience had risen high above our reach. Three days out of Brisbane and Darwin, the first peg on a climbing wall back to the UK was lost in fog.

The hunger we had for making miles vanished pretty quick. It was as if the elements cooking our tea took the form of some crazy vegan aunty. We were kids again sitting at the kitchen table, she smiled down at us through a swinging crescent of crooked teeth, 'Gluten-free rye bread,' the announcement, and with that screech-like pitch our expectations shattered. In it came, handed down with trembling hands of sincerity, with gusts that roared the words, 'I made it myself,' in a voice that damn near knocked us cold, with lips that spat and a snout that snorted. The breadbin's last crust was unleashed, thrown like a bone, a loaf so dry and weathered its density confounded us into a speechless glare. That was it in a nutshell, the outcome of our inexperience. We headed out boldly under engine, clubbing the table with pint glasses, chanting 'Fillet of beef!' at the horizon like a dinner hall full of drunk teenagers. There was no peaceful night spent beneath the stars for us, our chants hit deaf ears. We were handed down bird food and we ate it like dogs, fighting with the sails and barking at the waves.

With the light of dawn came our revival, the wind backed broadside, a dull grey sea changed in colour before our eyes, dropping the rags of a sleepless night over the side and donning a marvellous coat of sparking green. We rounded the sand point off Double Island grinning ear to ear, Little Coconut was singing at last, cutting fast across a harp shaped bay, knots falling from our gunnels as the whitewash of Widemouth bar moved out of the horizon and into the fold. The day was slowly opening her eyes, oblivious to the happenings of our maiden night at sea. We followed a fishing boat across a sandbar of breaking waves, motoring in through a channel of deeper water with large swell crashing either side. Our first port of call was to drop hook in the shallows, we slept out the morning on the feet of Frazer Island, surrounded by walls of mangroves, not a trace of civilisation in sight.

It had been an eventful run of days since our departure, even motor-sailing out from Brisbane in short eight-hour-day hops had presented challenges. One night we drifted anchor nearly hitting a low-lying road bridge, we woke to the knock of a fisherman's hand, the bump of his boat in our dreams. 'Bro, you're drifting.' Tap, tap, tap... 'You're drifting!' I woke with a start and nutted a cast-iron ceiling. Little Coconut was built in someone's backyard, storage space below the bow pulled priority, to sleep in the V berth was to accept the very real possibility of head-butting steel. 'Shit!' I shouted, rubbing my head. H was already up and chuckling to himself, Jamie not far behind, our anchorage just still visible way up the point, blinking with the slow sway of mast lights.

If our inhale was full of acknowledgment, it was an exhale which allowed time to contemplate, and this came in true seagoing fashion. With Widemouth's notorious bar crossing behind us and having spent the morning in blissful sleep, our feet were firmly off the pedal. 'That's the spot,' I said as we motored further into the channel, pointing across to a secluded tributary shielded from all wind by a scarf of green forest, 'What a cracking place for dinner.' H turned the wheel and gave Coconut some governor, we rushed off at 90 degrees and ran straight up onto a bank of mud. The tide was ebbing out and before long Coconut was on her side, beached high and dry. It was rather an amusing sight, three blokes sitting on the rail like birds on a wire, the sun was dropping down over the creak, bull sharks were picking off some unidentifiable prey, breaking up the brackish shallows with violent twists. There in the creak waiting for the tide to lift us off we had no choice but sit and be patient, to watch the colours change and the light drop away, the bent backs of trees reaching down to wash their leaves in the water. That once distant speck of wilderness, the one our modern world looks at through its double glazed windows, the one that walks off down the beach like a passing stranger, it stood over us. We had become the grain of sand and it had taken its rightful place as the mountain.

4

Running North

The leg to Darwin took around eight or so weeks. It was our equivalent of boot camp in the Brecon Beacons, minus any red-faced drill sergeant spluttering obscenities into one's grill. When H dropped his bag of ammunition on the hill and hit cruise control, leaving the regs to rust, really getting under an oil tanker's skin, there was no forced penalty march for the team come morning. I woke to the sound of an elephant's irritated trump, our radio bursting to life beneath the midnight oils, my sleep broken, our burrow breached, the thud and tremor of a big ship just outside our door, shining their industrial strength spotlight down onto our deck and yelling at us across the radio waves. H being a goofy footer had seen the tanker and headed for the wrong side of a tight inner reef shipping lane, shooting off left as one would in a car. He'd forced the tanker to go starboard to starboard instead of port to port, hedging his bets and sticking to his guns. I woke to that quick pulse of panic you get from time to time on a boat, it drifted off as fast as it came in, leaving us like a boat full of hedgerow rodents, squeaking in its wake. Getting the crew up to speed with seafaring etiquette was definitely the first of many checkpoints up Australia's east coast.

Balancing Little Coconut to move purposefully through the water in changing conditions was our next major hurdle, too much sail with the wind behind and she would start a heavy gin-soaked roll, too little and she'd wallow, it was that four to five knots through the water we looked for, that swoosh of power, that firm and gentle push, a motion which dipped slightly, or rolled just a touch when a wave swept past, keeping the mast central and steady with the ballast, popping back and driving forward as opposed to overcompensating and rolling the other way. That was the pulse we changed the sails by, not constant trimming like bay sailors do. We needed to be in that pocket of knots, nothing more and nothing less. Some days with the wind dropping in and out we might change the sails four or five times, other days we'd sit and not touch the rig once. To reduce sail fast downwind we came up with a system, instead of reefing the genoa we'd swing into wind and drop it for good. One person would crawl up the bowsprit beneath the flapping rag, lying on their back they'd wait for the helmsman to reach the mast and release the halyard, pulling the sail down by hand, bagging her up at the bowsprit before hoisting the cutter, a smaller sail closer in. Coconut would drop back to her cruising plod. If conditions worsened still, you were then running on the cutter sail which could be dropped with little effort, no need to turn back into the traffic, just drop it on the run and throw up a storm sail. In light airs we had a sail called Big Black, thin and vast, her delicate canvas holding form in just a whisper of wind, bellying out to pull Coconut through the water at about three knots. With regard to the main, we'd fly it if it didn't cast a wind shadow onto the jib. We tied in three slab reefing lines which enabled us to reduce sail area very easily from the mast. Violent squalls which once ripped in like tornadoes leaving behind a trail of devastation became great opportunities to grab the soap and take a long-needed shower.

H, being the most practical aboard, became Coconut's mechanic; the engine or any other moving device had his name on it. Navigation was my thing; I generally made the calls unless Jamie and H clubbed together and threatened to mutiny, the Hinchinbrook channel a classic example of this. Jamie's fear of night sailing coupled by H's adventurous spirit found some common ground. We were passing the entrance to the channel as night descended, 'It will be pitch black by the time we get in H, we could run aground.' The Hinchinbrook a pretty wild and environmentally protected area, a thin channel surrounded by thick forest and rolling hills. H disappeared below to confer with Jamie, who in a bid not to sail through the night had been doing some research. I listened in, 'It is one of the best cruising areas along the east coast,' said Jamie pointing to the guide, adding his own translation, 'that means world class.' H came up out of the gangway guns blazing, 'It is places like this that make me want to do this trip.' I backed down and we bumped in through the darkness and anchored blind in the pitch black. It was worth it; I woke beneath the trees to the sound of birdsong and a boiling kettle, popping open the hatch to unwrap our whereabouts, a reserve of untouched hills that reminded me somewhat of the Scottish Highlands.

In regard to sleeping quarters Jamie dominated the saloon, really marking his territory midships, H occupied the stern in an area nicknamed Harry's hole, the driest part of the boat. In the teeth of a gale, with a drenched forepeak and a soaking saloon, the words, 'H can I sleep in your hole?' marked the point at which morale dropped off the grid.

'Everyone always comes crawling back to the hole,' he'd reply laughing.

I took up residence in the forepeak for that first leg, we settled into a rhythm of sorts, hopping up the east coast with high spirits and in good time, pulling in for dinner, spending the odd day on a desolate beach, climbing a hill or walking in the forest. At Cairns it was time for Jamie to leave us, and he was sorely missed, he dropped down and kissed land for the last time, no more shouts of, 'That was yacht master material, H.' He had sailed with us a good way, debates like, 'What is the toughest beast beneath the sun?' featuring honey badgers, mountain goats, the big old grizzly, the pit bull, the rhino, and 'Don't forget the ram, not for a minute, never turn your back on a sheep with nuts.' Those debates didn't have quite the same edge when Jamie left, but with the ball now rolling straight it was time for our friend to leave.

Things ramped up a bit after Cairns, H went looking for some crocodiles on El Tenderino, our oar-powered yellow dinghy, and found some. We started to sail longer distances, dropping hook at dusk behind a headland or a patch of reef. We became more streetwise, throwing out deep diving lures close to the reef to catch dinner, snagging a rock cod or a Spanish mackerel. The further north we sailed the wilder and more remote things got. At night, there were no lights on the shoreline, in the day white lined beaches and green trees would pass without a break. With no handholds for vast kilometres, humanity had lost its grip on the landscape. We sat aboard our floating island and watched the coastline slowly change, dropping the quilt and donning the thistle, turning back the centuries. When the southerlies were in, rain or shine, Coconut was out on the water, making leaps north. It didn't take long to reach the top of Cape York, sailing in comfort for over 1,000 miles, gently and softly floating past the type of wilderness capable of holding off an army. The Australians didn't need bunkers and gun posts, walls and wire to protect themselves against the Japanese threat in the Second World War, they had 1000 miles of prickly bush, a swamp for a ditch and a croc for a foot soldier. As far as the Australia equivalent of Dad's Army were concerned, Darwin aside, it was 'Put another shrimp on the barbie.'

5

Ballard Of Mary Bryant

The year was 1787, England's West Country hills, stripped bare of trees, wrapped up in frost, wind battered, weeping silently in slow running streams. Down to the river they came, wrung out from a tired landscape by the white knuckles of an expanding empire. Brought across lowland flats by cart and barrel, pulled forth by blinkered horses that toiled beneath a cruel whip. Mary was in that number, marching a desolate road, convicted, the saint within her but a seed, sown deep beneath sheets of winter ice. Her defiance, that God given reckoning, it had taken off on the wrong gust of wind. Mary let go of the hill where she was born and tumbled, into a cloud of industrial steam, into the smog, into the roar and into the rumble. The landscape was changing, England had entered the Industrial Revolution, there was money to be made in West Country rock. Spending another winter beneath a dripping roof, counting rats and stitching up ripped sails, it wasn't enough, not with a new stream of cattle in town, sat in slow pools just beyond the mist. 'Instead of fighting gales of poverty,' thought Mary, 'Why don't I run with the gale?' She took hold of the darkness and fell into highway robbery, caught by the law, silk bonnet in hand, having dished out some minor beatings and stolen everything in the carriage bar Grandma's false teeth. It was death by hanging, she was barely twenty years old.

As Mary awaited the gallows, off in the distance, where the wild cats did howl, in the halls of Westminster, a new frontier came beneath the monocle. Australia had geopolitical significance in the Pacific, she was the new blue planet, the rising star of an 18th century night, one with gravity and atmosphere. King and country needed a harvest of adventurers, and fast. George III was on the throne, one eye in shadow, one eye in simmering light. History has found it hard to preserve a clear image of George. When we look from our stools, across the bar of time, it is hard to arrive at a conclusion. Preserved in the vinegar, shelved beyond reach like an ancient pub snack, sitting in the dim light, are we pointing at a testicle, an eyeball or an egg? Whatever the state of George, desperation was in the wind, that much is clear. Add to this nauseous mouthful, France, a competing empire, who stood tall on the beach, swinging wild, fighting England on sand, rock and ice. Then drop down the poverty, falling with momentum and mass, spinning with the Earth, a great storm that turned to slums those leafy valleys. The net result is an explosion of sorts, an industrial explosion. More laws equalled more crimes, more crimes equalled more laws, the noise streaming off the land was deafening.

'Colony,' shouted one minister, whose identity was obscured beneath a dull grey wig. 'Yes colony,' he repeated.

'What was that you said?' replied another minister, who was capped by the same fake mop, both were shouting above a furnace of sound. Home affairs at one end, foreign affairs at the other! 'Did you say colony or felony?' he repeated.

'Colony,' shouted the first, going red in the cheeks. 'We are here to talk about the new colony.'

'Can't hear you,' cried Home Affairs, lifting up his diary. 'Tuesday 10 o'clock,' he yelled back into the smog. 'West country convicts, I'm here to talk convicts!'

'Not convicts, colony, colony,' came a muffled reply. 'Not convicts, I'm foreign affairs you dimwit, it's Wednesday!'

Down dropped the pen, from another grey wig, a man who wrote in shorthand to save time, the minutes simply read, 'Colony of convicts, Home Office to Foreign Office.' With this, Mary's fate was sealed in 18th century Morse Code, her prayers answered. In that exchange of wind and word, a colony of convicts was indeed born, on a far-off reach of flat rock that sat larger than a seabed, a country called Australia. For the cat with one eye, winked or blinked, to the dog with one nut, as George, boiled like an egg in the heat of his time, nodded like a duck, struggling to lay out Cook's map, north up on his gigantic hardwood table. Eleven ships were bound for Botany Bay, and Mary was in that number.

Can you imagine a more hellish place for childbirth? 1788, the convict quarters of a First Fleet ship. Mary was out of wedlock and 23 years old, her child born in the deep, amidst wrecking balls of wind, swaddled in a blanket of sickness, laid down in a cradle of fear, a cot of havoc and heartache. Mary took the name chiselled into the timbers of that very convict ship and called her daughter Charlotte. It was as if her past had been laid to rest over the gunnels of the ship, sunk beneath the waves and beneath the sickness. Held there in the present, right in the jaws of death, Mary looked into an ocean wasteland, and dared to hope, she saw light out there somewhere, hovering like a spirit above the water. Make no mistake, it was a show of reckless defiance, to name her daughter after the convict ship, a name that means freedom. Mother and baby clung to each other in the darkness, that flame of unbreakable love, it lifted the convicts' eyes off their plight and into the journey ahead. For even in the pits of despair, there was a whisper, a quiet voice, a cord that could not be broken.

Both Mary and baby Charlotte survived the trip, they made it around the Cape of Good Hope dropping hook in Botany Bay. From the shadows of the gallows, from the teeth of a treacherous sea, land of any kind must have felt like a second lifeline. It would have been a crazy rush of blood, to leave the cramp confines of a ship lock up and walk beneath the trees, to feel the sun on your back by day and watch the stars fill the sky by night. Mary married William Bryant, a convicted smuggler, their wedding took place only days after coming in, the first marriage of a new colony.

Celebrations were sadly short-lived, the ship's sugar high upon arrival gave way to the sobering tones and cold realities of life adrift. The settlers were weak from nearly a year at sea, supplies were short, bellies empty and tempers hot. The colony would have fared better if the systems and iron framework of their old-world order had left with the ships, there was too much weight, too many guns and chains. Aboriginal contact did not start well, 'this is mine and that is yours,' a lost concept with the locals, who were colour-blind to cattle tags. The precious livestock that survived wasn't stolen necessarily, because like the rain and like the river, animals roaming the land, were not up for ownership. A child could be stolen, but not a goat. This obviously created a giant brick wall. A bunch of convicts forced out into unspeakable hardships for thieving items not half as dear. How could the officials have turned a blind eye? 'If that isn't stealing anymore, then what am I doing out here! Cut me loose before I go batshit crazy.' Blood was spilt and good relations lost, the settlers were alone in an alien environment, conditions deteriorated, and the colony starved. During this time Mary miraculously had another child called Immanuel. Mary picked a Hebrew name for her son, a name from the book of Isaiah, a name set like a precious stone into a land laid to waste, a barren world, a broken world, a land thirsty and crying out for God to deliver. It was the perfect name and true to the Old Testament story, Mary saw her child as a sign from God, but she couldn't wait for God to deliver, she didn't wait, the defiance in Mary drank from the wrong cup, a plan was hatched to become the deliverer, to steal one of the governor's open-topped cutters and make a break for it up Australia's east coast. Immanuel's father William and seven other convict seamen were in on it. Conditions must have been unimaginable to put two infants through the teeth of such a daring voyage. It was a well-planned leap, they'd acquired some navigational equipment and some very rough charts from a passing Dutch boat, their plan had the makings of a trip with legs. With regard to seasons and weather the team left two months too early on paper, March the back end of summer, not yet out of storm season further north, violent squalls and heavy rain more than likely in the great barrier reef area. The crew would have known the summer was not a good time up north, they probably waited as long as they could. With no big ships in dock to give chase, hidden by thick cloud and a moon starved night, they decided the window was open and snuck out across the bay.

Their voyage took somewhere close to 70 days and covered a distance of 3520 miles, a feat of endurance which almost beggars belief. Their destination Kupang Timor, part of the Dutch East India company, an important trading harbour in the colonial era. The first 800 miles should have been pretty straightforward, with no reef to worry about and presumably some food in the hold, they could have easily made Frazer Island between weeks one and two. Just above Frazer things start to change, you enter the Great Barrier reef, without channel lights this meant an enforced curfew, it would have been day sailing for the most part. Interestingly the governor's cutter was a similar vessel in size and draught to Little Coconut, with six oars and three sails, made out of wood, she would have been light and manoeuvrable, well suited to sailing down tight channels, well suited to scoping out bays and reefs for anchoring. This section of our sail had good fish stocks in 2011 so it must have been jam-packed in 1788 with no commercial fishing. The threat of hitting a reef was high, but this risk did come with some nutritional positives. Violent squalls common at the back end of a cyclone season dramatically increased their risk of shipwreck too, but again with the squalls came the drinking water. The hardest section of this voyage must have been when they turned west at the top of Australia, a leg of 1,300 miles, possibly attempted in one hit, undoubtedly low on supplies, tired and weak after two months in the saddle. They somehow managed this long uphill finish, posing as shipwreck survivors from a boat downed off North Australia, joining Kupang's expat community, a motley group of merchants, traders, military personal, officials and lost sea dogs.

Gossip was a dangerous disease, for an open-topped cutter full of convicts. Mary and her children had nowhere to hide, people would have flocked in to help the shipwrecked crew, fruit in one hand, damp towel in the other, whispering, 'Where did they come from? Two infants? What was the name of the wrecked boat?' The crew pulled it off for three months, the port extended their many hands of hospitality. June, July and August were theirs, when the trade winds blow in cool air, with a frozen blue sky and a head full of sun, baskets of tropical fruit at their feet, asleep beneath a shady veranda, or beneath the rustle of leaves, the sound of children laughing, that sea which nearly drowned them far away in the distance, a soft motionless carpet of green.

The river eventually hit its turn, September the month all bets were off and all cards on show. The escapees had got too comfortable, they'd waited too long, with the wet season fast approaching things took a massive turn. At the docks more open-topped boats were coming in, four in total, all packed with shipwrecked sailors. Not only had these sailors been in a real shipwreck, but their boat sunk off North Australia, exactly where the convicts claimed they'd gone down. To make matters worse it was an English ship, an admiralty one, the captain none other than Edward Edwards. If ever there was a guy you didn't want rocking in for the party, it was Edwards. Why? Because he'd spent the last two years in the South Pacific popping balloons and spitting on birthday cake, this guy was a weasel, hand-picked by the admiralty to go catch mutineers. Which ones? All of them, but specifically ones from the famous ship the Bounty. If you can remember that old film *Chitty Chitty Bang Bang*, Edwards was a sailor on the runs' equivalent to the child catcher, the man was an unrelenting law-abiding nut, the guy the Royal Navy sent out when their cheeks turned red, and their bottom lip started to wobble. 'What!' shouted William Bryant, 'Edwards, here in Kupang? You've got to be kidding.' The sad part is they weren't. Edwards's boat the Pandora had hit a reef on the backend of his mission, he'd been rushing back in the wrong section of water, sailing through the night where he shouldn't have, his boat went down in 11 hours, which at least gave everyone enough time to escape on four over loaded lifeboats. Their remarkable open-topped journey equated to the last third of the convict's marathon, scrambling across a few reefs, catching some fish and making a dash for it across the Arafura Sea to Timor, port Kupang the only option available it would seem, for any open-topped vessel lost somewhere in the region of Northeast Australia. It soon became evident who the convicts were, as the shipwrecked sailors recovered the Dutch governor kept the escapees under house arrest in his castle. Edwards's replacement vessel arrived a month or two down the line, a boat named Rembang. The convicts were clapped in irons and thrown in lock-up, their hellish journey to Batavia began. During this leg, relatively short in nautical miles but attempted just outside the trade wind months, baby Immanuel died and so did Mary's husband William. I didn't find out how, from reading a few accounts Edwards seems a man void of compassion, in the sticky wet season heat, without that constant draft from a trade wind, conditions for the convicts would have been unbearable. With the heat comes the storms, Rembang got hit on that leg and was nearly lost by all accounts. Mary must have been in the pits of despair, her and Charlotte made it to Batavia and waited for a ship back to England under the shackles of a cruel order. Upon that long, hard and feverish journey from Indonesia around the Cape and up the Atlantic to England, Charlotte died, Mary walked off the boat alone, she was escorted to Newgate prison, it had been over seven years since her feet hit English soil. Some accounts say she remarried an officer on the Gordon, the boat which carried them back. After a short spell in prison with her story gaining much notoriety, legal aid was granted and she was pardoned, returning home to the West Country.

Mary then vanishes from the records, leaving her story behind for us to sit and wonder. I can't help but picture Turner's famous seascape when trying to close this chapter, painted in the same period of history, marked by a little red buoy floating on a wild and storm ravaged sea, a buoy that somehow holds the frame together. The defiance in Mary, I can see it when thinking about this painting, tethered down beneath the deepest and darkest fathoms of human experience, a line that runs up through the abyss and into the light, to break the surface and dance in the gales, a line attached to an unsinkable buoy, filled up by the breath of faith. I suppose the joy of Mary's tale, with regard to things unseen, might just be the tragedy of ours. Take eternity from the picture and a ship will soon choke in the darkness. Suffering cannot be stomached when hope has nowhere solid to rest, it tears to pieces the human spirit. Paint over that little red buoy and the sky falls away from the sea.

6

Ducking into Darwin

Once at the top of Cape York it was time for H and I to start heading west. We had reached the northern extremities of Australia, ducking in as the sun turned red, dropping hook in the lee of a remote untouched island. H had snagged a rock cod on passage. Never have I seen such a mean-looking fish, dark and slimy with cloudy eyes and a mammoth's head. The fish would have fitted in well at the bottom of some deep ocean trench, snagged off a shallow reef in the coral sea we were a bit taken back.

'Man, that thing is ugly!'

'Ugly! What you mean to say is she ain't pretty.'

'It's a rock cod!'

'Are you sure it's a rock cod?'

'Nope, but the rock cod is the closest illustration in the book.'

We cooked the cod at anchor over our camping stove, looking out across an island too stark and wild for anything other than the birds, an island which had doubtless changed but a whisker since the Bryants passed by, back in 1790. They might well have rested in that very same stop on route to Timor, rowing a shore to forage the rock pools for clams and the thickets for bird eggs. We rose early, not leaving as much as a footprint ashore, our next stop Thursday Island. We made the anchorage early afternoon, settling for a spot a little close to the reef given the heavy blusters of onshore wind. The anchorage had a slightly restless feel.

'H, that fish is off,' I said as he came up with the leftovers. 'It's been sweating all night and all day.'

'The fish is good,' he replied boldly, 'I'm not wasting rock cod.'

'It smells of excrement. How can it be good? Throw it to the crabs.'

'You're facing the wind and smelling your own breath,' replied H.

'We got 700 miles to Darwin,' I snapped, 'is it really worth the risk, shitting through the eye of a needle, it will make the passage twice as long for the pair of us.'

H mulled it over with a few more mouthfuls then tossed the carcass over to the crabs. Since Cook Town a week or so back we hadn't seen another human, it was time to row ashore and blow off some steam. Thursday Island felt like an outpost town, corrugated roofs, rusty shacks and dirt tracks, was this still Australia or had we missed it and hit Papua New Guinea?

We wandered into a local bar, the cold fizz of a crisp cheap lager, after weeks in the heat with no refrigeration, it was too tempting to resist. Never have I walked into a more social boozer. H and I were greeted with beers instead of handshakes, one guy even offered us work, he looked down at Harry's bare feet, looked up at Harry's ripped T-shirt, read between the lines and said, 'You boys will be wanting some work then won't ya, I'll see what I can do, we need some good labour round here.'

'Pommies,' came another shout from behind my shoulder.

'Proper Pommies, all the way from Brisbane, no way!'

'I left with five pounds in my pocket back in 1960, haven't been back since,' said the man who offered us work. The head of the bunch was Cape York's equivalent of Crocodile Dundee, the real-life version. This old wiry dude used to sell crocodile skins back in the seventies, he'd catch them with a powered-up harpoon gun, a mask and a set of flippers, diving beneath and shooting up. We staggered out in the pitch black, stumbling back to El Tenderino, Little Coconut waiting for us somewhere out there in the night. It is crazy how things work, in a city or a busy marina we'd have blown in one day and left the next, no one would have batted an eyelid. In remote regions things are different, the sponge like nature of a community's social appetite is unsaturated out in the wilderness, thirsty for conversation. The sparse and barren surroundings, the dust and the wind, the waves of the sea, they have an impact. The city is a place drenched with speech and soaked with bodies, meetings locked in, dinner dates set, things to do and people to see. In Thursday Island they might well have sat and watched us come in, the whole pub, it had that slow feel about it. In the morning with our boat missing, they would have wondered where we'd gone. We met some great characters not because they were any more special than the people of Brisbane or Cairns, but simply because we had that opportunity to actually meet. 15:30 to lights out and doors shut, that was the length of a handshake in Thursday Island.

My head was beating when I woke, still half-cut from the blowout and fearful of a day's labour, the sun just starting to rise above an island still lost in slumber. Harry pulled the anchor up, I hoisted the main and Little Coconut pushed out into the bay of Arafura, a seven-day sail across to Darwin. No working cooker meant no hot food for the week, no auto-helm or wind vane meant hand-steering, which in turn equated to a dog of a trip, hours on the wheel fuelled by cold spaghetti hoops and short snatches of sleep. After two days I tried to take down a raw onion, eating it at the wheel like one would an apple, cracking a can of corned beef and spooning it in between bites, my stomach rejected it, 'Oh no you don't, 'it said,' I threw up violently over the side. For the first few days we didn't sleep, our bodies not yet numb enough to find rest in the broken motion of three-hour slots. I remember the forepeak hatch popping open one night whilst I was on the wheel, a confused and half-dazed Harry peeked out shouting back, 'What course am I steering?!'

'You're not steering any course,' I replied faintly with full lungs beneath the wind.

'I said what course?' he yelled back like a horse.

'H, I'm on the wheel and you're meant to be in the bunk!'

There was a pause, Harry looked around, the wind whistling, the night black, my head torch shining across into his eyes. Without a reply he shut the hatch and disappeared, rising up through the gangway two hours later. 'Did you get any sleep?' I asked.

'Must have,' Harry replied.

For the first half of that passage, we were like two ghosts, present but not there, surviving but not living. As the days passed, we found that beat and started to settle, sleep came in pinches then in puffs, we found our way out from beneath the hooves and up onto the horse's back. It all culminated with an amazing night sail, one of those soft milky nights, the wind sat perfectly on our beam, the moon high and full, the sea flat calm, Coconut so steady Harry managed to boil a kettle and dish out some cups of tea. We balanced the gib against the main and locked the wheel, the compass kept her course, our hands were finally free. I sat at the mast and looked up into the heavens, behind in our wake flashed sparkles of luminous green, Darwin just beyond the night, our last stop before heading out across the Indian Ocean. We'd made it, 2,000 miles of coral sea cruising, for me that was a milestone, we had earned our passage across the ocean, we'd earned the chance to have a go.

Darwin was a place to stock up and get ready. Our wind vane had arrived, a helmsman which doesn't take up space, that doesn't need sleep, that doesn't drink water or eat food. The greatest luxury of them all for a boat with two sailors, a necessity for a boat with one. The device we got was a servo pendulum wind vane, consisting of a blade in the water and a separate blade in the wind. The wind vane can be looked at like a simplified body, it has different parts which need to work together, they use energy from the wind to unlock more energy generated from a boat's movement through the water, a greater reserve of energy, turned off and on like a switch from the wind. It is this relationship, linked to the boat's wheel by control lines, which keeps a steady course. The boat must be balanced and the control lines must run smooth, coming in from a wide angle to the wheel. It had arrived in Darwin via post, we fitted it in a marina, the heat was on. Harry for the first time in twenty-four years put his nose in an instruction manual, we brought a spirit level, a tape measure and a battery drill, there were no ifs or buts, we had to get the placement right.

The next thing on the list was a cooker, or a modification of our camping stove, a hot drink in the morning and a hot dinner with the setting sun, the bare minimum required for a happy ocean crossing. Bunnings was our shop, a DIY megastore, a place where fat guts and tight denim shorts walk countless aisles in pursuit of their abstract dreams, clutching gardening ornaments, sticks of bamboo, tins of paint, anything that catches the light. H and I had much the same methodology, we needed stuff to hold our stove steady beneath the shaking hands of a moving boat. If you imagine how a bird goes about building its nest, flying the hedgerows looking for loose twigs and dry moss, that too was our assembly, running off separately and returning back to the trolley with an improvised trimming. Cable ties and duct tape, coils of metal wire and clutches of metal hooks, we grabbed some lengths of thin chain, blocks for the stove to sit on, metal strips for strength and balls of string. Back at the dock we spread them out and got to work, building a body for the stove to drop into, with a housing to hold the pot. We drilled a hole in the ceiling and hooked up the sum of our efforts. It looked like a piece of self-indulgent modern art, confused and complicated, forced and awkward. We stood back and watched, a faint wave from a passing boat hit Little Coconut and our stove started flying laps around the chain, we burst into laughter, 'You can be Laurel and I'll be Hardy.' The stove sucked, but we stuck to our guns drilling in some more holes and adding a few more lengths of chain, we coiled up some wire and twisted on two metal straps. They acted as arms, clamping down the pot's lid, sealing the show shut when cooking. A positive was the stove could be easily stored when not in use, the holes in the ceiling had hanging hooks, the stove was also small and light. After the adjustments H and I were confident it would do the trick, our days of eating cold cans at sea were over.

We stocked up, people get pretty geeky when it comes to ship stocks, they divide a passage into weeks looking at calories and nutritional needs, they ration and tally, they tick, cross, highlight and calculate. H and I are two brothers cut from the same cloth, it was refreshing not to even think of going to such lengths, it wasn't even selfish not to, we were free to sling in the potatoes without counting, shooting onions into the basket like a child would his or her penny chews, hauling trolleys of bottled water, grabbing the cheapest can with no thought as to the particulars, green coloured veg all the same to H and I. Sailing with a brother is so very different to sailing with a wife. Six years later I'd be confronted for picking cans blind and chucking them behind my back into the trolley. My movements weren't echoed with H's laughter, what followed instead was my wife's cries! 'Stop doing it like that, who are you trying to impress?' Miranda would say in disgust. 'Peas, mushy peas, they're horrible, just horrible!'

'You won't taste them in the stew babe, something to thicken the sauce with!'

'Put them back,' she'd squeak, tears welling up and bottom lip going. Miranda couldn't operate without order and thought, it was a meltdown unless I donned that jacket of compromise. H and I argued but at different times, we'd butt heads about when to crank the engine, what sails to use or if hanks were better than fullers, we'd argue alright but never in the supermarket. Stocking up was an exciting time with H, the adventure literally taking shape in an array of loose cans rattling around numerous trolleys. Outside the core body of drinking water, rice and canned tomatoes, a diet you can survive on for years, coupled by some vacuum-packed wraps in case the cooker was to break, shopping for an ocean crossing was an exercise in making the other guy laugh. It was a monstrous shop, we stuffed Coconut's pockets with a massive haul of sustenance. 4,000 miles of open water lay between Darwin and the next supermarket, we had nets filled with lemons and green oranges, coffee and tea, hot sauce and cans of beer, we had legumes, carbs, and canned meat, we were ready for the off.

The lasting image I want to leave you with, which I think best describes those two weeks in Darwin, was uncovered or revealed to me by a Brazilian sailor just before we went our separate ways. The night had drawn in and the bay was dotted with what must have been 100 anchor lights, bright white and yellow floating effortlessly above the sea as if suspended in an invisible spider's web, caught somewhere beneath the heavens and above the earth. The end of the winter had come, and it was time to leave, the length of Australia and the breath of the Pacific, they'd bottled together in a place where the Indian Ocean begins. Augusto looked out, 'I love that,' he said, 'each one is its own separate adventure, each light a living dream.' The Brazilians can pull off a statement like that, it was a fitting way to say goodbye to our friends. Looking out across 100 lights burning up the darkness, it installed confidence, we were the migrating heard of 2011, we had assembled under flags from the far corners, ambassadors of our tiny worlds, about to be thrown up like a handful of sand into the wind, about to disperse across millions of square miles of ocean. We'd started up the east coast like the whisper of a lone prayer in a dark-room. That bay in Darwin represented a cathedral filled with folk, we'd heard the bells ringing and found our congregation, joining together for a chorus of song before our work commenced and before our passage began. That was Darwin at the end of August in a nutshell, Little Coconut just one small light in the constellation.

7

Ocean Waves and Coral Sand

The ark and the light or the seabed and the darkness, life was that simple out across the Indian Ocean. Becalmed just one week in, Harry and I donned masks and jumped off the side to check out life in the middle. We leapt out of our tiny world, out from the creaks and rattles of a boat becalmed, out from the matchbox and into the whale's belly. I sat like a prop hung weightless above the curtain, suspended in that bridge of water still alive, still held by melodies of light. At the time there were no words to fill the void, I gazed down upon the set of Jonah's prayer and felt the weight of water. This is how Jonah penned the scene from countless fathoms beneath.

"In my distress I called to the Lord,
and he answered me.
From deep in the realm of the dead I called for help,

and you listened to my cry.
You hurled me into the depths,
into the very heart of the seas,
and the currents swirled about me;
all your waves and breakers
swept over me.
I said, 'I have been banished
from your sight;
yet I will look again
toward your holy temple.'
The engulfing waters threatened me,
the deep surrounded me;
seaweed was wrapped around my head.
To the roots of the mountains I sank down;
the earth beneath barred me in forever.
But you, Lord my God,
brought my life up from the pit.
When my life was ebbing away,
I remembered you, Lord,
and my prayer rose to you,
to your holy temple.
Those who cling to worthless idols
turn away from God's love for them.
But I, with shouts of grateful praise,
will sacrifice to you.
What I have vowed I will make good.
I will say, 'Salvation comes from the Lord.' "[2]

The wind came in one day as if turned on by a tap, slowly opened wide until our sails burst with life. 'The trades have arrived,' H cried joyfully as he scrambled forward to hoist the genoa. We ran for days and days, twenty to thirty knots of wind, big swells sweeping in across our beam from faraway storms in the Southern Ocean. One week passed and then two, our self-steerer didn't skip a beat, our hands were free and the heavens were open. There are no words to describe the difference a wind vane makes to life on a boat with two. Without a method of self-steering the wheel gobbles you up like a giant sleepless octopus, one whose tentacles somehow get everywhere all at once, holding any luxuries one might enjoy out beyond reach and grappling to take away even the most basic elements of human decency. The dynamics changed the day Harry bolted on our wind vane, the octopus we'd been fighting got knocked on the head and put in the pot, we weren't just existing out there we were living.

Every couple of days Harry and I would see some action, often woken in the middle of the night by violent squalls, we'd tag on and head out to pull down the genoa, adrenalin running through our veins as we battled with sails in the darkness. To couple the self-steerer things also changed when we got into the trades. Distance and time broke their chains and ran off like wild dogs, those links of endless circles shattered, the increments all gone. Africa for the first time felt reachable, the days melted together, one became ten, ten became one, it didn't matter, in the quiet of sleep they'd rush by, in the panic of a squall they'd stall. We kept no log or commentary of those weeks at sea, we cooked one hot meal a day, often as the sun dropped down beneath the horizon, we ate fresh fish and rice, canned tomatoes and oranges.

Fear has many faces in this world. Out at sea the face of fear is not misshapen, not frozen to touch, not a wicked stranger. Out at sea, fear is quiet and steady, fear is sure and known, not screaming or lashing out, not bent from the furnace, hooked or warped, injured or demented, but a respectful fear, a fear that knows one's insignificant weight, a fear that wants to protect life not crush life, a fear that comes from a positive and objective place. 'Tag on tonight won't you,' I'd say religiously to H. He'd piss off the side, one hand on the stay, head back looking up at the stars. I was frightened he might slip and fall. Regarding navigation I'd plot our position on a paper chart once a day, I was frightened our electrics might stop working, a rogue wave down the hatch or a lightning strike to the mast. We were careful not to use too much gas or fresh water, if our wheel broke or if our mast snapped supplies would have to last twice if not three times as long. Sailing out beyond one's comfort kept things sharp, the fear was there to protect our trip, to give us a fighting chance. One day we lost our genoa halyard and I had to winch Harry up the mast in a big sea. In that critical operation it was fear that kept me 100 percent focussed, the fear of H falling. There is a proverb in the bible which says, 'The fear of the Lord is the beginning of wisdom.' This is the type of fear I'm talking about, positive, objective and purpose driven, a fear which runs out from the destination to draw you in, a fear which prompts action not inaction, a fear that keeps the course steady and the boat moving forward.

After about twenty days we caught sight of land, the heads of the trees barely standing above the white caps of the sea. It was a grey and squall battered dawn, Little Coconut was flying, H and I had spent the night trying to slow her down, opting to enter the reef in good light. As the sun rose Cocos Keeling came to life, on the ocean highway to Africa this was one of the few resting places. Thick reef walls stop cold lumps of Southern Ocean swell, lines of Coconut palms shield the wind, a soft white sand lagoon waits with open arms. Little Coconut was ushered in by five or six black tipped reef sharks, they rushed towards us like a crowd of expectant porters. 'Worried stiff we were,' the sharks cried, 'been waiting for days we have, come let me take your bag. This way, if you please sir.' They lead us through multiple reef bombies right into the anchorage. The ancient crater of a volcano was our resting place, once raging with fists of blasted rock, with lips spitting lava and a mouth burping out toxic fumes, with ill-tempered eruptions and clouds of smoke, now reborn, unrecognisable, full of soft sand, vibrant colours and quiet water. We sailed through walled gates and dropped hook in the shallows, joining the wildlife to bask in the sun.

Cocos Keeling represented more than just landfall to H and I. Dad was flying in to join us for the big leg across to Mauritius. He left Jersey and flew to London, from London he flew to Perth, then finally from Perth to Cocos Keeling. He landed miraculously on the very day of our arrival, dropping down into heavy blusters of wind, landing right on a pin head in the middle of an ocean, it was surreal. Dad got off the plane like a coiled spring, it was a jackpot moment for us all, for over twenty years he'd been grafting and for over twenty years I'd been standing motionless like a Las Vegas slot machine. To the blue and gold chips laid down for a fine education I burped back a string of horizontal C's, waiting out my school winters with the playground starlings, with the arrival of the swallows

I knew my summer holiday was drawing in. I sat at the back with the dribblers and the nose pickers, with the window gazers and the class clowns. My absent-minded reasoning didn't end well, having picked university on proximity to the surf I was forced to quit, walking out of an exam in Ancient Greek unable to answer even a single question. I'd lost my trainers somehow, donning a set of wetsuit boots instead, squelching to my desk, dripping a stream of saltwater and stale piss. I left that exam hall to muffled laughter, 'Who is that clown?' I rang home to explain, in the cloudy recesses of my mind I missed the buck again, deferring university for a year, switching from ancient history to geography and landing a course even closer to the beach. The point being our Indian Ocean Crossing represented a time when the coins fell and lights flashed, none of us foresaw it or designed it that way, it wasn't forced or reasoned, they fell when they fell how they fell. Dad dropped the plough, we gave the reins to the wind, we let the waves carry us, we sat on Coconut's back with equal weight, we barely even touched the wheel, the big guy beside us in the bunk, snoring peacefully.

To see Dad on the dock, pale white and soft in the belly, half-dazed from the air travel but ready to rumble, it was a rush, he was energised like a wasp just released from a shaken-up bottle of pop. 'When are we off,' he smiled. Harry and I had to slam the brakes on, we'd only been in paradise for a morning. 'Give it a few days,' we reasoned, 'she's blowin a hoolie out there, let's wait for the squash to pass.' We took a small passenger ferry back from West Island then snagged a lift with some German cruisers to the anchorage. El Tenderino our oar-powered yellow dinghy hadn't the legs to take all three of us, we towed her behind, Little Coconut only just visible, a small white dot floating on a lagoon of magical blue. To see Little Coconut in her natural setting, lined by white sand, sitting beneath the green palm trees, warm sun and a fresh trade blowing, gently swaying on her hook, you couldn't ask for a better setting to join the crew. It took most of the day to wash our clothes, sort the bedding out and re fill containers of freshwater. We rowed to a neighbouring island to use the tap, soaping the clothes with rounded stones, rowing back and forth till the job was done. That evening we cracked eggs, ate spaghetti and drank warm beer.

We woke to a knock, 'Harry,' tap, tap, tap... 'Little Coconut! Are you there!' It was Martin, a single-handed Brit, a rare breed of adventurer, he had made landfall with the morning light, we rubbed our eyes and climbed out of the hatch.

'Is this it?' shouted Martin, his eyes wide like golf balls, 'not more palm trees please!'

'Is what it?' I replied.

'This,' shouted Martin, pointing to the crystal-clear water and deserted white beach, he spat into the sea, 'not more of this shit!' We looked down from Coconut's high rails, he looked fragile, ghost like, almost half-starved, his hands were shaking, '40 knots,' Martin continued, 'days and days of it, no one said it was going to be 40 knots!' There was almost a reflux reaction going on, the spoon full of medicine that is Cocos Keeling was flatly rejected, 2,000 miles alone had clearly been way too much for Martin. 'Coffee?' said Dad.

'I can't stop, Customs are on their way, I'll come around later.' With that he pushed off and started to row back to his boat, shouting in a final cough as if to clear his throat, 'I'm off tomorrow, this place is horseshit! nothing here, absolutely nothing!'

That was Martin's magnificent opening address, it was an alarm call like no other, he'd offloaded two weeks of worry in a flurry of hot words, then dashed off abruptly leaving us chucking on the rail, his oars erratically punching the water with heavy spades of heat. A cruiser once joked, 'Never look a single hander directly in the eye,' what she forgot to mention was how utterly impossible it is to walk past and not. Martin was classic, one in a million quite literally, beneath the rants and almost constant disappointment there was a true spirit of adventure alive. 'South Pacific,' he would say spitting, 'rubbish, absolute rubbish, worst place in the world,' or 'If I ever try and do anything like this again kick me, won't you!' There was a childlike quality at play, a bike running downhill with no way off, travelling too far and too fast. Martin was in that boat till he hit Britain, there were oceans more palm trees lining his white-knuckled ride home, no doubt each one receiving an earful of abuse as he whizzed by in a hot gust of wind, the tyres of his light weight Bavaria skidding round the bends as he fought to keep his rig on the road.

Once the medicine went down, Martin chilled out, we all spent at least four days on Cocos Keeling, leaving on the very same morning for Mauritius. My one regret from our stop was not rowing over that last evening to pick up Martin for dinner. His tender was stored away, lashed down ready for an early start. With the wind blowing east our sterns faced the setting sun, I looked over at Martin as Dad, Harry and I ate our last supper at Cocos, we ate with laughter and conversation, he ate alone. Landfall for a single hander, especially in remote anchorages, must sometimes feel even more lonely than life out at sea.

It had been light for some hours when we rose, Martin already long gone. Harry pulled up the chain and we motored out for our next 2,000-mile leg to Rodrigues, a small reef bound island close to Mauritius. By the time Dad joined us Harry and I had things pretty dialled. Everything was kind of set up, the solar panels gave us the electricity we needed, fresh fish provided daily sustenance, Harry had stuffed the lockers with coconuts, the wind vane was steering, the temperature beautifully warm. With a crew of three things became social, three hours on six off gave that extra bit of time for conversation and reading. Our days took form, starting with morning coffee, after coffee we'd relax, read or simply sit and watch the waves whistle by. A spot of lunch would follow, maybe a boiled egg wrap or a bowl of cereal with long life milk. We'd nap in the afternoon, a fish would take, we'd prep it for the evening meal. H would cook it with coconut milk and spices, with rice or with pasta. We'd eat outside on the deck and watch the sun slowly fall. I liked to wash in the evenings, stripping off on the rail, pouring out some fresh water in the clean bucket, before running it over my skin to wash away the salt. Night would begin, passing way faster than the day. During a night watch I'd listen to a lecture, art, history, philosophy, we had it all. At times I'd simply sit on the deck by the mast gazing up at the stars. There is nothing quite like it, to skip across the black sea so effortlessly, powered only by the wind, the stars and the moon softly shining as Dad and Harry slept below.

When the isobars of a high-pressure weather system push together things can get rough, sailors call it a squash. During an Indian Ocean crossing they often knock on the door, unwanted but not dangerous, uncomfortable but not confrontational. On Coconut this meant Dad might spill his morning coffee, a few minor burns for the crew, he might knock his head or graze a knee. We'd drop the genoa and sail with the cutter, cooking would be hard work and one would have to crap in a bucket at the bottom of the companionway stairs instead of outside off the bowsprit. The squash could run past before long, dashing off to badger another neighbourhood, life would go back to how it was before the interruption, perhaps this time with a greater appreciation of the mundane, of the Joe average day on the trade wind highway.

8

Small Island, Big Hill

Dad's voice came in like a wave, one which for many days had been dreaming of crashing upon a soft bed of sand. 'Land ahoy old boy,' he called, and there out beyond his outstretched arm and pointed finger, unmistakably, was the faint outline of a volcanic island. Rodrigues was hiding in a thicket of white horses, totally unaware of our arrival, the sparkle of her coat catching our eyes from beneath the undergrowth. 'There she is! Look! Two fingers off the bow!'

In a crossing ultimately bound for Africa we'd just stumbled across an off shoot, a chip off the block, a child of the great continent, fragile almost when set against the scale of the sea. We ran in like a boatload of distant uncles, with arms wide and smiles beaming, and like any child interrupted by three exuberant relatives, and like any child busy playing make-believe games in the woods, Rodrigues paused kindly, looking up at us as if to say, 'Not more uncles!' Her siblings Mauritius, Reunion and Madagascar were nowhere to be seen, she played out of sight and earshot, her hills dwarfed by the waves, her head down and her heels dug in. For three weeks prior we had sat in the elements, perched upon an open palm and placed out beneath an undisturbed wilderness, a creation held together by laws far beyond our reach and understanding. Cutting the apron strings and heading out alone was a moment of release, like a noun unbound from a stake in the ground, from the tether and the wake of its own description. Psalm 23 simply writes, 'He makes me lie down in green pastures and leads me to quiet waters, he restores my soul for his namesake.'[3]

'Man, you've lost some timber,' I said to Dad when we came in, he must have shed close to two stone. When we spotted Rodrigues on the horizon, she wasn't just anyone to us, we'd been out in the galaxy, we'd been thinking about her for 1,000 miles. It was a special moment in the life of our voyage, to greet land again on the far side of the sea.

To say our first beer hit the spot would be a gross understatement. Beers were invented for moments like coming in. Decade upon decade of artisan toil, 4000 miles of tropical ocean with no fridge, these two mighty tides met head on, in a torrent of icy bubbles. They clashed in a space as small as the human mouth, can you imagine the explosion? It was hands down the perfect beer. Out of all the lagers drunk in my life that was the one which counted, a bottle no bigger than a human fist, our ocean crossing crowned in the most generous of ways.

The café was shaded, its tattered coat of lime green paint was half-shed, the chairs were cheap and plastic. Outside a happy street buzzed beneath hot rays of sun, it was break time at the local school, the sound of children laughing filled the air. We sat like three stray dogs, we hadn't yet washed or changed our clothes, our first luxury was that ice-cold beer. The bubbles washed away weeks of thirst, each mouthful had been paid for ten times over, it was truly justified, it tasted sweet, we didn't try and soften the sensation by ordering a second, instead we backed it up with plates of sea food. The islands of Rodrigues must have greeted many sailors over the centuries in this way, our cold beer was their giant tortoise. It wasn't discovered by Europeans until 1528, and colonization didn't start on the island until 1691 some 163 years later. The location of Rodriguez and its relatively small size are key factors behind her uninhabited past. She lies just off the beaten track, with bigger neighbours like Mauritius and Reunion offering greater potential downwind. Once the ships sailed past, getting back to Rodrigues in heavy trades was a serious endeavour. A small group of Huguenot refugees found this out the hard way, seemingly dumped out in the far reaches, right on the turn of high water, just as Europe's waves of exploration cut loose the cargo, and just as Europe's great ebb of exploitation began. A man called Francis Leguat was stranded on that beach, right as the tide turned. He was a Huguenot, a French protestant who had fled persecution on home soil. He travelled under a Dutch flag, volunteering to start a new colony in the East Indian islands. Like an ember spat out from the mouth of a burning fire, Francis and his Huguenot comrades sailed off, behind them roared the flames of a troubled past and in front of them lay nothing but smoke and water. Things didn't start with any degree of definition for Francis. Reunion, the island they set out for was off limits, the French had taken it over, an establishment whose iron hands were frantically swatting anything Dutch and throttling anything protestant. Unknown to the volunteers it was agreed they'd be left on an island called Rodrigues instead. I can almost picture the scene, the dark candlelit room, full of shadows and sharp voices, a low-lying table, lost in darkness beneath the scrum, officials stooped tightly around a new world map. 'Last thing on the list then, this business of Huguenot volunteers, where are we putting them!!' In the time it took the fat guy to finish his glass of brandy a decision had been made. 'I simply won't have these poor devils butchered by the frogs, not again, they can land here.'

'But sir no Dutch boat has landed on Rodrigues in years, the only thing we know about that island is it has an abundance of tortoise.'

'Splendid, make notes to cancel their rations.'

'You do realise the island is uninhabited?'

'And?'

'Well, the volunteers are all male, how will a colony flourish with just males?'

'What is wrong with you today, Charles?! Please stop asking so many questions, put a footnote down if you're that bothered, women to be sent later.'

'Great idea sir, trouble being the next ships are all booked up.'

'Booked up already! Well then, put them down on the trip after next.'

'On the trip we've just labelled as mere speculation due to lack of funds?'

'Today's speculation is tomorrow's endeavour Charles, you of all people should understand that.'

'Poetically put sir, a bunch of lady Huguenots pencilled in for a maybe landfall at the back end of the decade.'

'Perfect, now roll away the map, I'm off for dinner with the governor.'

And with this the fate of Francis was handed back to the mercy of the sea. They left from Europe on a mammoth passage to the Dutch colony of Cape Town, spending three weeks on land just as the grape season began. Francis writes in his book, 'those of us that were afflicted, landed at the cape, as soon as we arrived, to cure ourselves of the scurvy, staying at land being the only truly and sovereign remedy for that distemper.' When strength had returned on the 13th of February 1691 Swallow weighed anchor, her crew saluted the fort and they sailed out again, the fruit of an unknown island paradise just beyond their reach.

To get the line required to make Rodrigues under sail the Sallow had to travel in the Southern Ocean for many leagues. One month in on 15th of March at 40 degrees south, a violent storm hit, Francis writes, 'The wind became impetuous in very little time, and the sea foaming and lifting up its waves, formed mountains that seemed higher than our mast, the air appeared to be all on fire, lightning struck us almost blind, and the waves howled dreadfully in upon us. But our crew were most of all terrified at the sight of St Elmo's fire, which stuck to our masts, our ship so little, that people were amazed at the fight...'[4]

With St Elmo's Fire burning, Francis and company hung on, trimming their sails and arcing north to the East Indian islands, spotting land on April 3, 1691. Weak from sea the volunteers were surprised when their captain didn't put to shore. He had miscalculated their longitude and hit Reunion, the scent of land filled the air, green capped hills broke the horizon and yet they carried on. Beating back against the trades to Rodrigues took another twenty days, the volunteers were weak and frustrated, one member of their party had died on passage, beneath the surface simmered pangs of discontentment and hot flushes of anger. Sitting on the deck, their bodies depleted of strength, their throats dry and their legs heavy, one can only imagine what the sight of land meant, spirits must have soared! Onto the shoulders of a little remote island out in the far reaches of a troubled word, our friends leapt, and upon these shoulders they would hang, totally cut off from civilisation.

Of his two years in Rodriguez Francis writes, 'I lived like a prince at ease, and in abundance, without bread and without servants, I had been rich without diamonds, and without gold, as well as without ambition, I had tasted a secret and exquisite pleasure, and content in being delivered from an infinity of temptations to sin, to which men are liable in other places. Collected in myself I have seen there by serious reflection, as plain as if it was within reach of my hand or eye, what nothings the inhabitants of this wretched world admire, of this world I say, where art always destroys nature, under pretence of adorning it, where artiste are worse than art, hypocrisy, fraud, superstition and rapine, exercise a tyrannical empire over mankind, where in short everything is error, vanity, disorder, corruption, malice and misery. I cannot help adding here by way of advance, that whatever inconveniences might have attended a longer stay in this island, I would have never left it, had I not been forced to.'[5]

Good decision making, ability to hunt, physical fitness, teamwork, thinking on your feet, these attributes were all optional extras on Rodrigues. There were no poisonous snakes or spiders on the island, there were no lions or bears, there was no need to constantly keep warm. The turtles came in at 500 pounds, the giant tortoise so abundant one could hop from A to B upon their shells, the biggest juiciest bird also flightless and tame. Land crabs and coconut palms, one could dine out on that alone, wood for the fire, oil to keep it lit, meat and vitamins, all within a few yards. If one's throat got a touch dry, if the melons and coconut water weren't quite hitting the spot, no worries, just pick up a clay pot and pop down the stream, bag a giant eel for tea while you're down there, it was that type of paradise. Manta rays and manatees swam above sandy corridors of sea grass, there were rolling green hills in the backdrop covered in thick trees. The volunteers hiked in their spare time, they planted seeds from Cape Town, they played chess and made palm wine. Francis writes, 'Hunting and fishing where so easy to us, that it took the pleasure away, we often delighted ourselves in teaching parrots to speak.' In another extract Francis describes the effect of shouting in the open. Instead of putting the wild animals off as one might expect, it would help bring them on. Worried by all the commotion these gentle creatures would arrive on the scene, walking up to the agitators like a squad of St John ambulance first aiders, tunics full of shining buckles, eyes a blaze and hearts full of good intention, black buckets in one hand and magical yellow sponges in the other, ready to softly soothe a hot weathered brow. The shock of it! rocking up to help only to get knocked on the head. There is no enjoyment in that type of kill, it was for survival purposes only.

As the months passed it became evident there was something missing, something no amount of talking parrots would change. In their hot stumble out, in their stretch for Eden, our poor friends forgot Eve. Not even a pristine ecosystem filled with exotic wonders, not even freedom in the raw and untampered sense could fill the void. A year passed and the volunteers hadn't spotted a single ship, Francis was close to losing his company, he was fifty they were in their twenties and thirties, he voted to wait, and they voted to leave.

A plan was hatched, a raft would be built and if after two years no news had come from the outside world, they'd launch out themselves and head for Mauritius. Francis couldn't persuade his youthful comrades against it. When faced with the prospect of a future alone he was forced to join their struggle. The old saying, 'you can't just live on a full belly and a good view,' rained true, a fruitless future outweighed everything else in the paddock, the sweet turtle meat, the fish, the water melons and even the palm wine, none of them came close to Eve.

It was a mammoth undertaking; 350 miles of open water lies between Rodrigues and Mauritius. Armed only with two hand saws and a pocket full of nails they sat like wing clipped ducks beneath the bark of countless tall and stout trees. I wonder how many times Francis and company crouched down to draw out their plans in the sand. The volunteers didn't split up into little groups, if they sunk then everyone sunk, if they succeeded then everyone succeeded. Whatever prior experience gathered in their lives, however distant or unrelated, it was needed now more than ever before. The seafarer, the carpenter, the boatbuilder, the navigator, the engineer, the architect, the tradesman, the medic, the astronomer, the fisherman, the weatherman, whatever cords present, no matter how weak or frayed, they had to be picked out and followed. Everything gathered up then needed to be bound together and spliced tight enough to withstand the sea. Not only did the rig need to float like cork but it also needed the accuracy and direction required to hit bullseye.

Two years came and not a single white sail had passed Rodrigues, it was time for Francis and company to leave. There had been no major rifts or arguments in his party and no reported cases of sickness, everyone was in great health, physically strong and ready for the journey. 365 days of preparation, in work and in thought and in prayer, all for what could amount to as little as three days on the water.

Attempt number one was a disaster, their vessel hit a rock upon entering the outer channel, and 'if not for the miraculous intervention of God,' Francis writes, the whole party would have perished. The wind changed direction, their sinking ship was brought onto a reef studded outer island, they spent a night in temporary shelter, before an improvised hop back to shore come morning. One member of their party, a young man called Isaac, was cut badly by the reef. He caught an infection and became very weak and swollen. A heated argument followed; some wanted to draw out the infected blood, others didn't, the company narrowly voted in favour of the motion, incisions were made with a pen knife and the patient's condition worsened still. For three weeks Isaac suffered before finally passing on. Francis writes that in the last week of life he reclaimed some senses, finding his voice in times of prayer and worship. They buried him and got ready for attempt number two. Strangely the death of their friend seemed to increase the party's resolve, it was now a do or die passage, the chaps had tasted defeat, they understood the forces and the risks. Before leaving, makeshift buoys were placed in the channel to act as markers. With their boat repaired and restocked they waited for a fair day then made a clean break out into the open ocean. Their passage took nine days, triple the time anticipated, it was a passage fraught with worry, one which took them right out onto a spearhead of suffering. Their food turned bad and had to be chucked, they got hit by angry squalls, with rain that dropped mercilessly in thick cold sheets, and then came the wind, with fists of fury, a tropical storm swept in, blowing Francis way off his anticipated course. On the morning of the ninth day, as the sun broke through, Mauritius was spotted. If not for the storm, which actually blew them back on track, they might have missed the island completely. The volunteers were overjoyed, they made landfall at black river on the south western tip of Mauritius, the date May 1663, finding a small colony of Dutch families. Francis writes in his dry witted style, 'I believed my companions, who had been so long away from women, would not be able to contain themselves when they again beheld those amiable objects, or at least that they would surfeit themselves with looking on them, but I was not a little mistaken, when I found they were no more moved with them, than with the sight of cows.' [6]

For one whole month the crew recovered. Once strength returned the next move was to notify the governor of their arrival. This was no small feat; it involved a long trek up the west coast of Mauritius to Port Louis. It is here things really start to go downhill, and I must confess, in reading the account I can't quite put my finger on exactly what happened. It is as if the pulse of this story changed hands, their suffering wasn't attached to the natural world anymore, the vice switched, and the only thing darker and crueller than a hurricane is an unchecked human heart.

Like all acts of evil things start small, the heart is a divided place, the laws of God are written, and the chambers of surrender and rebellion set fast in the landscape. Free will falls from the clouds like rain and our choices move on the ground like running water, they can only flow into one of two basins, surrender or rebellion, the watershed between which is often very hard to spot. If one basin gets fed then the other starves, if fed too much the scales will tip and the battle will be lost. Pride and guilt are bound together like a chain gang, they work outside the prison walls, one swings then the other follows, they dig fast deep channels, everything which falls in gets taken with, even things which would be better suited to the service of God, used to fuel the rebellion against him. Francis's account of suffering is harrowing because the wickedness is both perpetual and personal, the dilemma is written on the walls, right across time, in every home and on every heart.

For five years Francis and his four surviving comrades were left to rot on an island prison, a patch of reef elevated just above the sea, probably no bigger than a couple of tennis courts, sharp dead coral heads full of dangerous holes, a few hard prickly shrubs and an old stone hut, that was their keep. Relations with the governor had gone from bad to worse, the milk had turned sour. What started as a gust of confrontation over a precious lump of Ambergris found on Rodrigues, an argument which landed our friends in house arrest, turned into a hatched plan to commandeer one of the governor's boats and escape to Reunion. This foiled plan resulted in all five survivors getting clapped in irons and transported two miles offshore to their island prison.

'But are you sure about the location sir! Two miles offshore on a coral shelf, they'll be dead with the first summer storm.'

'These dam frogs wanted to steal one of my boats,' replied the red-faced governor, 'it would be within my rights to have them hung.'

'In truth only two captives are guilty sir, the other three are innocent.'

'Bar humbug to that, you mark my words, those Huguenots they're thick as thieves, guilty by association!'

'That aside was it not us that impounded their vessel in the first place, if you can call it a vessel, and was it not us that cut up their sails to clothe the villagers.'

'Our villagers need cloths Mr Keeling, we have to use everything within our means, I took that boat to teach those fools a lesson! Confronting me! Over a lump of Ambergris, that rascal Huguenot had the audacity to raise his finger.'

'The rumours are true though sir, it was our smith that tricked them out of it, he told them it was worthless.'

'I don't care about the particulars Keeling, your wages came in this month didn't they! These French scoundrels don't deserve an inch of protection, we're at war with their countryman, now get out! You've just volunteered yourself to row over once a month with the offcuts and leftovers.'

With this exchange Francis and company began a new chapter, it was a season of captivity which cost another life and brought the team right out onto the brink. Two years in the wilderness on Rodrigues had got them ready for the challenges ahead, a rusty nail was tied to an old flagpole and used as a fishing spear, the fish meat cut fine and dried out in the sun. On the full moon they could swim over to a neighbouring island at low tide and scavenge for birds' eggs. Any spare foliage gathered was used to make sun hats and sold to the guards for extra rice and bread. Francis and company clung on, as the months and years passed things got more and more desperate, they got left on the shelf like untethered cliff climbers, with hands failing and feet scratching to hold, with their strength slowly fading and their beards blowing, like ribbons in the wind, weightless whispers, their legs dangling loose, cut like string their bodies thin not much more than sticks of sunburnt skin, hanging on the wire, with white-knuckled fingers above a shark-infested sea.

It was only a matter of time before one fell; the pain was simply too much. Francis tried to persuade his young friend against it, he knew it was a flash in the pan hack, not endorsed or thought out by the team, a solo effort, a lunge or a stab in the dark. But alas there was no way of telling him, he left one night, January 10, 1669, on a few branches of lashed together driftwood, he was never seen again. Killed not by the reef or by a storm, not by the hardships of sea, but through the negligence of a wicked governor, killed within earshot of a rooster's crow, within reach of generosity and charity. No one came to their aid, the island turned their heads and looked away.

The trip across to shore was successfully accomplished twice, on both occasions it was attempted because the prisoners spotted an anchored ship down the coast. If their plight was revealed to a passing captain then word might get out, an order for their release might come from across the water, from Holland or from Batavia. The first crossing took twelve hours, only two prisoners attempted it, Francis was deemed too old, and out of the remaining four, two captives were found guilty of trying to steal. Innocence and mistreatment were their appeals, so they sent only the innocent to plead. Parched but breathing, the men made it across.

Perseverance was the name of the boat at anchor. You don't just happen upon a boat called Perseverance, not in the perilous moments of an attempted escape, not given their history of prolonged suffering, and not from our elevated seat of hindsight either, can anyone conclude with a sober mind, these prisoners just happened upon a ship with such a name. It was indeed the signed letters of that appeal, handed over to the said officers of Perseverance, that consecrated their release. The seed was planted in that exchange, the envelope hit the glove, it was placed in the belly of a boat and in the hands of the living. The governor was nothing but a dead rag, their reach out was a bypassing bolt, his sphere of influence was breached at last. As Perseverance let loose her white sails and set off with the wind, their appeal left the confines of that damp dirty prison for the first time. What left that day as a seed returned as a basket of fruit, but it took five years, five years of perseverance, five years that cost one broken member his life, five years of fighting for survival, five years of unspeakable hardship. In 1669, eight months after their comrades failed attempt, they finally got a reply. Francis writes, 'On the 6th of September a vessel called Suraag arrived with a special commission to take us to Batavia. Our good and generous friends, the officers of Perseverance, of whom I have already spoken, were so kind as to present our letters and petition to the director general in Holland, so that when the governor found he could detain us no longer.'[7]

That was their ticket out, a real ticket but not a golden ticket, until the Dutch authorities in Batavia looked into their case they were treated like convicts. On that crossing to Batavia, a passage running directly against the trade winds, another member of their team died, they were down to just three. Upon arrival the Dutch authorities pardoned Francis and his surviving friends, they were put on a soldier's wage and eventually sent back to Europe as free men. Francis settled in Britain and lived to the age of 93, a staggering achievement given his yards in the saddle.

When we sat on anchor in Rodrigues, we did so in another life time to those that first set foot on the island. They saw the raw untampered majesty of nature, the 500-pound turtles, the thousands of tortoises, the manatees, the giant flightless birds, the sharks, the rays and the eels. They hid from cyclones in holes and caves, shivering in the rain with fear. Dad H and I went to the tortoise reserve and watched these giant and ancient creatures chill beneath the shade of tropical trees, we sailed in with dolphins and watched the sea birds swoop. The island was fertile and full of life, but also poor. I remember a villager trying to sell us some reef fish, they were tiny, about the size of a gold fish, faded in colour but beautiful, not something to be caught or sold, barely enough meat to feed a kitten. The rich valleys were cultivated, the magical lagoon stretched out with vivid colours for many miles. We rented motorcycles and ripped around the island. Tourism hadn't exploited Rodrigues when we passed through; it was free from the type of luxury hotels you get in more accessible destinations. I suppose in a way Rodrigues still holds the same thread as it did back when Francis landed on the tapestry.

One of our final evenings on Rodrigues was spent aboard a boat called Conversations. We rowed across, H carrying his rusty guitar. As the drinks went down the axes came out. Ethan was first, a technical young American, he played fast and frantic runs. 'No!' he would shout smiling, 'Not again, I always miss that note,' doubling back to replay the piece perfectly. 'Man, I can't play when I'm drunk.'

'Sounds pretty good to me, champ,' or, 'Run it through dude, just keep going.' Ethan finished the song, he was too young for it, wolfing her down stalk first before the shoot had time to flower, playing with technical ability and talent, but not quite netting the fish.

Next was H, H who croaks with the best of them but doesn't sing. He rolled out the flour and laid his tune on the table like a leathery run of uncooked dough. 'Chow down troops, she's ready to go!' The audience looked out bewildered, H started to strum.

'Deep in the woods where the birds don't sing
there is a snoring bear that will wake in spring,
he'll rise real slow this grizzly king,
while all around the sound will ring,
the sound of melting snow,
who knows where this hungry bear will go,

just a single glimpse of a story told
a single grain of sand in this shining dune of gold.'[8]

H had sung the bear tune many times on night watch, a six-versed classic, I'd hear his rusty guitar between the crash of waves, he wasn't practising when he played, he played for the sheer joy. I looked across the table to see what people made of it. Harry's guitar was a touch out of tune, his playing unschooled and his voice rough, but the song landed, with a heavy thud it hit the deck like a big old wild tuna.

Egor, a sixty-year-old Scandinavian then reached across and took H's guitar. 'Can I play you a song?' he said, his hands were like shovels, he thumped the strings, listening right down into the guitars belly, gently and softly turning the tuning screws. He played using only the low E and A strings, steady and slow, his voice rich and soft. He sang in Norse, a folk song from his childhood, even the wind seemed to pause and listen. Egor's voice was like a flood, one that carried us back off to the mountains where he was from. 'I'd sing as boy,' he told us, 'Back in the village they'd ask for me to sing.'

In a strange way, that night can be related to Francis and his company. It was the old head who held the floor during those years of suffering. Francis had the timing, he knew when to move and when to wait, he didn't need all the notes or all the words. Looking back in slow motion, right into the punch, into that black and broken rock face, you can see where Francis hung his troubles. He pinned them on the cross of Jesus Christ. You don't get to 93 on Frank's paper round without some help, not in the 17th century. The doubter will point to his grave and say, 'Dig it up then, let's see if the old dog died with a straight back.' The critic will point and curse in offense and judgment, of the time and of the people from the time, but through it all, looking off in a totally different direction, are the single letters of a bigger story, that like tiny grains of glass glisten because they face the light. Isolated in their spot on the ground, dung in between the dark decades, embedded in thick cold walls, they look not down the grain of their generation, as those around them did, but instead they face God, that eternal beacon, whose righteous light will never fade. That is the part of Francis's story that still lives.

9

A Cove in the Current

Mauritius is that place in an ocean where something from everywhere washes up, it has a cove in the current and a rock where rusty things stick. Countless Asian fishing boats were rafted up in a mysterious land cloud, they'd drifted in on the wind from God knows where, exiled from the orient, half-sunk and constantly pumping. There was a rumble and a clunk to these vessels, they moved with a limp, they rattled like a beggar's cart, when bound together they lost their identity and became indistinguishable. One raft remained, China, had landed in Port Louis.

Across the water stood another floating super power, a giant and solitarily American warship was tied up, sleeping like a dog in the sun, just a thin length of string hanging from its collar. She ate alone with cannons for company, the barrels of which looked like they could shoot down the moon. Between the red corner made up of hundreds and the blue corner made up of one, there was us, the middle ground, the travelling boats, all boxed up on a shallow wall. The harbour by day was in direct contrast to the harbour by night. At night everything would scuttle back into the docked shells they washed in on. The streets were deserted at night, a skeleton of bones remained, sitting by the water waiting for the sun.

When we entered Port Louis we arrived back into reality, somehow managing to run aground on a hidden rock just a stone's throw from the dock. It was 2011 and the Indian Ocean just didn't feel big enough. Somalian pirates had commandeered a huge stretch of water to the north using mother ships to attack boats 1,000 miles out. The road up through the Suez Canal had been shut off. Mauritius was a bottleneck, with the South African winter not yet finished the harbour was fast filling up, we walked into the cattle shed, no dogs required to herd us in, a cheap dock and a fresh water shower was more than enough.

'You call those udders? Check out me trotters,' shouted the pig to the cow.

'Pig's milk,' the cows replied laughing, 'you poor devils have spent weeks living on pig's milk.'

'I don't drink any milk at all,' added the shed's token goose, 'not at sea, doesn't sit right in me belly.'

'Well, what do you eat then, goose?'

'Grain, that's what I eat, God's very own grain.'

To which the pig replied, 'How do you carry the grain then?'

'I put the grain in a feather bag then tie it around my foot.'

'Feather bag?' stuttered the mule perplexed, 'well us mules don't have feathers for bags and milk is for kittens.'

'Well, how do you survive out there then mule,' said the goose, the cow and the pig.

'Straw, I eat a barn full before I leave, then I lash the leftovers on me back, us mules, we sail for months just on straw.'

'It was so windy out there wasn't it, did you find it to be windy?' Squeaked a rat parking up. 'Never again, I can't do that again!'

'Windy? That wasn't proper wind, rat.'

'It was windy for me; my rig is small and light don't forget.'

'You shouldn't be out there on those wheels,' coughed the donkey to the rat, 'you're asking for trouble!'

'Donkey has been carrying me for years,' clucked the chicken, 'she knows a thing or two about the sea, why don't you sail on with us. Rats and chickens make for good company.'

'I don't carry rats,' spat the donkey.

'Well, I don't want to ride on a donkey anyway' replied the rat, 'poor man's horse is a donkey.'

'Do you want to ride with me,' said an old shire horse with a slow sigh, 'I'll take anyone, even a rat, lonely out there, so awfully lonely, we could sail for the cape together!'

'Sounds like a plan to me,' concluded the rat.

'Here he comes,' bleated a chorus of sheep. 'At long last, look at that coat, still glistening, as white as when he left.'

'How does he keep that coat of his so perfectly white?' Questioned the pig.

'Well, he doesn't roll around in his own shit for a start,' gobbled the shed's turkey.

'Gales for breakfast,' whispered the goat, 'that ram eats gales for breakfast.'

'He better not raft up near us,' said the chicken, 'I don't care how many times he's sailed around the world; those dam hooves will squash us.'

'Rams don't raft up, and if they did, they most certainly wouldn't come alongside a stinking barrel of battery chickens,' scoffed the sheep, 'he'll anchor off in deep water!'

You can picture the scene: the port was a place where crews reshuffled. The herd came in and found a degree of order, the lonely found company, that bad tempered captain, clapped in irons for weeks at sea with his slanderous crew, got a chance to catch his breath, the troubles of his passage over for a while. Disputes dissolved into the herd, into a mass of talking mouths and listening ears. Boats we'd bumped into months back kept rocking in. Over the course of time, slowly and steadily a community had formed around us, one I wasn't truly aware of until sheep met cow and horse met pig. The ties that bound us all to the sea were strongly founded, the shared experiences and sundown beers melted together like hot wax, we all chowed down on the fodder. Most boats heading to Europe were on the back end of a circumnavigation, they were the cream of the crop, the characters who had that dash of salt in their blood, who could keep the fire burning years in.

We said goodbye to Dad in Mauritius, it was an emotional goodbye, you could tell deep down he wanted to sail on and reach Africa. When he left there was a moment of numbness, we had become a working body, a proper team, it felt like losing a leg when the big guy got in his cab. H and I were partners again. Later that morning we teamed up with a young

American chap and a Norwegian dude we'd nicknamed Rory, we headed off to go climb a mountain.

Climbing with H is a hard experience to relate, the agony of watching him, the euphoria one feels when he makes it down. In life we are all born with certain gifts, they are not the same and they are not equally portioned. H has a raw strength about him, not the type that comes from time in the saddle, with age or through training, but a strength which runs much deeper. I remember visiting Harry in Hong Kong on the way out to Australia, he'd lost the keys to his apartment, instead of cursing or kicking up a fuss he said with hands in pockets, 'I'll climb in from the fire escape.' I followed him down not knowing what that meant. To my surprise there was a level on the twenty something floor with no windows, a skeleton of bare concrete walls. H hopped on the rail and clambered up to his apartment from outside the skyscraper, his balcony only a level or so above our heads, but an intense climb to say the least. We were up at altitude; the tower block was so high it seemed to almost sway in the wind. Peking duck and Chinese lager made the whole parade a slippery dish, the searing heights boiled my bones, high above the cold spaghetti roads, wrapped up in a neon broth, that light and foam whipped froth, that floated like a cork at sea, as I clenched the rails and watched H wrestle and joke with gravity, fish hooking the night in his iron paws, unlocking the door and welcoming me in with the humorous saying, 'Cup of tea vicar!'

Everyone back home has a story about H growing up. 'He dived down for over two minutes,' one might say, 'with a knife between his teeth, it was early spring, freezing water, absolutely freezing, I couldn't believe it when he surfaced! Two lobsters,

I'm not joking, he came up with a bleeding nose and two lobsters.'

These tales grow their own wings as the seasons turn, they develop a life of their own, but the fact remains, H is a wild dude. Aboard Little Coconut I found myself grafted on, strangely bound to his wild jumps, my feet firmly dug in, my back stretched, dragging like a foul anchor. Climbing a mountain with H was no ordinary day out. On this occasion he had spotted the peak from Port Louis. 'Let's go for that one,' he said pointing off to a hooked beak of bare rock.

'A little intense for a Tuesday,' I replied.

'I'll pack a coil of rope;' H relied, 'they always look worse from a distance.'

Off we went, with two friends, jumping in a bus and driving out of town. We reached the back of the mountain but couldn't find a trail up. Unwilling to give in we fought through the undergrowth, climbing higher and higher until the shrubs and trees lost their roots, until the incline was too much for the earth and the ground sat bare beneath our fingers. Two sides of a mountain met in a knife edge ridge, the side facing out to sea was sheer, way up there in the sky, high enough to make my hands shake. Our American friend was waiting in the shade of the tree line, Rory looked across and said, 'We don't have the equipment to attempt this.' We stopped and H carried on, passing out of sight up a wall of giant stairs. Before long a muffled shout bounced back down from his lofty prison like a loose pebble. 'I'm stuck,' he yelled.

I caught the echo and repeated it to Rory, 'H is stuck, this must be bad.'

'Can't see the foot holes,' Harry shouted, 'past vertical.' I looked across at Rory, what do you do in that type of situation?

'We got to head down and get the Swiss guy,' Rory said, 'he has climbing equipment in his boat.'

'Will we get back up here before dark?' I replied, 'I doubt we will!'

In the heat of a tropical climb time froze. I'd never in all my years heard H shout out in a voice which spelled, please help. He'd literally never asked me for help once in 24 years. He didn't say the words but there was a hidden intensity in his voice, I dared not try and picture the knot he was in. As Rory and I debated the crack, each throwing back and forth a series of worried expressions, H's arse came back into view. 'Thank God for that,' was the cry. Luckily Harry had packed a spare halyard, taking it out of his backpack, he snagged it in true amateur fashion and managed to lower himself down off that shelf of doom. Never have I been so relieved, H might have scaled the mountain, but it was only by a hair's breadth, the rock face had won. We found the trail on the way down, making it back to Port Louis for a sundown beer.

After a couple of weeks in Mauritius it was time to make a break, Reunion was our next stop. We skipped across in the night, in a trance of soft stars, pushed on by a steady wind. There was a luxury game fishing boat pumping out jets of salt water, tied up against the dock. The two white short Mauritians running the boat had half sunk it, they had called Mayday and got airlifted off, the boat had been recovered later and towed in by the coastguard. 'Rough out there wasn't it,' they said. I looked across at their motor cat, 'must have been in that,' I said, 'You really don't feel much heat on Coconut.'

'The waves swamped us,' said the man, 'our pumps failed straight away, then our engines stopped cold, we span broadside, and the waves came in, we started to fill up like a welly boot, I wasn't risking it,' he said, 'I hit that red button.' It suddenly dawned on me, a badly made boat is no boat at all. Lakes and oceans are very different places, out in deep water a sailor needs genealogy in the lines of a boat, the hull has to come from that hard mould of history, you can't just create one off the cuff on a computer screen. Something shiny to take overweight tourists game fishing on just doesn't cut it.

Reunion was a magical place; it was a paradise really, where else in the world can you gaze up at a lush green mountain peak, then gaze out into a perfect blue sea, then pick up a freshly baked French croissant, take down a soft and generous mouthful beneath a cloudless sky, put the croissant down, pick up an ice cold glass of freshly squeezed orange juice, the shade of whose tree you're sitting under, then look across at the most beautiful waitress you've ever seen, her skin soft and brown, her hair jet black and her eyes wild and green, a daughter of both Africa and Europe. H and I were just not used to it, paradise had come early, our childhood hood was spent holidaying in Scotland, sheltering from screeching squalls beneath dry stone walls, constantly on the hoof, Dad's nose dripping in the rain as we ran, be it from midge or be it from weather. We learnt to rest on the hoof, marching to distant hill locks. We could not have pictured that café in Reunion, not in our wildest dreams. Pulling that stunt in a West Highland town, not a chance! No board shorts, no T-shirt, not likely! You'd be clothed in the wool of ten sheep and waterproofed by the black tar of a Dundee shipwright, you'd be munching on a Scots egg and swigging a can of iron brew, looking down onto the featureless plain of a white plastic table, staring out with vacant eyes, caught inside a prison of thick pebble dashed walls, just one arrow slit for a window, sealed shut with heavy pains of double-glazed glass. Hiding in the only bolthole available, hiding from the black skies and freezing rain, actively avoiding local interaction, talking in whispers, 'That waitress, she was an extra in Braveheart, I'm sure of it, she's big Hamish's missus.'

'Wrong again, Rob Roy, she was the clan's trusty Caber thrower.'

'Let's agree to disagree; if she goes for the rolling pin, we'll drop a fiver and run!'

Our first move in Reunion was to stock up and sail down the coast to St Pierre, a pretty fishing village at the foot of the mountains. There was a decent wave to surf just off the harbour wall, a powerful right hander, every morning we'd paddle out for a couple just after sun rise then find a quiet café for breakfast. Life doesn't get much better, everything was within walking distance of Little Coconut.

The end of October was fast approaching, another passage across a vast stretch of water dawned. Before leaving we headed off into the hills for a change of scenery. Two boats joined us for a few days trekking in the mountains. It was the break we needed, the landscape was striking, the lines of the hills sharp and free. With heavy breaths and beating hearts we climbed, our legs burning and our backs straight. It was a fantastic escape, no roads or buildings just miles and miles of untouched wilderness, it was a blaze of inspired desolation, rugged and hard. During colonial times the spartan landscape of Reunion's interior had the same effect. Plantation slaves often broke free, they ran to the hills and lived in mountain communities, cultivating patches of flat ground, fishing in the rivers and hunting for small game. These hill tribes survived for long stretches of time, right across the span of those dark centuries, the hills were their escape and their protection.

Towards the end of October everyone was glued to the weather maps. Like swallows we gathered on the wire, gazing off into the distance, one foot kicking out into thin air whilst the other clung to the dock, half jumping half hanging on. Cyclone season was around the corner, just beyond it, some 1,500 miles away, a South African winter was letting go. The flock was twitchy, our journey notoriously difficult, wrecking balls of wind come crashing around the Cape, they run into the Agulhas current, a huge body of warm water flowing down Africa's east coast. Getting the approach to Africa wrong was not an option. Those days before our departure felt like the night before a fight, we'd be dancing in the ring before long, beneath the white lights, taking shots from all angles, the massive waves I'd read about off South Madagascar rolled into my imagination, rising high and crashing down hard. We checked the rigging, lashed everything down and got ready for the marathon ahead.

10

Slow Water off Madagascar

One white sail passed us, then another, then another, the giant green hills of Reunion soon became small and grey, even the highest peak lost all colour, once proud and strong was withered then gone, and we, we were alone again. Psalm 103 writes, 'As for man, his days are as grass, as a flower of the field so he flourisheth, for the wind passeth over it, and it is gone, and the place thereof shall know it no more.'[9] Coconut's mast stood like a bare stalk in the breeze, our petals had fallen, they lay back in a shallow grave, buried behind our stern in fathoms of saltwater. The markets, the cold beer, the proud weeks of celebration, the locals and our friends the sailors, none of them could reach us now, our bow was pointing off across the water.

Seven days in and we were bearing down on South Madagascar. It was evening and Harry and I were eating dinner on deck, gazing out at the most incredible display of colour I've ever witnessed in all my days and nights at sea. A river of light, that cosmic stream of energy spanning back 93 million miles to the sun, it dispersed like a slow crest, in currents and torrents of pink, orange and red. Burning like a furnace, crashing with a mighty splash, clothing us in light, then softly drawing back out into the tide. Clouds of tiny dust particles get lifted high into the atmosphere above southern Africa, rising up from the baked earth in thermal currents. Our new dawn was written into the evening sky from 800 miles out.

In a bid to reach land quickly we cut the corner short off South Madagascar and sank into a counter current. The water became thick like clay and our boat speed over the ground slumped to three knots. Our impatience soon turned into complacency. As we trudged through the thick water our bodies grew increasingly tired. Have you ever watched a sparrow eating grain off a bird table? Out in the open their world is one of calculated checks, their survival depends on it, their eyes are never off the sky for long. Aboard Little Coconut we had forgotten our station in the hedgerows and got tame, with nothing but open water on the horizon for days, and with giant legs at sea behind us, we became a touch deluded, perched on sparrow's feet we pecked at the seed like farmyard roosters.

The visibility was perfect for prey on the morning our world turned into a cloud of feathers. Not bad enough to cause any anxiety, but far from good. The horizon had no definition, we sailed into a gentle haze, into a soft and distant cloud. With no AIS or radar to watch for us, cut alongside a leg sapping counter current, the trap was set, all it needed was a catalyst. Harry pressed play on our lap top, he picked a thoughtless comedy, something intentionally scripted as an escape. I sat below and watched for too long. When I eventually surfaced, in a slow climb up Coconut's companionway stairs, it was almost too late! We were right beneath the ship's clogs, so close to her blunt steaming bow one couldn't see her giant wheelhouse tower. Rows of containers sat as silent spectators; they blocked out the executioner's face like a black scarf. Pistons of fear erupted from somewhere deep within. I wailed down the radio, 'Collision imminent.' H jumped up and scrambled to turn on the engine, I rushed out to disconnect the wind vane, we slammed down the governor and followed the tack of our boom, rushing off at right angles, gunning for clear water, every bit of horse power cranked, all five knots of speed, our sails loose above our heads, flapping like a set of startled wings in a wild wood. We let out a squawk and a cloud of black smoke and just missed the bus. As she steamed by, I could see the officers, they'd run out onto a viewing platform, they looked down at us and we looked up at them, their faces were white with shock while ours burned red from the panic. How had an ocean of time flipped off the table and smashed to the ground so fast? Our world exploded into a shower of broken glass. Death by comedy/container ship nearly had us, a gag, a laugh then a wallop.

As we pulled out of the counter current, after a few violent squalls, the visibility got better. Coconut returned to her steady four-knot plod and H and I settled into life at three hours on, three hours off. The next incident of note was an encounter of polar opposites. Out from the blur of perfect wind and blue skies, a black sail was spotted on the horizon. It got our attention in a fairly major way because the boat was in front of us not behind us, we couldn't quite believe our eyes. Ten minutes on from H's first sighting we started to get a little worried, 'Something is up with that boat,' I said, 'we're gaining too fast.' We had never experienced the thrill of overtaking on Coconut. Boat after boat would sail past and leave us for dead. To see a sail in front of our bow was unprecedented, we were on a one-way road.

'We should head right up and have a look,' H cried. As we drew closer the sail went from black to maroon, our radio then cracked and a Dutch voice came in from across the airwaves. You could tell a lot about the man on the other end from his voice, there was no filter, no muffler, no pretence, he wasn't copying or acting, his personality bled out like juice, reaching across the water in a strong arm of sound. '80 days,' he bellowed, 'I haven't seen land since Australia, I just go man! Where you guys heading?'

'Richards Bay,' we replied.

'I heard on the longwave there is still plenty of spaces at Richards Bay, I go to Durban.' Hank had been out for so long he seemed kind of anxious about coming back in. 80 days straight from Australia on a 26-footer, alone. It felt epic to bump into a journey like that, we had been scripted in, we met Hank in his element, right there in the present, sailing up close enough to drop the radio channel and start wailing. 'Little Coconell,' he shouted with a thick Dutch accent, 'nice boat man.'

'What is your boat called?' we replied.

'Songni d'oro! It's Italian, it means dreams of gold!'

'Good name!'

Hank refused when we asked if he would like some canned food thrown over, we figured he'd been out for so long stocks might be running low. 'I have plenty,' Hank replied. 'I should have scraped the hull after crossing the Pacific! Maybe I see you in Durban, we meet up for a beer!'

'100 percent,' we cried.

With the cold ones on ice, Little Coconut cruised past and out of earshot. In my entire circumnavigation that was the only boat I ever overtook, Hank had taken our crown, it was rightfully his, he came in last on the smallest so he was first and the biggest. For us and the others who crossed that year there was no need to roll out the red carpet or shower the poor Dutchman in champagne, a slap on the back and a cold beer would do. Sailing a 26-footer alone was doubtlessly a harder road than sailing a 32-footer with two or three onboard. Hank hadn't seen land in 6,000 miles, he was travelling just over two knots when we passed by, his experience put simply was much deeper than ours, his trip more radical. It was Jesus who coined the concept, when in the gospel of Mark, he said, 'Many who are first will be last, and the last first.'[10] Now obviously he was talking about life as a whole and not just isolated endeavours, but at least on the ocean the nature of life is unveiled. The sea is a real place with real consequences. When Jesus said this, he wrapped it all up, he took the line and the lure, the past and the present, then cast out his line of truth, deep into the future. He then showcased this in his ultimate earthly landfall, the biggest and greatest in history. Jesus rolled into town on a donkey, the highest of high priests, the saviour and the king of kings, pitched up to bridge the covenants and redeem humanity, right at the turning point of history, on a donkey! Our little crossing and all the other ones before and since are just droplets, barely visible and significant only because they hold a glimpse of truth. In each journey of note, the sailor makes land with a strand of donkey hair in his/her cap. When a small white light floats across a desert of dark wild water, and makes the safety of shore after thousands of miles in the saddle, there is meaning in that type of journey, the metaphor is both physical and real.

After a good spell of weather my old man told us a bomb low was flying in, 'Better to stay out in deep water and slow down, let the low pass through,' he said. Our approach was delayed by a day or so as H and I worked to sail as slow as possible without stopping. Heavy showers of rain blew across us as the low swung by, it just missed, that steel toe cap boot flew past and we caught but a loose lace, it bounced redundant off Coconut's hard shell. As we got 100 miles out electricity filled the air, by nightfall we were right beneath an electrical storm. Black clouds of fork lightening surrounded us. A giant oil tanker off our port flank took a bolt of lightning, I witnessed the strike, it hit like a Henry Cooper left hook, knocking out their lights. H and I waited to get clipped, with eyes scrunched up and elbows tucked in, with chins down and paws over our temples. We did a range of things, some backed by science others wrapped in superstition. We put our spare handheld GPS and sat phone in the oven, we then wrapped electrical tape around Coconut's metal wheel and steered the boat wearing flip flops. Little Coconut walked straight through the storm without taking a shot, as bolts of lightning rained down, we slipped by unscathed.

Day 19 and there she was, Africa, the water light brown from days of heavy rain, the visibility pretty poor, the wind on our beam. Landfall came in like a pulse of adrenaline in this instance, not slow and heavy but full of energy and electricity. During that 48-hour approach we got very little sleep but I don't recall feeling tired when we got in. Africa reached out and took us by the hand, marching us in through the finishing tape. The fatigue of endless broken nights hadn't managed to catch me, I celebrated our landfall all night, climbing back into Coconut as the sun rose up. I slept out the morning like a snoring bear, waking to a fresh wind blowing through an open hatch. Little Coconut was so still, tethered peacefully to a harbour wall, not a sound came from within her shell. For our entire passage there had been rattles and clicks, shaking sails and the constant bang of loose things hitting metal. Our weeks at sea had been plagued by a need to just hang on and out last the weather. Having sailed away from the trade winds there was nothing steady or safe about our environment. That night of celebration was the last gasp of a frantic leg, I was on land but still connected to the wild crashing seas. When I woke, I truly landed, my surroundings had changed, we lay in such a state of peace it is hard to describe. Anxiousness and worry had been lifted from my shoulders as I slept, the violent squalls, the bolts of lightning, the oil tankers and container ships, none of them could harm us now; Little Coconut was safely in. The Indian Ocean had been crossed at its widest point, from the spartan and desolate coastline of North Australia to the wild and wave-battered reaches of South Africa. It was a landmark moment on our journey home.

11

The Cape of Good Hope

The peace I found upon landing in Africa was short-lived. As I rose from the bunk, my head started beating, a skin full of beer the night before had wrung dry my throat. Our wallets were near empty, I was thinking about currents and weather patterns. I climbed out from Coconut's hatch and looked upon her weary deck, it had been a good 8,000 miles on the hoof, she was dressed in rust. I turned my eyes up upon the harbour wall where H was sitting in the sun, his feet bare, a set of salty trainers left by the wheel, his T-shirt looked like it had been torn up by a pack of hungry dogs. He was talking to a sailor on the boat behind us, shouting down to a blond chap from Sweden. 'We kept off the coast and let it pass through,' said H.

'Poor Martin,' replied the Swede. 'He came in with eyes like golf balls, white like a ghost.'

'That wasn't the storm,' replied H, 'that is just Martin.' They both chuckled. The water in the harbour was full of logs and sticks, our sheltered shallows had been turned by the rain into a brackish swamp.

Richard's Bay was a perfect port of entry, the Agulhas current runs slow off that northern section of coast, not yet in full stride, this ensures the sea state doesn't go from rough to nuclear. All we, the little boats, had to do was wait for a northerly rip and make tracks to the Cape in short hops, with wind and current. Richards Bay, Durban, East London, Port Elizabeth then Simon's Town. Only five ports along that whole east coast stretch. It doesn't take long to get a feel for the current en route south. The main body of moving water lies miles off the beach, out where the contours drop. If a band of weather was to hit unexpectedly, a sailor should head in not out, they should hug the sand with short tacks, the exact opposite of what one might expect. We found this out on passage from Durban to East London. Hank on his 26-footer, covered in weed and barnacles, came in before old Norman on his 65-footer. Hank headed straight for the deeper water, he was first to reach the current, Norman stayed in close and picked up a fraction of the speed. H and I watched Hank disappear, then followed his track. Little Coconut was soon in the mix, running at 12 knots, it was an in-house record not to be beaten. The sea was alive with dolphins, whales and shoals of fish.

Our trip from north to south down the east coast of South Africa, brought in many a creature great and small. Low pressure cells which roll around the Southern Ocean in wrecking balls of wind get pulled north by a dominant Atlantic high, cold currents sweep in from the west and the Cape becomes home to Africa's only penguin colony. In contrast to the east, you have this fast-moving current, a huge body of warm water heading in from the Equator, redistributing heat from Mozambique. Leather back turtles and bull sharks enter the fray, the sea rich with flippers and fins. I remember surfing in board shorts, sailing for a week or two, then getting ice cream head aches and cold feet, shouting over to Harry! 'What just happened?' In just a few hundred miles of coast the oceans meet, the wrath of the South, a freezing fist, explodes on warm sun-baked cliffs. There, floating above the surface, in the spray and the haze and the mist, where hot meets cold, where light strikes upon a drum of broken water, a rainbow nation is reborn. As with the birds and the animals, swept in from far off fields, so to with the nations. Dust coloured bands of Bushman, armed with wood and bone, Bantu tribes from the north, and gusts of white settlers, pushed high and dry by southern storms. It is in this meeting, in the turbulence of a rough and headstrong embrace, we catch a glimpse of the rainbow, marking the sky where rock reaches out into a troubled sea. And the gates of hell will not prevail in such a place, let that be known, for invisible is made visible, the fullness of light, split into bands of colour, drawn like a bow and raised high like a flag. Hope set like a sail upon a dark horizon, so that the human eye can see the light of God for what it is.

The story of my trip down to the Cape was one of light and darkness, a passage of contrast. I caught my first glimpse of what was to come on the beaches north of Richard's Bay. It had been a night of heavy drinking, and my head had not hit the pillow, I picked up two surfboards from Little Coconut, giving one to a Navy Seal, who for many an hour, I had been trying to out drink. We walked to the beach, half-cut, staggering along a winding track of sand. As the sun hit the horizon, I heard the sound of hollow waves, pounding against shallow banks of sand. The inheritance of that beautiful morning was not mine; I had squandered everything the night before. Upon that beach was the face of a different house, a house filled with peace. A preacher was leading his friends in prayer, I walked right past, and he held his gaze, his skin dark and his eyes full of light and warmth and love. That picture of contrast, it bit right through me. I knew in that moment I was captive to the current, and I knew he was free. The red sun wrapped around him like a halo, I entered the water to be steam rolled and smashed, half-drowned in the whitewash, wipe out after wipe out, till I staggered back up the sand, to sit in a wet pool of conviction, watching the Christians praise God and the sober surfers catch waves. It would be a long time till the chains of binge drinking were broken, not for years, but a lasting picture of light and darkness entered my shallow world, contrast and colour, etched into my memory. What a meeting of different currents that was, a bubble floating to the light sails past a stone sinking to the darkness. 'Let go of the weight,' says the cat on the bubble to the dog with the stone in his mouth. It was a band of red light and a band of orange light, red for the rising and red for the warning and orange for waiting.

The street children of Durban gathered in numbers like a slow flood of courage, their bodies were empty and desperate, sapped and in need, they sat in circles sniffing glue out of paper bags to escape the pains of hunger. The world to them was a jagged edge, a thirsty stone, a pick of ice, it lay over them, it consumed them like a breaking wave. That wave which threatened to drown them felt like the same wave H and I were riding on, we shot past so fast, locked into the barrel, riding and gliding over shared ground, over a sea bed which pulled them down into utter darkness, till every cell in their bodies cried out for a breath of clean air. To my shame I did little to help the children, bar hitting a fast-food joint and dishing out a round of burgers. The darkness surrounding them was abandonment and poverty, it led to addiction, crime and violence. I am reminded of the words Jesus said in the gospel of Matthew, 'I tell you the truth, when you refused to help the least of these my brothers and sisters, you were refusing to help me.'[11] A blue band of light rises off the Cape, for the crystal waters of their eternal rest, for the quiet and peaceful pools of restoration that lie beside the mighty river of Zion in paradise, and for the tears that fall on earth, that are seen by God and that will be redeemed.

There was the face of fear too, it sat on the ground like a fallen cape, tossed from the horse on a hot day, a cape with no choice but to sit still and wait for the rain, a shiver of fear hiding beneath a skeleton of shaking grass, the fear of someone with nowhere to go and everything to lose. 'Don't walk over that bridge!' He shouted to H and I with blood shot eyes as we headed off under foot to look for surf, 'it is the most dangerous bridge in South Africa, they'll rob you with guns on that bridge.' We walked off like a gust of wind, straight across the bridge, into the woods and up over the hill. We came to an empty wooden bench, it sat on the hill like a frozen tear drop, marked with a name and lined up to face the waves. Life with love and death with tragedy, a shark bite, a cloud of blood and a bed of countless shells. Violet and Indigo, they are the next bands of colour off the Cape, split from white to take one's eyes away from the fears of a broken world, the fears of sharks or guns or any other suffering, the fear of death, or loss, whether blood or wealth, reputation or titles. A colour that shows God in his rightful majesty. For it is God who should be feared above all else, when we revere the Lord in such a way, all the other fears bow their heads, they are bundled up and brought in by a rope, to dissolve beneath the furnace of his love. If blue was for the poor, then violet and indigo are for the rich.

We made good time down to False Bay, playing cat and mouse with the south-westerly bomb lows, picking up a buoy on the outside just before new year. The Cape was wind battered, at times it was too strong for El Tenderino to carry both H and I ashore from Little Coconut's mooring out in the bay. We flicked coins for who had to row and who had to swim, the water was cold and the threat of great white sharks was always in the back of one's mind. We had two friends flying in, first Cousin Tariq, on a flight from Dubai for a holiday. Second, Jersey man Daniel John, in from Perth for a leg on Coconut. T-Rex was first, he brought good company, but also money and wheels. H hadn't bothered to pack his driving licence and my licence had been commandeered by the authorities back home. It felt great to be on the road again with Tariq behind the wheel. He took us into the landscape of South Africa. To have sailed by and missed the rolling hills and dramatic scenery of the Cederberg mountains, would have been akin to enduring the sting of the salty waves without tasting the honey of land. We came back from our road trip to spend new year in Cape Town. The city was wild, a maze of dark shadows surrounded the streetlights, it was a land of moonshine filled waterholes, with vultures watching and hyenas laughing, jackals waited out where the grass grew high. My empty pockets got pilfered by pick pockets numerous times, gangs of young teenagers were working the crowds. There were no trains back to False Bay until the morning, Harry, cousin Tariq and I had to outlast the night. A large group of sailors were in town, each boat connected by another, Danes and Swedes, Norwegians and Americans, we met in the mayhem, halfway round the world. I remember all the skippers, young Daniel sailing solo, Pair who had lost his love in the South Pacific, and Alex Rust, the captain, sitting in the bar like a large planet, moons and meteorites hung about his belt. The city felt empty when dawn broke, the sunlight came in and swept everything clean, we boarded a train and slept out the journey back to Simon's town, it was the last big hurrah for us travelling boats. Cousin Tariq said goodbye, his holiday had covered the wine region, the Cederberg mountains, a surf on the Atlantic coast, a surf on the Indian and a big New year's shindig in Cape Town, what a blast! We bid farewell to T, then waited for our friend Dan to arrive, a new season in the South Atlantic was on the horizon. The last colours we gazed upon in South Africa flowed out around Simon's Town in long robes of weathered grass, shades of green and gold. Green for the wind-battered hill grass, studded with wild flowers, and gold for the light that reflects off the bare rock down on the Cape. Out at sea, a sailor's heart jumps when looking upon this beautiful Cape of Good Hope. Green and gold are for provision and promise, raised aloft right through the squall, to lift a sailor's eyes off the compass, to push the show on, across the water and in the other side.

12

Dunes of Sand

He came aboard having never sailed, yet he came aboard having grown up by the sea. Outside Dan's childhood kitchen window, right there beneath the double glazing, lay the beach. Wild crashing winter gales almost seemed playful when you gazed out at them from Dan's house. His kitchen was warm, the lighting was soft and Dan's dad Terry, whose favourite room in the house was the kitchen, liked to sing. The sea gently danced in the moonlight, it hummed harmony behind a constant stream of Sinatra covers, white horses rose and fell behind the cereal packets and hot toast. One could quite easily sit and watch a ship go down and not even realise what had just happened.

Harry and I had been waiting for Dan since before the beginning, until Cape Town he was the bride that never showed, we'd awaited his arrival from the altar of a dozen distant ports.

Jamie had arrived and gone, Dad and taken his bunk for a time, cousin Tariq flew in for a holiday and all the while Dan's seat on Little Coconut lay vacant. What started in the months prior to our departure as very definitely in, slowly turned to quite possibly out. The traffic light above Dan's comings and goings changed from green to flashing amber, there was nothing anyone could do about it. Life quite simply got in the way. To his credit Dan never gave up, arriving on Coconut a little bashed but in working order, dropping in as if by accident, right before we rounded the Cape of Good Hope and let ourselves loose into the wastelands of the South Atlantic. Dan flew in with no real reality of what was to come, he was born by the sea and he jumped for the moon, landing like a lost longlegs, two midges for company and an old rusty boat.

The sun was shining down upon the cafes of Simon's town when our friend eventually arrived, we spotted him from afar, pigeon-legged and barrel-chested, a true Jersey man. Dan slotted right in, his keep aboard, the wooden bench between Harry's hole at the stern and my lair at the bow, the midships. Dried fish scales were stuck down so fast by that stage in the game they almost seemed engrained in the woodwork, hanging nets of fruit lay above and engine parts below. Dan arrived right into the heart of the wolf pack, he wasn't an outsider or a hitchhiker, he was one of the team. Our first job was to stock up the boat and get ready for a leg ultimately finishing on the other side of the ocean in Brazil. The South Atlantic would run off into endless days, the breeze would be constant and gentle, blowing softly around a dominant high-pressure cell, taking Coconut across the ocean as it naturally would if we were cut loose and rudderless. H and I knew what to expect, but Dan didn't. It was exciting to have a fledging onboard, someone who was experiencing life afloat for the first time. H bent down in the supermarket and bear hugged a generous horde of pasta, bailing the packets over the side of our shopping trolley in one hit, Dan let out a squawk of nervous laughter, he was under the wings of two Bonn boys with no way out, his head was full of theory and his heart full of doubt, but the meeting had taken place, he'd landed on the surface, he was coming with whether he liked it or not. 'I can't quite believe we're heading off tomorrow,' he said, 'it feels a bit like we just went shopping for a Sunday barbeque, is this real? Are we leaving tomorrow?'

'Upon first light,' the reply.

Every generation seems to land that big fish at least once in a lifetime, that song which cuts right through its surroundings, echoed back through the atmosphere in broken beds of off notes. To look back at Africa from outside having left, it was an awesome experience, she rose up from the sea like a redemption song, her cliffs, they cast down no shadow, she was iron like that lion roaring in Zion, giant walls of bare rock stood tall in perfect light, tablets of stone, without blemish, flawless like a diamond. The continent seemed reborn upon our departure, she stood larger, bolder and clearer than ever before, the waves of two giant oceans, with all their wrath, with fists like spoils, couldn't wet her feet. We felt so very small, Dan turned sheet white, he lay at the base of our downed cutter sail, he couldn't even raise his eyes to say goodbye, all Africa saw of him on that day was his two bare feet, they sat above the rolling sea like distant grave stones on a bare hill, pale and lifeless beneath the branches of our full sails.

It is hard to step into Dan's shoes because I have never been seasick, and it is hard to step into his shoes also because I've never jumped off the ledge and taken to sea without some insight into what the road ahead entailed. My older brother Ed and I were frogmarched into dinghies as children. As a boy, I remember praying for the traffic lights to be red, praying we'd miss the boats and arrive to an empty harbour, to a line of vacant red buoys. 'Boats all gone Dad, never mind, look there they are, white sails way off down the bay, too bad, we'll catch them next time, now let's go down the park and kick a football.' Dan however, he'd never drunk from that cup of cold and salt drenched suffering, he had only his imagination to go off, both warped and romanticised. Upon sundown on our first day Dan was sick as a dog and inconsolable, I had to insist he go down for the night. Hugging the bucket, in a cold shell, feather pillows turned to blankets of lead, the reality of life adrift blew in like a cold fist, knocking down the idols, knocking them down in violent waves of sickness. There was no escaping the wrath, nowhere to run and hide, no comfort zone, black water swirled just 5mm past his ear, the rattles and shakes of a boat on the move were never ending. That first night was one to forget. Nothing changed come morning, he was white as a sheet, 'Is this it? How long will it be like this? What do you do all day?' These where the first series of questions. H reached down below Dan's foam lined wooden bunk, 'What you doing?' Dan called out as Harry roughly pretended to search out the pea. For three days Dan puked, as the hours peeled away, he became silent and disheartened. The conditions were perfect, probably the best patch of sailing in 6,000 miles, 15 knots of wind max, full sail, ripping up the

Atlantic at five knots, heaven only knows the state of him had we actually hit some weather. Upon sundown on day three H and I decided our friend wasn't going to make St Helena. 'If we miss Namibia he's screwed.' We got out the books and decided to head in, the closest port a place called Lüderitz on the Skeleton coast, one of only two good harbours in 1,000 miles of desolation, 'He's had enough,' we concluded.

Dan had arrived on the dock carrying just a schoolboy's rucksack, inside it barely enough gear for a change of clothes, to top this his one luxury item was a book entitled something like *100 Worst Stories at Sea*. Who rocks up for their maiden voyage carrying a book about death and wrecked boats? As the days progressed and the sickness took hold things got ugly, in Dan's head everything merged together. 'I saw it,' he said one night, 'an old galleon with full sail heading for the Cape, right against the wind, every boat who sees it goes down, we're doomed!' I'll never know if Dan was hallucinating or acting, if he was offloading his discomfort somehow with stories of ghost ships, or if he was slowly losing his mind, either way he clung onto that tale for days, he just wouldn't drop it, nothing I could do would pry it out from his jaws. Maybe the fear of ship wreck was the only way out from his sickness? Maybe he needed it? Maybe bringing that type of book aboard wasn't rebellious or cocky, maybe it was genius? Either way it must be noted, Dan spent those opening days either puking, complaining or spreading rumours about ghost ships. Catching a shark two days out from Namibia was definitely the moment things started to change for Dan, the excitement of a thrashing fish on the surface seemed to somehow shake away the cobwebs and awake the primitive hunter gather within. 'No way!' He shouted. 'Go H, you got this, you got it!'

We pulled the shark in beside the boat, travelling at four knots a relatively small shark felt eight feet long, it was gnarly and weathered. H reached down and grabbed the metal lead with his bare hands, 'No H,' I yelled, 'cut it off, cut it off.'

'Not a chance,' H replied.

'Dude, that wire could go through your hands, drop it.'

H wouldn't, he wanted the shark, either freed safely or out cold and in the pot, I ran around with a set of pliers and cut the lead myself. A heated argument followed, a brotherly flurry of hot words, in one ear and out the other. The shark sadly got released with a hook lodged firmly in its mouth. The fear of having a sick mate to my left and a fingerless brother to my right was too much. By nightfall everything had simmered down, we sat on the rail all three of us for the first time, eating our one cooked meal of the day out of pint-sized cups, rusted and chipped, full to the brim with rice and fish. The sun sank away and Namibia, a country we never intended to visit, awaited our arrival just beyond the night.

Dunes of sand looked like snow-capped hills from 30 miles out, they caught the light, reaching out above a dark green sea, a cold and unforgiving sea, a sea where big fish lurked in murky water. We'd snapped two fishing rods; we'd lost countless lures, every six hours something monstrous would strike, the reel exploding into life. It was a place unlike any before, even the northern extremity of Australia stood as hospitable and warm by comparison. We sailed up close then ran along the desert until Lüderitz came into view, a natural harbour which parted a never-ending line of white capped waves, waves which broke down onto bare shelves of black rock. The only two palatable things on the menu where oxygen and fish, the miles stretched out hundreds long and thousands square, no fresh water, no trace of humanity, just a sparse and daringly beautiful desert. The sickness drained out of Dan upon seeing this Skeleton Coast, moving bits and loose parts all clicked back into place, that long and tiresome expanse of nothingness had a sudden reboot, it was now sharp and focused, the bare bones of an uncharted hill somehow relit the spark within. A man called Blind Willie Johnson penned the scene with a song called, *'Trouble will soon be over and sorrow will have an end.'* [12]Landfall came in like salvation, albeit comically.

Little Coconut rolled right into those sand dunes of gold, the chains which had bound us, were busted in the night, there was no sickness and no sorrow, the crew had been delivered, not once but twice! Land had been taken, land had been promised, then land had been dually given, between the two, a savannah of desolate wilderness. Such was the nature of this double-edged journey within hours of landfall Dan had forgotten all about the hardship he'd just endured, he couldn't remember anything. We found an oyster bar between some storage sheds, the beer was cold and the seafood just off the boat, 'Twenty dollars this would cost in Perth!' Dan said, as he washed down a small side of cocktail oysters and a cold beer, paid for with pocket change. In a matter of hours our friend had spun 180 degrees, 'I'm not bailing now,' he smiled, 'this is awesome!'

I draw on this landfall because ocean sailing is about coming in. That small sharp leg from South Africa to Namibia was a mock exodus, albeit a week in the wilderness instead of 40 years, albeit from the monotony of privilege instead of from the oppression of slavery, and albeit for the promise of land, any land, instead of an exodus for the promised land herself. Our trip saw many similarities, we like some of the Israelites, had called out for the dock we had sprung from. Sure, that thought might have been just a murmur in H's mind or a passing gust in mine, but it clouded around our friend for many days, it wrapped him up with iron hands. In both tales there is suffering then deliverance then suffering, before finally making landfall. Two sets of chains must be broken, the first to shatter, the old world, the physical connections, the iron framework, the touch, the sight and the smell. Once out in the wild a new battle begins, an internal battle, a battle against sickness, and the wilderness is the perfect battleground because folly can't win, you don't get to front up to the wrath of the sea and make ground. On the old dock you might trick and lie, you might bully or you might hide, none of that is possible when you're fighting the elements, you eat manna and you pray for fresh water. When land comes it is a feeling of profound joy and thankfulness. A sandy wasteland, a shed full of oysters and a cold beer, that was our milk and honey. We couldn't have been happier. It was a moment of sheer joy, it felt like sitting on the summit of a mountain without having to walk back down.

13

St Helena

The next leg was one where we made ground, Little Coconut took us as we slept, the wind was perfect, light and soft, the sea got warmer and warmer, the days fell away, like drops of water, like passing waves, one on top of another until out of the abyss, with hunched shoulders and a high brow, St Helena came into view. At first glance and from twenty miles out the island looked inhospitable, like a solitary boulder left alone, bare stone with nothing to give and nothing to take. As we sailed closer her character changed, her skin warmed and we started to see patches of lush green. Life had somehow leapt across the pond before us, we were sailing in the wake of blown seeds and beneath the tracks of migrating birds. Strangely the character of landfall changed again and again before dropping hook, it returned back to a rocky wasteland as we got beneath her giant cliffs. Nothing of the hills was visible, her stone dark and black, it was if the depths of the sea had given rise, breaking the water in knuckles of molten shelf. As we turned the corner and made our way to the anchorage the sun caught hold, the rock got smoother, and the caps of green hills once again rose up above the volcanic cliffs.

To jump back for a second and explain our route home, Harry and I decided to sail for Brazil. As previously mentioned, in a boat like Little Coconut we needed help from the elements to cross the Equator. In the middle of an ocean, the doldrums are thick and violent, raging and churning, nothing then everything then nothing. One can't sit and sleep in such a sea, there is noise but no movement. Light hulls and large fuel tanks can welly through unhinged, but I had my reservations about Coconut, a vessel whose engine parts had lost their touch, united not in the sweet science of combustion nor the art of propulsion, but instead united with idle chatter, sitting in the mess hall of our engine box like a cackle of council workers sheltering from the threat of possible rain.

'Too much heat!' The would-be shout of our Thermostat.

'Not another day!' The whisper from one Cylinder brother to another.

'My shoes are wet and my missus didn't pack any sandwiches!' The echo bouncing along empty copper pipes in the vacuum of our laid-up heat exchange.

'We're done here!' The shout of our starter motor. 'Not now, not tomorrow, not beneath this dark sky and not until my heat exchange gets his sandwiches!'

I saw the script unfold 500 miles from the arena, I saw it in the splutters and coughs, in the hot head of forty minutes under steam, in the black smoke and in H's resolve never to crank the engine. Our passage back home would pass both St Helena and the Ascension Island before making landfall at Fortaleza in north Brazil. It was there we'd pick up Dad and sail for the Caribbean, we'd pass into the northern hemisphere with water spraying off our gunnels, beneath the banner of a full sail, we'd drop off the old boy, then arc north and run for the Azores, stopping for a pint and bacon sandwich before punting out for Blighty. St Helena was the first stop in a gigantic zig zag up the entire Atlantic. Reaching land so far offshore, in the middle of the ocean, was the first of many boltholes on our climb home, we could sit and rest, we could look down and back or up and forward, we were homeward bound well and truly, there was no going back, no retreat and no surrender.

The anchorage was deep and blue, the type of water one only gets in the middle of an ocean. We dropped at around 50- or 60-foot, H disappeared down the chain for some minutes to check our holding. Two of us rowed ashore and one swam, we tied El Tenderino up on a stone wall and walked ashore to clear in. From first glance St Helena reminded us of home, a slight false sense of security given how far we were in reality. Jersey before the banks landed with their strings of financial workers, Jersey before the tourists and before the cod fishing, Jersey before the farming really took root, must have been somewhere close to St Helena, albeit the local residence of our bailiwick not by in large as pretty, coming in from one or two Breton families total, instead of from a gene pool spanning the whole world. Napoleon wasn't the only one banished out onto a rock in the middle of the sea, hundreds of plantation slaves were brought in, slaves from Madagascar and mainland Africa, from Indonesia, from Taiwan and China, all far corners came to reside at one time or another, even 600 Boers from the Anglo-Boer war in South Africa, were shipped to St Helena as prisoners. The island is so remote that everyone fell beneath the hammer, the guards themselves captive to the hands of geography, even the sailors were banished to some degree, even the governor and his officials weren't free.

For those employed by the British Empire it must have been grim reading, a summoning come sentence, side lined to a pit stop, to a remote rock, dropped down the latitudes, thrown and slung, sent off clutching a cannon ball with just a single length of string tied around the ankle, slapped on the arse and blown through the stable doors with a, 'No worries Jack we'll pull you on back just as soon as you've given us 10 good years.' It was out from beneath the eagle's wing to an island of prey and talon. There is something of the saved and something of the captive engrained in the soil of St Helena, the recluse and the rescued reside side by side, those choosing isolation, those banished, those passing through, they all get lifted up above the waves in the same paw of black cliff.

The first sailors rocked up in 1502, dropping hook on the sheltered west coast, they were the first humans to look upon the island. Elevated above their weary heads, a pristine and untouched ecosystem, an ecological paradise, packed to the rafters with ancient African gum trees. To lift an entire forest out of the depths in such a way, so far from land, not as a chain or as a collection of islands, but as a single entity, it is mind boggling. How did the seeds from the continent arrive and how did they make it up the steep cliffs? Parachuted in maybe? Taken by the wind on the wings of ocean-going birds perhaps? Or transported across the water in the body of a fish, to be hooked out from the deep by the forked beak of a diving bird? A seed deposited onto dry land safely, like the remnants of a chicken Jalfrezi, in the mouth and out the bowels. Maybe the stomach acid of ocean birds can act like an alarm clock, waking seeds up from their slumber, breaking down the walls and gently nudging the soon to be sapling out of bed. Or maybe no vessel was needed? Maybe life can be ground down into a cloud of particles, so small and light each element gets lifted into the atmosphere on molecules of evaporated water, maybe plant cells have chromosomes which split and merge, joining back up in the clouds to drop with the rain thousands of miles from where they left? Or perhaps when God created the trees he did so more literally, could life have shot up from the rocks everywhere all at once, planet wide? No one can detail exactly how it happened or how long it took, to turn rock into forest so far from land. Our history begins right at that moment where the cycle reverses, where humanity enters the fray and that delicate and fragile ecosystem gets opened up like a can of baked beans and swallowed whole, gulped down in just a century or two, down into the bellies of 1000 ravenous sailors.

The first person to settle was Fernandez Lopez a disgraced Portuguese nobleman, the year 1513. Fernandez had defected over to the Moors whilst serving as a soldier in India, he married a maiden of Islam. He was caught by his old firm eventually and put to the knife, they took an ear, they took his right hand and his nose, they cut off a thumb from his left hand and scalped him alive with clam shells, sending him away as a walking example. There is nothing more hideous than an unhinged imperial governor, we learned that much in Rodrigues, a man whose anger is burning, a cat whose wheels just fell off, who can't escape the flames, who sleeps on a bed of tinder, who works so diligently for his fuel, storing in great barns the unstable disposition of his wicked and human nature. Lopez, no doubt a hit with the ladies, whether absentmindedly or whether unknowingly, had dealt this crazy governor a crisp and very public backhand when he jumped the wall to marry in. The very things Alphonso took pride in where dropped, his hard-earned pearls got cast down like aged copper coins, like void currency, thrown beneath the running hooves of herding infidel. Decades of toil out in the sticks fighting for king and country, not even traded with or bargained for, but binned. Loyalty, hierarchy, religion and king, given up in a heartbeat. Such is the nature of pride, the root of all sin, no mercy was given. God, however, he had his own plans. He planted an island paradise for Fernandez, who on his way back to a life of humiliation in Portugal snuck away deep into the forest. For Saint Helena this was the start of her golden age, a time where gardens got tended to and fruit trees blossomed, where ships took away full branches of lemons, where quiet footsteps walked beneath the rustle of countless ancient trees. Fernandez became something of a legend in the sailing circles of his time. In a world so caught up in sickness and suffering, it was Fernandez who embodied their plight, he wore the wounds that blew across the water, he took up his brand when they bit down their knives. The sailors didn't mock and scoff like the courts of Portugal might have, they too were weak and broken from the sea. Fernandez tended his St Helena gardens tirelessly for the sailors; he doubtlessly saved many men with his provisioning. The very man they mutilated, the very man they sent off as an example to be mocked and ridiculed, became an example alright, but not their example, God's example, not of anger and violence but of provisioning, service and self-sacrifice. The news of Fernandez got home; some accounts say he was called back to Portugal where upon the pope himself sought to absolved the transgressions of his past. Instead of staying in Portugal Fernandez opted to return back to St Helena, he'd found purpose and meaning to his work, an island positioned with pin point accuracy, sitting in a sea of loose words like a full stop, right in the perfect place for boats to rest and replenish. A place where the old sentence finishes, where breath is drawn one last time before the new sentence begins.

Skip a few centuries and we land right beneath the cliff, Napoleon Bonaparte is left on a bare hill, guarded by 2,000 men, locked up in a desert of blue. Long wood forest with its mighty army of African gums, felled! The branches of Napoleon's courts, scattered! The blossoms of his victories all gone, split for fire wood, stripped bare into planks and nailed up beneath the grey render of faceless buildings, or bent fast into the belly of a slave ship, dunked in tar, and shot out like a plague across the water. Napoleon lived out the remainder of his life on St Helena, forced upon a rock of non-negotiable peace, the wind he'd been chasing whistling about his ear.

Between the sighting of land in 1503 and Napoleon's burial in 1821 everything about landfall changes, the blunt stones are now sharp volcanic ledges, the green is now grey and the sun has turned to shadow, the sea is kicking up against the land, we jibe the boat, swinging the sails through the wind. For me two big things happened which changed the course of St Helena's history, lifting us out from a rocky wreck to a sheltered bay. Firstly, the abolition of slavery in 1833, secondly, the body of a local population, rising up from the weary soil. The chains of slavery busted from inside the empire, and what stood after was what had grown before, their eyes blue and their skin brown, not solider, not sailor, not prisoner and not slave, but free citizen. Our landfall in 2011 retraced the steps of every ship passing, in doing so the island's past was opened up, we sailed in shadow past the black cliffs until the sun broke back through. So happy to drop hook after 10 days on the ocean, resting our frail bones under the wings of an island which gave its last gum tree for the provision of seafarers. There were maybe 10 other cruising boats sharing the anchorage. Everyone climbed the stairs of Jacob's ladder, standing above the tiny community of James Town, nestled like a spring between the steep hills. Dan's Dad Terry was flying into Ascension Island on a RAF plane, we didn't have long to breathe it all in, our next leg, some 700 miles, would be the last passage with Dan aboard, he'd somehow come up with a genius plan, organising a holiday for Terry and a plane home in one hit.

14

Golf In Ascension

Above the sea was the sand, above the sand the rock and beyond the rock a bare hill, there was no trace of fresh water, all nine holes of Georgetown's golf course were laid bare, each of the flags out of place, floating above an avalanche of Lunar rock, flickering away in space, struck down into the dead earth by the hands of some bygone Apollo mission. Hole number One cried out, 'Lord have mercy, Lord won't you grant us some rain, not one golfer in a whole month, we need greens, we need fresh grass, they just won't play in this dirt.'

'Month,' shouted over Hole Nine shaking his head, 'the cheek of it, you do realise they never finish this course, they start but they don't finish, they get to six and seven but they don't make it to nine.'

'They get to eight,' replied Hole Eight, 'I got a bridie six months ago, landed straight in off the hands of the wind.'

'Liar, shouted Hole Seven, 'not a chance, not with your fairway of crushed rock, not with your putting green of baked earth, not under the rays of this hot sun.'

'It was an egg not a ball you idiot, with a beak not a club, a real birdie, one landed two flew away, they lined my hole with a mass of feathers and nested here for nearly a month, the greatest moment of my life.'

'Stop bragging, I can't listen to this,' continued Hole Seven, 'I cop the sun all day, right on the nut, while you bathe in shade, my shade, snoring happily in the backwaters of your good neighbour's scorched brow. They don't come near me, they fly over and crap down, but they don't land in.'

'And what a blessing that is,' piped up Hole Six, 'east west running holes have 70 percent more chance of copping bird droppings, I lie south to north, the traffic all flies across my fairway not down it. Look how much algae you have as a result, albeit lightly scattered, albeit isolated and patchy, albeit a broadline green, but algae none the less, a rare privilege out here. To top this there are legitimate rumours flying around about a pet lizard, are they true? Come clean now!'

'I don't tell secrets about fauna to holes hording rare species of flora, your north facing ridge is offensive, rocks in shadow, garnished with great crowns of golden lichen, you'll never find my lizard!'

'Stop this right now,' snapped Hole Five, 'we're in this together, things can and will change, we need to be silent and wait, we need to take strength from green mountain!'

'Wise words, Hole Five,' added Hole Four, 'we can't move but we can wait, faded but flying we will one day flicker above banks of lush grass, let us dare to hope, let us look upon the mountain!'

The holes all turned their backs to the thirsty sea, they looked inland to a green hill far away in the distance, the highest hill on the island, a hill dressed in forest.

'How did it go from rock to tree?' questioned Hole Four with a slow sigh. 'How did it go from nothing to thirty, then from thirty to sixty, how did it produce a harvest 100 times what was handed down?'

'Seeds fell up where the clouds pass,' said Hole Three, 'I heard two elderly fellows discussing this very question but two years ago.'

'The same two that collapsed with heat stroke?' questioned Hole Six boldly, 'the same two which got wheelbarrowed off my fairway in a state of delirium? dried and pickled by the midday sun.'

'It was me that did the damage that day,' owned up Hole Five with his head down, 'I triple bogeyed them, I triple bogey everyone, no plus sixties unaccompanied on hole five, we all agreed it, why did I let them on alone.'

'Never mind about the old boys, said Hole Three, 'they lived and anyway it wasn't just you that triple bogeyed them. Now what of those clouds, what of the seeds and what of green mountain.'

'The seeds came in from out beyond the sea,' piped up Hole One. 'In each speck, the makings of a giant house, a house with roots, a house with many rooms, a house to shelter and a house to water, a house filled with rest and peace. The seeds came in the bellies of creaking boats, rattling across the waves in empty envelopes, tied up to bare stalks and bound down in dried out leaves. They got marched up the hill, planted where the clouds pass, where the rocks are filled with water, where ears can hear and where eyes can see. Norfolk Pines, groves of ginger, thick reeds of Bamboo, ferns and grasses, Eucalyptus and pomegranate, apples and oranges, rock to forest in 100 years.'

'All very well but that hill is up in the Heavens and we are down here on Earth, we don't have the reach or the stamina, we don't have strength or ability, we live with the rocks, those wretched golfers, they scoff with shards of blue language, they spit at us, curse the very ground they drive from, ''Bastard of a hole,'' they shout, on a good day. So, what of us? What of the hemmed in and sculpted out? What of the empty and the cracking, the thirsty and the lost?'

'Yeah, how do we reach green mountain?' Repeated Eight and Nine.

'We can't reach it, not on our own merit,' said Hole Two, 'that much is clear. The forest must somehow find a path to us.'

'I've heard this story before,' said Hole One, 'a body of people waiting in the desert, the chaff and the remnant side by side.'

'People in the desert without a club house questioned Hole Four, 'this can't end well.'

'A slightly different breed granted, but folk none the less, their leader held a staff which when struck down, turned the rock into a stream of water.'

'Now that is what I call an iron. Get that man here now,' barked Hole Nine, the most desperate of holes.

'No can do Nine,' said One, the man is dead, his bones have turned back to dust.'

'This gets even worse, even him who turned rock into water is now dust, so we are doomed.'

'Not necessarily Nine,' said One, 'for the power was not of the man but instead of the club.'

'Can we loan it, is it still on Earth? let us loan it for a while, just to get things moving.'

'Loan?' questioned Hole Eight, 'what good is a loan? The sun will dry us back out, it will be worse than when we started, to know all that was gained will one day be lost. If we get the staff, we must find a way to keep it!'

Hole Seven was deep in thought and had been for a while. 'I can't help thinking about brother Charles.'

'Don't do it Seven, we promised never to speak about the death of brother Charles.'

'The worst golfer but the best of men.'

'The kindest and jolliest.'

'With a putt for a drive and a drive for a putt.'

'The kindest and jolliest man that ever walked this course, why rake up such memories Seven, why trouble us in this way.'

'It was a grave mistake, rebranding this forsaken course as a pilgrimage of humility, nectar on a red rose petal, is that for the God-fearing man, pitching golf as a walk through the desert was a total misjudgement, they are not one, they are not the same, and we have all learned a valuable lesson. It is not my want to bring back brother Charles's death and cast us into guilt again, but right before then end, on that dreaded 17th day, still nowhere near making the ninth, right before he fell, brother Charles cried out for the staff of Moses, the same staff which turns rock into water, he called out for it by using the name above all names, for brother Charles, the staff of Moses was Jesus Christ.'

'Still not helping,' cried Five, 'brother Charles obviously didn't get the staff from his Jesus or he would have drunk and lived.'

'Not so Five,' said One, 'I can't believe it took me this long, I can see it.'

'See what?'

'Our place in the forest.'

'Not a chance One!'

'Roots beneath our feet and flowers above our heads.'

'He's losing it!'

'Fruit on the branches and fruit on the ground.'

'Medic, call a Medic!'

'The whole story, it surrounds us.'

'Tell us then, where are these roots Hole One?'

'Buried beneath the rocks of this world, beneath the dead sand and parched ground, beneath this very course, the roots are the roots of his resurrection.'

'And the flowers?'

'The flowers. Look up there, look at green mountain, look at the heights we can't yet reach, they are the flowers of ascension, his ascension, an ascension which blooms for every generation, a branch in flower for every soul that turns to look, for they shall see, even in the darkest valley, the revelation of his promise!'

'And what of the fruit Hole One?'

'Rolling down the hill, tumbling in on the waves, pushed up the beach with the tide, righteous fruit, fruit that grows out from the unseen vine, from his abundant and ever living spirit. Fruit like joy in the desert and peace beneath the baking sun. Fruit possessed by one for the sustenance of another!'

'Keep going.'

'Drink from the water of this world on Friday and you'll thirst Saturday, if the water is taken away, you'll whither Sunday, if your shade fails, you'll be dead by Monday. Jesus brings a different type of water; he speaks of water like a spring welling up to eternal life. Living water that flows out from deep within the rock, from a place where neither man nor element can reach, a place too deep even for hands of darkness. Brother Charles might have looked blistered and beaten from the outside, but he was full of peace within, we all saw it, death had no hold on him, he wasn't thirsty for the world, he drank from the cup of salvation, a cup only God can fill, he cried for the staff of Moses, that lance of light that strikes cold hearts and turns rock into water!'

'Can we eat this fruit? Can we take shade beneath these branches? cried the holes.'

'Lord,' spoke out Hole One in reply, 'it was said that out from these stones you can raise up children of Abraham, well here we are, buried in the desert, shrouded in worry and bitterness, here we are, arguing about shade and lizards, cussing and slandering, envious of everything beyond our reach, even bird droppings. Lord, will you strike us and turn us, lead us to that place in this desert where we will thirst no more. Nothing is impossible for you, you who gives without measure, you who speaks in existence, who draws down time with a single breath, you who blows eternity in through the eye of a needle, through the revolving storm of your own suffering and sacrifice. You whose love is reckless, who weighed up the cost and paid the price, who took the weight of our sin, who walked that slow path up the mountain in his prime and who willingly laid down his life on the altar, Lord have mercy, Lord find us where we stand, Lord reach down and write us in, upon this bed of hot sand may we never thirst again.'

"For the righteous flourish like a palm tree, and grow like a cedar of Lebanon, they are planted in the house of the Lord, they flourish in the courts of the Lord, they bear fruit in old age," they are ever full of sap, they are ever full of green.[13]

***

We couldn't hear the holes when Coconut landed, they sat still and quiet, I must confess to pointing and laughing, playing an actual game never even entered our minds. The nucleus of the whole show was the green mountain. To stand back and look out at it from the rocky shore was supernatural, but to enter beneath the trees was the most natural thing imaginable. The forest whispered and moved in the breeze, it was cool and soothing, the contrast between sand and tree, between the baking sun and the natural shade, was such that for those brief and precious moments we landed clean, passing through untouched, right between the letter A and the letter S, past the word and into the very heart of Ascension. There was no ambition for the future up in those clouds, and there was no contamination from the past, we had landed back in the garden, rags and riches all outside beneath the sun.

A forest of Bamboo up high and a gentle wind blowing, what a sound, each stalk hollow and ever so slightly different, each stalk catching a note, bringing into the light an unseen face, the face of the wind. Countless leaves letting fly the gusts like kites with runs of melody. Leaves and branches like an open palm, offering up to us, the weary traveller, what so often slips through the fingers of man, what we feel but can't catch or see, the bounty of the wind! To chase after such a thing might well be meaningless, but to rest beneath it certainly isn't.

Upon beaching our little yellow tender, we had walked ashore hastily to find Dan's Dad. With only one road and a handful of houses, it didn't take long. Terry was sat like a day time moon, just visible beneath the shade of an open sided inn. Our engine had failed five miles out, it popped and hissed then shot out a cloud of black smoke. The seven days from St Helena, it passed like a breath, we had sat aboard Coconut like elderly monarchs, present but not fully there, our eyes off with the stars, our toes dead on the seabed. The engine failure woke us, we sailed up close, then wailing out on the radio, a fellow cruiser heard our call, they chugged over in a rubber duck, kindly coming alongside to bring us in.

Our landing was both a logistical success and a proper seafaring rendezvous, a moment of heart jumping celebration. Dan's trip had somehow flown through the uprights, it swerved and spun, it hung up in orbit, flying in slow motion for much of the time, then it dipped and like a rock it dropped, right in through the sticks, three points on the whistle. There was energy transferring, from the sky and from the sea. What started with a doubtful but weighted punt, hinged with heavy arms of longsighted anticipation, ended with Terry

Arthur, light footed and waltzing, microphone in hand, backing track blazing, smoothly belting out Mac the Knife, one of his kitchen classics, out sweetly from the mouth and into the ears of a half-empty but fully pissed bar, with flicking lights and punters seeing double. Terry nailed it, he crowned Dan's trip. H and I swam back to Coconut the long way, turning circles in the black sea, the stars softly shining.

15

A Short Stay in Brazil

At sea it is the road that sets the seats apart. First class a gently moving boat, a sail full but not flapping, a wind vane steering, warm weather and clear night skies. Or a book whose pages are turning, open hatches and unspilt tea. First class the sound of big H out cold and snoring at 10 am or simply when you don't have to lift a finger to get over 100 nautical miles in 24 hours. The reality of all this hit me on route to Brazil, I was barely clothed up top, Big Black our light wind genoa was flying so steady it was a celebration just to sit and watch. The South Atlantic was a season of sailing where every element ran smooth, flowing quietly in unison, flat water and steady wind all the way across.

The plan was to pick up Dad in Brazil and sail with him to the Caribbean. He'd secured another holiday, albeit slightly shorter. To top the problem of timing there were added logistical issues. Our engine was down but as it turned out not totally broken. Old diesel Kubota engines are built to last; the heat exchange anode had worn out, probably a while back because we never checked it, the copper pipes then corroded, which in turn stopped the cooling system. Our engine had overheated, it blew off some hoses and shed a cloud of black smoke, but the breakdown was not a major one, the combustion components albeit flogged, were still operational. From that day hence forth, fumes would seep out of an oil overflow pipe into the cabin, the engine became a last resort, a luxury to be used sparingly. Harry had rung home with the part number and Mum had amazingly sourced a new heat exchange, the very same one, from a Kubota factory in Florida, Coconut's country of origin. It arrived the day before Dad's departure, he simply bagged it with his washed smalls, popped a few books in for good measure, then boarded the plane.

As we approached land the air became thick and hot, a haze floated above the water. As night descended small faint lights were spotted, lights H and I hadn't seen before, naked flames like fire flies above the black sea. Beside each naked flame a naked fishman, napping out the early hours. At dawn these little mysteries came into the light of the day, they were wooden rafts, each with a sail and a seat. The boats chugged out using resurrected outboards, engines somehow brought back into the realm of the living, engines still clothed in the drapes of the grave, covered in rust and part buried, limping and chattering, spilling out smoke, but amazingly parting the water. They fished away then sailed back home with the wind to conserve fuel. So constant and gentle the elements, a driftwood fleet had formed across the generations. Boats which wouldn't last a week in the North Atlantic were happily and safely fishing, some 100 miles out, boats not much bigger than a canoe. Our eyes were scanning the water all the way in. Lines or nets, plastic bottles for buoys, sticks of dynamite, we never did figure out exactly how the practice of fishing came to be, all we knew for certain was these guys were barely floating. Coconut was a ship by comparison, and we who nearly got flattened by a tanker in the Indian, had some insight into their fragile state, we kept clear where possible, not wanting to disturb or worry them.

Around Africa the ocean had started out with life in it's veins, the water ran in erratic circles, the wind hit with bluster, one couldn't predict past three or four days. By Brazil the ocean body felt old and predictable, the sea sat quiet in the same seat, for weeks and weeks. Land came in like a never-ending line, like a deadline, unmissable, a sure thing. With the wind so steady, with all the forces in nature gently pushing our backs in, it was a certain. Land was flat and wide, the ocean ended, we didn't escape it, we didn't turn in through towering heads of rock or swing in past a sand point. We kept one course and sailed right up onto the beach, cranking the engine last minute, picking up a buoy and shutting her off before she even drew in any heat.

Dad was flying in and H was intent on picking him up under foot. H had been at sea for weeks and wanted a jog, being a practical guy H decided to jog for a purpose, the purpose being, meeting Dad at the airport. He didn't want a map and refused to plan his route or even acquire some basic directions. He simply donned a set of salty trainers, then looked up at the sky to see where the planes were dropping low, he gauged time by the sun with an outstretched thumb. 'Dad should be here soon,' H said, jogging off like crocodile Dundee, off into a maze of alleyways, into a labyrinth of twisting roads and spaghetti junctions. Two hours later H was back with Dad, they were grinning ear to ear, our road to the Caribbean started in celebration.

We took Dad for a swim in the sea to wash off his air travel then went to find some food. Never in all my days have I eaten in a joint like that one in Fortaleza, and that says something given I once witnessed H pulling out a rodent's rib cage from his curry, he threw the bones to a stray cat then took down the dish. Growing up we were spurred on not to complain and to be grateful for any food handed down with a smile, I always struggled with this. As a child I remember shouting up to my grandad, 'Hey Grandad look an earwig in your salad.' He looked back at me with intensity, then ate it whole before my very eyes. 'Lucky me,' he said, 'they never served us earwigs in Korea, only bullets.' Dad looked disappointed when his order came in, H and I burst out laughing, until that is, our food entered. Dad had ordered fish; one would be hard pressed to dream up a better way to spoil fish. Cook it beyond repair, bake it from soft flakes which dissolve in the mouth to a cube of chewing fat, serve it on a bed of melted cheese, a thick mattress of cheese, off smelling cheese, cheese like mud, different nations of cheese all melted together under one broken banner, cheese that has already enveloped and part digested what was left of the fish. Then add to this dangerous tide, a fistful of old banana. The dish entered our world like a Tsunami, crash-landing onto the table in a giant wave, fish bones bouncing like broken glass or felled trees, mercilessly set loose in a torrent of oil. Dad knew instinctively not to touch it; like the wild animals his appetite ran for the hills, play around with it, smile, make polite gestures but don't eat it, Dad knew straight away this was a dish which wanted to eat him. I however didn't read the warning signs in that place, bending over a toilet sink I drank straight out of the tap, the water was brown, pumped in straight from a Brazilian gutter, one mouthful and I knew trouble was coming, I dry-retched, it was only a matter of time.

We walked the seafront after dinner then went back to the boat, my stomach was starting to cramp, H took the reins on best route back. 'Shouldn't we stick to the main roads?' I said, 'things are a bit more visible!'

'Course not,' replied H, 'the harbour is down here.'

Dad and I followed H into the favela. Before long Dad had secured a following of beggars, he couldn't blend in, white, soft around the edges with a smart shirt. They surrounded Dad as H and I tried to navigate back out onto the main road as quickly as possible. With no purpose in that neighbourhood by all rights we should have been robbed, we looked lost, we didn't have a name, no one from the neighbourhood was showing us round, we weren't visiting anyone or anything, it was rudderless and to make matters worse my stomach was cramping up fast, I felt weak and faint. 'Don't you dare even think about finding a place to go.' I told myself. 'Not an option Hugh, not your dumping ground, now get a grip!' The diarrhoea was coming, H and I somehow pulled Dad out from the tight clutches of desperation and poverty, we made the main road, we walked it down and got back to the safety of Coconut with wallets in hand. For two weeks nothing but liquid passed out of my body, I didn't feel right until Barbados, 1800 nautical miles away. We only had a few days in Brazil, I can't begin to describe a place after such a short pulse of time. It was sad not to have sailed properly in Brazil, sailors like Alex Rust had explored the Amazon, others had visited beautiful islands, or dropped hook outside lush countryside and stayed put for a month straight. For us, we picked up our Dad, caught a stomach bug, shook hands, said thank you, and left with a boat stocked full with the most amazing delights. Back out into the drink, into a different passage of water, one heading off fast, across the Equator and into the northern hemisphere.

16

Caribbean Punch

The door was indeed open, there had been a change in clothes up above our heads, a new beginning that went far beyond fresh stocks and clean T-shirts. The natural forces were shifting, we were right there, as the pull of one magnetic pole lost its grip to the rival hand, we were in that bank of conversion, a belt of latitude where ships have tossed and turned until the brink of madness, with eyes on the horizon, with a working compass and a course in mind, but with no power or propulsion to make it through. Let it be said, to change hemisphere without extreme suffering takes more than just will, it takes a moving body of water, one has to sail into the right current, into the right spirit, one has to know the forces at work and the limits of human endeavour. It is as much about the run beneath the gunnels as it is about the working boat above. The southern hemisphere, it slowly shrank away, Brazil, a country we had only just met, quickly became our greatest friend, banking up all the energy drawn in by the trade winds, and deflecting it north in fast currents, currents fuelled at both ends, by the draw of rising Equatorial air to the north, and by the push of a gentle trade to the east. Like a changing baton, or a torch passed on, a new carriage of water was awaiting us on the other side.

It was the easiest doldrum crossing on record, we drank sundowners, Harry cooked up fresh tuna, bled and delicate, pink in the middle, with lime and finely cut Brazilian chilli. Our angle to the wind had altered, we were due north, this meant a full main, there was no shadow on the genoa. Coconut was flying the whole 1,800 nm, she never went below four knots, not once, averaging a steady five, breaking into the sixes a lot of the time. We were only two days out from South America, land just a short limp away in the unlikely event of breakage. Stunted squalls swept past us, but they lacked the intensity of mid ocean doldrums, and between them, instead of no wind and black skies, was a fresh breeze and blue skies. Never have I felt such peace at sea for such a sustained time, it was a joy, just to watch the clouds pass, they were held up high in a golden light, it was the fastest run since riding down Africa on the Agulhas current.

Barbados greeted us with a carpet of white sand, her east coast sheltered, her palm trees gently waving in the breeze. The water was a milky blue, we dropped hook after clearing in and went swimming with turtles. The leg had been so quick Dad had a good ten days with us in the Caribbean. It was March, after the bustle of Brazil even a strip of sand tailored for cruise ships and tourists felt quiet and settled. Out in the anchorage, our world was detached to some extent, from the comings and goings of life on the beach. Coconut had sailed into a different drift, we didn't see any of our old friends anymore, we were an Australian boat in the North Atlantic, Dad, H and I were a tribe unto our own.

The first major stitch up of our landing involved Dad and a few glasses of Caribbean punch. H and I had never seen him drunk before, not in twenty-something years of living. There were times during our childhood when his senses would dip but they'd never go. Misplaced spectacles a prime example. Our house always made strange noises when Dad lost his specs, a good sixteen stone let loose on the landing, our dog Whooper would calmly make tracks back to her basket under the stairs where she'd wait for the blizzard to pass and for the sound of Dad's feet outside on the gravel. Then there were his trips to the dentist, another fine example, true paradoxes in their own right, certain but never foreseen. 'Not another molar,' or 'liquorice was more prevalent than toothpaste in post war Britain, wasn't it?' Poor Dad would go about his business with a totally numb mouth. I'd get a glimpse into the nature of his early childhood in these moments, a boy of seven, waiting for a train back to boarding school, sat alone at the station, missing his mum, freezing cold, dressed in grey shorts, a cricket bat in his hand and a mouthful of liquorice.

We went for a sundown drink at the yacht club, H and I sticking to cold beers, Dad, lured in by his sweet tooth, went for the punch. There was a band warming up, we sat and listened. The alcohol seemed to hit on the same crest, the first glass caught up by the second, which in turn got swamped by the third, they all rolled in together, crashing ashore, a mass of stumbling hooves. Before long H and I were under his shoulders, one to the left and one to the right, Dad innocently spiked by sugar coated rocket fuel. We walked the old boy out; it was time to evacuate, if Dad connected the beach to the band's drum kit or the full sails of Coconut with the lyrics of his youth, things had the potential to get wild. With a jungle of curls around his ears and a bone-dry desert from forehead to crown, it wouldn't have been pretty, with big clubs and a heavy gut, there was potential for damage, with sight blurred and co-ordination gone, the outcome was likely, with the brakes cut and gas pedal down, the likelihood was beyond reasonable doubt and with his iron frame and massive feet, the consequences were far reaching. H and I, from a health and safety prospective, were liable, the dancefloor was simply not an option. A song like 'Sailing' by Rod Stewart, just too big a risk, if it dropped so too would innocent bystanders, Dad off like a wrecking ball across the oily floor, scuttling people like skittles, into the air with their cold drinks. Getting the big guy back out to Coconut was a challenge in itself. El Tenderino looked up at H and I with a panicked stare, our tender had the eyes of a family Labrador, just before some exuberant relative drops down their excited toddler. The ringing door, the loud embrace, the footsteps, the squeals, the points, the nods, then down into the basket he goes, peace robbed from the dog, a finger in the ear, a clumsy foot, a loving eye gouge. Once aboard, we waded Dad out past the whitewash. The stars above our heads helped distract a barely comprehensible protest about not being allowed to swim. Everything gave way to the milky night, Dad looked up in awe at the heavens as one son rowed and the other swam, napping out the early hours, waking up fresh faced from a deck of dew, from an anchorage bathed in morning light.

***

Two spires of hard rock stood tall above the town, the first a sharp peak, standing like a wave turned to stone, a wave frozen just before it breaks, with enough rock in its crest to fill the canyon and to bury the town. The second peak sat further away, it was slightly flatter, just ramping up, a wave not yet ripe for catching, a wave just moving upon the shelf, a wave which to, had been turned into stone. The rock was young but the town and the forest seemed old, the bay was beautiful, it was quiet and covered in forest.

As we sailed in it was this landscape that took our gaze, rich beyond all measure. Out from the grandeur, from a lush and plentiful land, came the next meeting. Boats of locals spotted us; they raced out in different open-topped vessels. It was around 10 o' clock, we were the only travellers in town. Our greeting with humanity was totally different to our greeting with geography, the people were poor, they were poor in spirit, not visibly hungry, but desperate. Coconut rolled in like a cold can of coke, it took us by surprise. Different locals seemed to have rights to different buoys. Anchoring was simply not an option, to deny their moorings would be like denying the existence of their village. I can't remember how we ended up on what buoy, but after a quiet night beneath a gentle breeze it was somewhat stressful.

We rowed in on a barely floating tender, dressed in threads that had been beaten by the sun for two oceans, there was nothing worth anything upon Coconut's deck. In short everything was going well; we were beneath the radar. It lasted till about lunch on that first day. A small group of children approached Dad, 'Excuse me, good sir,' they said, 'have you any money for food?' Without hesitation Dad reached down into his pocket, I looked over with wishful eyes, 'Please just give them enough for a loaf of bread.' Out came a wad of American bills, the kids started to dance, their eyes lit right up, one punched the air, it was a jackpot, the rusty machine paid out. How much money did Dad give them? I can't say, it was enough to secure a following where ever we went. I remember eating dinner one night in a restaurant, outside the open window a collection of youths called up, 'Can we have more money? We need more money!' They were high on drugs, voices all slurred and full of gravel, they were outside in the darkness and we were inside beneath the lights. They waited for us, longing to eat the scraps thrown down from our table, old T-shirts or foreign coins, it didn't matter. They waited by our tender, they waited outside the restaurant, they were there waiting on the jetty in morning and still up when we rowed off for the night, waiting to take us on a hike up the mountain, waiting to take us out for a day at the cricket. It got heated, such was the desperation. On one occasion I said yes to a local who wanted to take me climbing up the mountain. H and Dad had also said yes independently to another guide. My guide, built like Evander Holyfield, just happened to spot me with H and Dad's guide at the foot of the hill. He was working to clear bush, armed with a machete, bare chested and covered in sweat. 'Far out,' I thought, 'busted by a furious and desperate Holyfield look alike, one carving shrubs up with a blade, I'm in for it.' He approached me bellowing, 'You said I could take you up the mountain!' The dude was super aggressive, I explained it was my intention to go for a swim and H and Dad who wanted to climb the mountain, he walked off in a huff back into the bush and I walked off to the beach.

The story of St Lucia, make no mistake, is the story of the rich man and Lazarus. One lived in luxury dressed in fine linen, the other woke from a bed of sores and waited by the rich man's gates for charity. Such was the state of things even the dogs took pity on Lazarus, licking his wounds. It is a story filled with chasms, comfort above and torment beneath. In death everything is flipped. 'Father Abraham,' the rich man cries, 'have pity on me and send Lazarus to dip the tip of his finger and cool my tongue, because I am in agony in this fire.' But Abraham replied.

'Son, remember that in your lifetime you received your good things, while Lazarus received bad things, but now he is comforted here and you are in agony. And besides all this, between us and you a great chasm has been set in place, so that those who want to go from here to you cannot, nor can anyone cross over from there to us.'

He answered, 'Then I beg you, father, send Lazarus to my family, for I have five brothers. Let him warn them, so that they will not also come to this place of torment.'

Abraham replied, 'They have Moses and the Prophets; let them listen to them.'

'No, father Abraham,' he said, 'but if someone from the dead goes to them, they will repent.'

He said to him, 'If they do not listen to Moses and the Prophets, they will not be convinced even if someone rises from the dead.'[14]

Lazarus is named by God, the rich man unnamed by God, Lazarus saved and the rich man condemned. Bones beneath the clothes, truth everywhere, real characters from the past and real-time souls on the line in the present. 'If they do not listen to Moses and the prophets, they will not be convinced even if someone rises from the dead.'[15] That verse is reinstated, not even Jesus in the heart of his ministry could make them see, nor the miraculous tales of his resurrection to come, nor the life changing testimonies that followed. Saul blinded on the road to Damascus, it means nothing to them. We sat at the rich man's table for much of the time in the Caribbean, the gates where shaking, wooden shacks on one side of the stream, massive luxury hotels on the other.

***

Dad's big goodbye was a day at the cricket. A local chap who I'll call John, took us up the coast for a princely sum. We went by way of water, tearing to the game on his old open-topped run around, dropping in to pick up crew from various villages en route, mates informed most likely about a free ride to the game. Australia beat the West Indies but it didn't seem to impact the crowd in the slightest, they were in good spirits all day long. After the game we walked back towards the harbour in a sea of people, we hadn't seen John for hours, his cousin had come and gone, our ride back to

Coconut at that point seemed unlikely. Sitting on a grassy knoll, some way from the stadium, we heard a dude hollering. 'Hey there, this way guys.' The chap was a friend of John's, full of fake gold and white teeth. 'I'm taking you back to the boat.' He knew us, we had never seen him, he was waiting as if by accident, waiting like a fisherman does for shrimp, a man who knew the currents, the incoming tide of people slow and scattered, the outgoing herd, a mass of water. He waited by his chosen rock and swiped us out from the crowd without having to think. We followed him down to the harbour, joining his friends aboard another rusty motor, cranking up and chugging off into the night. Dad left the next day, John sped round and picked him up from Coconut, it was farewell again, our trip into the northern hemisphere complete. H and I sailed on, we stopped at one more place in St Lucia, an anchorage far beyond the gates and well inside the walls. Dominica was our favourite island, its saving grace, no white beaches, all tourists searching for sand and sunbeds left sorry, there were no big ugly four-star hotels on the island, at least not where we dropped hook, no swimming pools and no swanky bars. The forest was thick and rich, full of natural fruit, the island was wild and rugged. We kept up a steady march north until our salt water pump gave up the ghost. The blowout in Ascension had axed the cooling system. Our new pump took ten or so days to arrive. We sailed into English harbour Antigua, H walked Coconut deep into the anchorage, he dived down the chain, picked the anchor up, running it ten feet across the sand, rising to take a breath, then repeating the exercise until Coconut sat pretty between an armada of boats.

Freeman's Bay in English harbour, that was our anchorage, two fingers of rock almost pinched the bay closed, we'd entered the mouth of a mini waterway, an aquatic cul-de-sac. There were boats everywhere, the masses all anchored off in the fringes, the smart boats tucked in close. Nelson's Dockyard was the focal point, H and I rowed over to clear Customs. English harbour was an easy place to sail into but a hard place to leave, we got slow cooked, seasoned with salt, stirred up with all the other crews, washed around by an endless stream of booze. We woke up one morning with itchy feet. I walked past an English skipper, he'd been drinking so hard for ten days he didn't even recognise us, walking past like a ghost. Crusty hitchhikers by the juggling tree were threatening to start a new dance, dreadlocks and fireballs, a bad combo. Everything seemed off, the regatta had finished and the German dude on a neighbouring boat had lost his speedos. 'Let's bail,' said H, and with that we stuffed El Tenderino with oranges, fresh water, canned tomatoes and rice, then punted out for Europe.

17

Homeward Bound in the North Atlantic

That patch of sea between the Caribbean and Europe, that is where the famous song *Amazing Grace* began, the shoot hadn't surfaced obviously, the song had no face, it was leafless and without root, but there deep beneath the skin of John Newton, held tight in clubs of white knuckle, fed by blood beating out from a heart gripped with fear, caught beneath the blanket of death, *Amazing Grace* was born. In the cradle of a storm, in the creaking and splintered hands of a sinking ship, in the soul of a man who knew just how wicked he had become, a man who in that moment, was so deeply frightened of death. Newton cried out to God just as Jonah did, from the roots of the mountains, with engulfing waters threatening and the deep surrounding all walls, he cried out for

God's mercy, because like Jonah, John knew, 'Salvation comes from the Lord alone.' Newton at that time was more Ninevite than Israelite, persecutor not prophet, he dealt in the trade and exploitation of human beings. With his living cargo traded for sugar and spice, the pockets of his ship were full, dark clouds of sickness rolled over the boat, weeks at sea fighting gales had ground his pride to flour, then the spearhead of a storm off Ireland drove it through, something cracked in John, the mountain fell to the sea and another Christian journey began, one crowned with those famous lyrics, 'Amazing Grace how sweet the sound that saved a wretch like me.'[16]

Back upon the beaches of the Caribbean, bound and chained, another part of the song drew heavy breath, the part that gave up its earth to build the mountain, voices in the darkness without shame. 'Blessed are the poor in spirit, for theirs is the kingdom of heaven.'[17] Out walked the blessed, not enthroned but shackled, betrayed first like Christ was, from deep within, by a rival tribe or by an earthly chief. Into the hands of Arab traders they went, tethered to horses, marched in lines down to the coast. From the coast they boarded ships bound for the colonies, from one master to another, from one plantation to another, in each exchange, the earth above their heads towered higher and the valley beneath their feet sunk lower. There in the darkness, there was nowhere to run, when the truth eventually tumbled in, when Jesus entered their world, the fear of death, it shattered into pieces. 'Swing Low, Sweet Chariot, coming forth to carry me home, swing low sweet chariot, coming forth to carry me home.' That spirit of Elijah, it lives in *Amazing Grace* too, not in lyric but in melody. It is the melody of those who dug the earth and not those who built their world on top of it, a melody sung generations before it was ever written. When the two meet in *Amazing Grace*, the valley is filled and the mountain flattened, Heaven is brought down, both parties are reconciled together, the last then is first now, lifting the lyrics up and walking the whole show out past the bullshit, out into a different hemisphere of living.

H and I would follow a similar line to John Newton out from the Caribbean, ducking into the Azores instead of arcing wide for Ireland. It took us all one month to cross. We left the Caribbean and the sun stopped shining, the waves turned, they crashed and splashed and foamed at the mouth, they turned the water, the fish left and everything around us got cold, we were entombed, in a barren world, in a dead sea. H, Dad and I, we tightened our bonds. Dad would ring with weather updates every day, sometimes twice a day, he was glued to the live data, to the happenings of the present. H was busy reading the historical records, the wind patterns of the past. 'Further north,' H would say, 'we need to get deep into the westerly stream.' Dad would reply back in the morning to the decisions of the night, 'too far, head back down, big lows coming in, the jet stream has moved, start heading south.' We ended up sailing a track between both lines. With Dad in one ear and H in the other, Coconut was strangely balanced, catching the edge of some rolling storms, but staying in the stream.

Opposition from the outside soon became opposition on the inside. Our self-steerer gave up the ghost, it wouldn't hold our line for love or money, not for more than 20 seconds. Out there in the wind 1,000 miles from anywhere, it was our time to do a medley, to 'Get one's nut down and go in.' H and I rolled out the watches for 31 days straight, by the end we lived off canned tomatoes and rice, it was bare poles at times, no sails up, Coconut driven through the water at hull speed, maxed out, breaching sideways when the waves crashed down upon our deck. We strapped ourselves to the wheel and hand-steered for 2,000 miles straight, pushed hard the whole way. We ate like prisoners, H would throw the hatch open, passing the food out in a flash, he'd slam the hatch closed before a wave could break in. Coconut has no cockpit, 30 foot of hull in the water and a flush deck, we were in the elements, it was like trying to eat dinner in a giant washing machine. It took us one month to reach the Azores, at times the wind came in on the nose and we had to heave-to, sometimes for days straight. The ocean was a mass of white horses when we finally arrived, the Azores stood tall, green hills waiting for our arrival. The smell of land hit us and our hearts started to beat fast. I was fearful of the entrance, the deep gave way, her white crests crashing hard upon steep black cliffs. 'The wind will swing in that hollow,' I said, 'we should gybe, safer to stay in the heart of the channel.'

'No need,' said H, 'it's fine.'

'Not fine,' I replied, 'Anything but, we're heading for the cliff, look at the shape of those hills, the wind is going to move in there.'

'Bullshit, the wind will swing,' replied H. 'Let's stand firm and sail tight.'

After a month at sea without one argument, it was only fitting to let off some steam given the finish was within reach and we were under the cloak of landfall. I was strangely anxious to come in, 100 metres looked like 10 metres, what I thought was 2 minutes was 2 hours, my mind was recalibrating, the hills looked like mountains, we could smell the grass and the mud.

As we got closer, it became apparent we had crossed a chasm, gone from an empty world into a full one, crossed from suffering into safety, from sleeplessness to peace. We had a landing party at the Azores, made up of two special people, Mum and Madeleine, they had flown over from Jersey to see us in. Our sail home was dedicated to Madeleine's son Ben, a family friend and a marine who died tragically whilst training for the SBS. Nick and Madeleine set up a charity called Challenge4Ben, our trip just one of the many other challenges. Madeleine flying over to meet us was a big moment on our journey home. They stood up on the cliff that morning we arrived, staring out into the white horses, wondering where we were and when we would land.

Ben was a true soldier, he'd toured in Iraq and Afghanistan. By true soldier I mean, at that young age, when you have it all, he gave it all, not to selfish pursuits, but to service and sacrifice, like a knight of old. I can't speak into the loss his family live with, into that grief, into that void, but I can write with hope. I can point to the footsteps Ben followed, out from a comfortable island home, into the wilderness, to walk a frozen mile beneath a broken sky. I can point to those ancient footsteps and see a host of fallen sons whose valour the decades cannot decay, their faces forever young. To fall in those footsteps, out in the barren heights of human endurance, for a glory far greater than one's own, is to reach a hilltop crowned in light, a hilltop few find. 'Where I am, there also my servant be.'[18] Set apart, not to isolate or to glorify the servant, but to wake us up, us who live at the foot of the hill, us who age and us who groan, to call us on, into a bearing of substance and purpose. That is what Challenge4Ben meant on Little Coconut.

Royal Marine Ben Poole serving in Afghanistan

The book of Revelation writes, 'He will wipe every tear from their eyes, there will be no more death, or mourning or crying or pain, for the old order of things has passed away.'[19] H and I, we took down just a taster of that promise in Peter Cafe Sport at Faial. Everyone crossing that year had been pushed hard, everyone was in safe. One captain was heralding it the worst in all twelve of his Atlantic crossings. The old order was gone, the suffering over. Cats couldn't contain themselves; it was cloud nine. Our friend Daniel, a solo sailing Swede, he resurfaced like a wartime submarine, we hadn't seen him since South Africa, he walked along the harbour after 70 days alone at sea, opened the bar door, beer spilling and Johnny Cash blaring, he closed the door softly and walked back to his boat, knocking on Coconut come morning for breakfast.

'He will wipe every tear from their eyes, there will be no more death, or mourning or crying or pain, for the old order of things has passed away.'[20] This line can never be fully grasped this side of the grave, like a letter it can be carried but not opened yet, carried across the waves, carried in songs like *Amazing Grace* and *Swing Low Sweet Chariot*, carried through suffering, grief and loss, carried in shallow hands, like the hard passage we endured. We must never drop the promise, never let it fly out of our hands, never let a cruel wind steal it, or a heavy wave rip it from our hearts. Romans 8 v 38 goes, 'For I am convinced that neither death nor life, neither angles nor demons, neither the present or the future, neither height nor depth, nor anything else in all creation, will be able to separate us from the love of God that is in Christ Jesus our Lord.'[21] Christ suffered with us, he was in the boat remember, asleep in the storm. Christ was begotten not made, that means from a place of glory into a place of brokenness, from the safety into the pit. He suffered death, he cried out 'My God, my God why have you forsaken me,'[22] he was tortured and mocked, pieced for transgression, such was the state of distress, his sweat was like drops of blood. He suffered in every way possible, mentally and physically, he was the man of constant sorrow, pinned up between the joker and thief. Christ suffered and died for us, because he loves us, because he wants us to partake in his glory, he wants us to share in his inheritance, he is a God that loves recklessly, a God that cares so greatly for our eternal future he has already done the work and won the spiritual battle for our lives. We struck him at his weakest, we struck him to make sure he was dead, with a lance, a wooden rod with a metal spike, yet when he strikes us at our weakest, it is with light! A light that can pierce into the deepest and darkest moments of human experience.

18

Grandma and the Sea

Grandma was old as the towering pine trees of her garden in my eyes. The planes that zoomed above her head as a child, they were bombers and spitfires, dressed in brown and green. She was a Buxton from Norfolk, the land flat and the sea cold. She was raised on the broads, beneath the rustle of reed beds, with roads of still water, shimmering silver, catching the light and parting fields of wheat and barley. The natural landscape of her youth, it was alive in Grandma right up to the very end. She would frequently proclaim, 'Look, another pheasant!' aged 86, confined to a winter house, pointing up at a white ceiling, her spirit resting deep in the marrow of her fragile body, wrapped up beneath the blanket, lost at times beneath the fog of her deteriorating mind, cracking by the fireside and waiting for her celestial spring.

Dad approached Grandma about making the trip over from Jersey to Cornwall for our landing, he gently dropped the trusty pitchfork favoured to persuade other herdable family members behind the door, he walked into the kitchen and announced, 'The boys will arrive back sometime next week!'

'Just brilliant, and what boys are these?'

'My boys.'

'Young Edward?'

'Not Edward, Hugh and Harry, in from Australia on their boat.'

'In from Australia! Splendid, I should like to be there for that.'

'Then so you shall,' said Dad.

Grandma could have waited one week and seen us land in Jersey but she wanted to travel out to see us in, she couldn't wait, she'd been sitting in the same chair all winter. If H and I thought the weeks were slow sometimes out at sea, what of her world? When the sun rises up at Grandma's house, it hits the same patch of white rendered wall, it sets behind the woods outside her kitchen. Was Grandma not residing in a ship of sorts? Had the details of her surroundings not been blown flat by the wind? Had the world outside her walls not become an ocean? If one reads then naps, then wakes to do nothing more then read, that person is in transit, that person is sailing! When a veteran pensioner travels out to an ocean sailor, it is an embrace from one seafarer to another.

Mum, Dad and sister Dawny journeyed over with Grandma, travelling out from the Bailiwick, across the channel then down the A30. The counties of England along the South Coast, they don't change much untill you cross Tamar River and rise up onto Bodmin Moore. Cornwall stands alone, like a rough old coat pegged onto a single hook, Devon pulled back east of the river, yoked in with the softer threads of Dorset and Somerset. Cornwall hangs its cloth out west, dripping wet on the outside, still warm on the inside, pegged out beyond the warmth of England's kitchen, out in the Atlantic draft, a coat lined with waxed and weather-beaten shrubs, with tin cliffs that rise at the collar and fall down upon a floor of golden sand. The China Clay pit hills of St Austell catch the light like shining buckles, the coat hangs heavy, pockets of copper drummed down deep into the rock, with a soft underside patched in calm woodland bays and winding rivers. The entire county studded with strange sounding names like Nanquidno and Nanjizal. You don't sail past, that first coat in the corridor, it is the warmest and the most weather proof, you're guaranteed shelter, before any other garment gets donned, you come out of the ocean and make landfall in Cornwall, you take off those wet cold socks and warm the cockles in a pub right on the waterline, with Cornish ale and hot pasties. If we headed straight for Jersey, it would have been a pint of cow's milk and a cookie, a remedy for tired babies not weathered seadogs! H and I didn't want to go straight home, Cornwall was the only shout for landfall, nowhere else came close.

Dad assembled representatives of our clan with heightened enthusiasm, brother Ed came down from Oxford, Aunt Mary from London, we had big Uncle James with a vice for a handshake and Cousin Tor for her sins, beckoned in by the big guy, given no option but an early start. Dad hired a fishing boat, he woke everyone up ridiculously early, they all headed out to find us. Summer was in full bloom; the fields were green;

the ocean was calm and settled. H and I had a fast passage over from the Azores, we got hit by one band of wind and cloud, it ripped through like a giant eraser and washed everything away, it ran off before long and we were left beneath blue skies, flying with just our cutter sail up. We hand-steered the whole passage, spotting the Lizard lighthouse in the darkness before dawn. We met them all somewhere off Helford River, a blue hull steamed towards us with a collection of waving quests. There is something fragile about meeting on the water, beneath the hum of diesel engines, with waves running past and a gentle breeze blowing across one's bow. You can shout but they can't properly hear, you can frantically wave your hands but you can't reach across for a bear hug. A cold can of beer slung through the air, that was about the only thing we caught clean from their fishing boat, the meeting had taken place, we were joined by an invisible thread, steaming in together. After the initial buzz everyone settled down, Coconut had a full main flying, we were motor sailing with our jib rolled in. Sharing that last furlong, it was a peaceful moment, it was enough, just to look out and see them looking back at us, we parted the water together, we tied up on the same dock, the fisherman dropped off our party and we united on the pontoon.

Grandma got lifted up like a child, over the rails and onto Little Coconut. Coconut and Grandma were from the same world, when they sat there together you could see it. Coconut's ribs and Grandma's stomach, made of the same steel. Grandma had a keen eye, she'd pick her summer gooseberries months early, no messing around with prep work, in they went with whole leaves and twigs, bark and loose flowers, down with gusto into her wartime crumble, glazed together, a thick mass of acidic magma, piping hot and pig sour, simmering like the earth's core in the vaults of her cast iron aga. Above the foraged fruits, a thick impenetrable crust of deep larder biscuit, called in last minute from the far corners of some high and dusty shelf, bashed with a rolling pin and let loose like a sand storm. Grandma cooked her puddings for long sustained periods of time, they were tectonic, they arrived on the table ready to pop, she would then unleash great ice-cold bergs into the bowls, her two hands wrapped around a dull silver serving spoon. Wedges of whatever diary product her fridge freezer could muster, broken off from an ancient raft of wartime ice, from the great ice sheet itself, a frozen store that served Grandma faithfully right through the decades, from the cradle to the grave. To eat such a dish, it took character, to nod approvingly with a piping hot garden gooseberry in the mouth, that doesn't come naturally, one has to keep at it.

A night watch aboard Coconut wasn't far off from an Oaklands gooseberry crumble, bare steel ribs cold to touch, a thin foam mat on a wooden bench, awake in a cold sleeping bag, oil skins dripping wet on the floor, forty minutes till you're back on watch, three knots across the water, one week in, three weeks to go, no sleep, Coconut chewing through the chop like Grandma would her own cooking. 'How delightful, my what great berries we have this year, we did get some good days in March, how lucky we are.' Coconut would smash the miles, weeks on end, head down, H and I just had to hang on, our work, the gentle and cautious art of separating fruit from stone, humour like spoons of sugar, down into the dish with unceasing regularity. We learnt over time what part of the deck one could safely walk out on, where to start and how to politely finish. Some days we just had to suck it up and take down an entire plum stone, there were times when we had no choice but to throw everything to the dogs, stopping the watches, lashing the tiller and going down for some undisturbed sleep. We learnt not to fear the dark twigs in our pudding, pretty soon we were picking our teeth with them and laughing. Grandma and Coconut, they never complained, endurance and simplicity that was their world. Grandma's character didn't just raise acidic berries from the mud; it worked the other way too, you could get the best chef in Paris to cook pudding, in Grandma's world, it was on par with her crumble, they were both 'delightful,' the same word with the same sincerity, used to describe two dishes that couldn't have been further apart, it was awesome. For Grandma it was all about the heart, about the people around the table. 'Give us this day our daily bread,'[23] God never promised fine dining, he promised sustenance and love, that was Grandma's cooking, she really did try, and that was Coconut's sailing, both carried us safely across.

That morning in Falmouth, it was a break in the clouds, a time where we sat beside Grandma and shared a moment with her in full. The occasion served to preserve the memory, it silenced the world around us, all the noise was drowned dead. Climbing down into the cabin with Grandma, sitting beside her inside the ribs of Coconut, it felt like sharing an empty church, like a bare cave or a quiet tomb. Years later I was sailing in the South Pacific when she died, I never got to say goodbye to her, God gave us that moment instead, a moment sown in weakness, but one raised with power. There was a decline to Grandma at the end of her life, she hit a band of fog like many seafarers do when they approach land after a long road, her spirit knew what was happening, it left the wheelhouse and went down to rest in the marrow of her bones, down in the deep chambers of her heart. Occasionally she would rear up above the fluster of voices on deck and say things like, 'Keep your eyes on me!' Her mind got muddled, the ropes knotted, she waited in the fog for her landfall, her daughters took the reins and cared for her diligently, keeping her in a bay of calm water till God, in his perfect timing, called her in.

Fog on the water, it rips up the rug from beneath one's feet. Back before GPS the nerve and seamanship of a sailor would be greatly tested in the fog, today we get off lightly. H and I left Cornwall and hit pea soup, we had no AIS or radar aboard, Little Coconut couldn't see the big ships in the Channel. We sailed home in a cloud, in a smoke-filled bubble, the bellow of big ships echoing through the night. The tide off Guernsey, it ripped up the broth, the water swirled and gushed, it was getting funnelled over a shallow seabed, reefs of grey granite, rocks like teeth, they reared up close by, we could picture them in our imagination but could not see them, the environment had changed, the fog couldn't conceal it, we had entered the waters of the Channel Islands at last.

We arrived mid-week, friends of Dad wanted to organise a group of Jersey boats to come out in celebration, we were too impatient to wait till the weekend and the fog served to ensure only the hardiest of boats were out beyond the harbour walls trying to find us. Just as a pink granite cliff came into view, two good friends, big Josh and Rich steamed up to us through the mist. Sat beside big Josh, a blond-haired girl who H and I had never seen before. Shortly after another motor vessel found us, filled with a deck of waving cousins and family friends, we motored across St Aubin's Bay into the marina. Right on the sea wall as we came in Jamie shouted down to us, he was on a bicycle, he'd left us in Cairns over a year ago. To see Coconut bust in on the tide, to look down and see the old crew coming in, that was a rare and beautiful sight, I do believe Jamie had a lump in his throat. I can't remember anything else of the day other than there were a lot of onlookers and well-wishers, it was noisy, the local rag showed up, there was a bit of fuss, hot air really, by the time the fog burnt off everything had settled down, the pensioners on the sea wall went back for their afternoon tea and we, reunited with our beloved family Jack Russell, got in a car and went back home for a well-earned steak dinner, our journey from Australia, it had nowhere left to run, the wick hit the wax, our candle was out.

Once you break the tape and eat your fill of cake, what next? After a few days my bones got restless, I was twenty-seven at the time. Borrowing cash from the old man to go down the pub, it didn't sit right, the feeling I mean, not the beer. I was starting to go bald, sponging with a bald head, whilst sat in a pair of your old man's washed smalls, five pints down, it was over the line. 'Mum!' I shouted one morning from the top of the stairs, 'Dad's out of boxers again and I need ten pounds immediately, no more milk!'

It was too much, it didn't add up, it couldn't add up because nothing about anything was justified or justifiable, no amount of ocean crossings mattered. Our granite farm house felt small and Jersey, I just couldn't picture staying. I rang up a contact back in the mines, he promptly lined me up with an underground gig in no time at all, he even paid for my flights back to Australia. Within three weeks of landing, I was off. It felt nuts flying across the oceans without being able to experience them, without having to lift a finger. Harry in true maverick fashion married the first girl he laid eyes on upon coming in, literally. That girl in the rib sat next to big Josh, H and her got hitched, they fell in love, they met in the mist, their worlds had been concealed up until that moment. Our homecoming, for H especially, was a collision of providence. When Coconut hit those pink granite cliffs, H truly landed. I like to think the spartan sea and my ugly mug played an extra role in that divinely authored script, even if our desert trail through the blue only draws light on a small section of the picture. Either way, H saw a bright future back home, like two fish swimming upstream in the same run of rapid, once we hit a patch of quiet water, the pond drew us apart, it was only natural, for brothers it was no big deal, we didn't give it a second thought, we landed and I bailed before anything had the chance to sink in. A slam dunk on the whistle, a boot to the sports hall's double doors and away I went, into the fresh air, head back and arms a blaze like Eric Liddle. 24 hours of air travel and I was right back at the start line, dressed in mining overalls one week and board shorts the next, flying between the desert and the beach.

19

Spire above the Grass

L imbo is a place between two worlds, a muddled mind in the air and two pairs of shoes on the ground, a wilderness one side of the hinterland hills and a land of milk and honey on the other. Limbo is a tin-can plane that bounces between the honey and the dust, a plane that rattles in the turbulence, a plane riddled in rust. I was back under those wings, in a carriage packed with miners, their heads were down, they sat quiet like stones, we were flying in for work and I wondered if the propellers could handle the weight.

This was a mine hanging on, a mine lampooned to an ore body running dry, a mine too deep for the spoils it was chasing. Mapping it, blowing it, trucking it and pumping the stope with paste took everything, there was little fat left, the company operated right beneath the brink of collapse. Under this heading a troop of fielders took their instruction, with a squad of young engineers that bounced around like summer crickets, nutting the rock, dizzy and pale white. They flew around our offices with their scribbled plans, constantly trying to float a sinking stone, they had to run everything pass King Kuma, the mine's resident Geotech, who could be found napping out his afternoons in the tech services bus, sleeping off a heavy lunch, aware of the situation, but equally aware of his inability to change the outcome. The mine ran 365 days of the year, all day and all night. Christmas was a paper plate and a plastic cup, white bread rolls and a box of wet prawns. We stood in our overalls and ate quietly. The pit was connected to a small town by a long straight road, the town connected to a far-off city by a runway. It was a landscape that reached out wide but caught hold of little, not a hillock in its hands, dressed by the comb of a bone-dry wind, the burning sun was its only true and lasting companion. We had to fit half a day's work into a full day, six hours into twelve hours, I had arrived into a rigid structure, one couldn't reach across and help another department when things got slow, that would be like stealing eggs or stepping on another man's shoes. We caught our bus out in darkness and we returned in darkness. I worked as a surveyor, I was alone for much of the time, mapping tunnels and scanning stopes, I'd set up the rigs with grade and line to keep things roughly on script. My camel was a thirsty Ute, a Toyota Landcruiser, we'd rock around underground between the different crews. Our shifts lined up like hurdles, seasoned miners had the race down, three long strides and over each hurdle they jumped. Others, lesser miners, ran blind and red-faced, stumbling and cursing, drinking beer long into the night, then cracking a can of Red Bull as the bus drew up beneath a rising sun, heads beating and eyes red. Off the bus they went with startled looks, 'What on earth is that distant heavenly body rising from the dust?!'

'Quick, run!' They'd snarl, 'not the sun.' Across like ants on a dirt track, they went, mullets and tight rugby league shorts the order of the day, flip flops and baseball caps, into the dugout and down the hole for 12 hours, 'Best place for them,' the old boys would cry! Fly home day, that was the promise that kept the beat going. Those leaving would head down early and set things up for the cats coming in, we'd pack our bags, have a cold shower, then depart with high spirits, five well-earned days the reward, coupled with a generous haul of cash.

There was a line in the sand where the wilderness got stopped cold. Flying back to the coast I'd see it in the landscape and my heart would jump. The dirt and the dust turned into green pasture, then a tide of Hinterland hills broke the flat earth, they rose up to take the moisture from the sky, hills covered in thick forest. Each basin had a creek and each creek stretched out its hands to touch the sea in a finger of still water, to lay its cargo down on a series of sand points. The geology was set up for rich and diverse life. On the ground between hill and coast, a soft mattress of sedimentary earth, a vast run of alluvium sand, this bed stalled the fresh water on its way to the sea, colourful birds filled the branches, bats hung asleep beneath the leaves, tropical fish hid behind sunken stones. On a pushing tide, salt water from the ocean moves in shore, the brown ebb beaten back by barrows of Pacific blue. Each sand point had a perfect right hander, the waves broke hard and reeled down the line, it was a paradise, a geological marvel, an enclave in the wilderness.

We made this coast our home during my years in Australia, when I returned from sailing my English comrades still hadn't made a single Australian mate, they lived like my ancestors did, like a tribe of wandering Jews. Red meat and cold beer aside, the culture of the Gold Coast had not penetrated the clan. Paul Salmon's skin was still white like the white cliffs of Dover, his hair a rusty mop a crimson top, not burning red, not flaming like an Australian red head, not bleached at the edges, but the colour of an English country lane in November, full of cracked chestnuts and dark puddles, brown bark near the roots with a mud red canopy leaf! Salmon came over on a gust of wind and looked perpetually lost, he was a pot-bellied coot or a country pigeon, there was nothing tropical about Paul, no bright feathers or giant nut-cracking bill, no plumage to speak of, he'd look across at the parrots and flaming galahs with a side glance and a poker face. You could track Paul through the roost by the drips of his teabag, he'd walk it to the nearest window and lob it straight out onto the street below, he would smoke indoors if he could get away with it. When Salmon got booted out of Christian flat share, he tossed his unmade bed upon the tin roof of his motor, mattress and frame hanging on, sheets and duvet flapping in the breeze, off down the highway they went, off to find a new abode. He was impulsive, 'Man I'm driving to Sydney to pick up a mirror dinghy, see you in three days.' Salmon was sensitive to, sensitive and rarely satisfied. The only part of his entire body tuned up were his hands, Salmon was a guitar player, his fingers like a squad of marines, gristle and bone. He had a natural frame, a wiry strength, but this side of Paul was not cultivated, Paul would not touch the plough unless his life depended upon it. After about one year of mining, we moved in together, we lived a stone's throw from the beach beneath old Mikey, our ground floor flat faced the ocean, the sun rose up and sent a flood of light straight in through our front door. Given we were only back five days in a fortnight we camped out. There were no soft furnishings, no books on the shelves, our cupboards bare, our fridge ice cold but empty. Salmon collected musical paraphernalia, every square metre of floor had something sprawled upon it capable of letting off sound, a full drum kit was set up in our kitchen, there were amps everywhere, with lesser instruments hiding in the shadows, shaking musical eggs or rusty tambourines, boom boxes or bongos. Salmon's world swallowed up our tiny flat like a great big musical whale, with a tongue like a drum, metallic tonsils banging upon hollow walls, with a heart that let fly its beat, off down the spine, down a neck of tort strings, out to the flippers and down to the tail, ripples of sound, through the window and out into the street. Going for a piss in the middle of the night, especially for none musicians, was alarming and hazardous, with an array of loose cymbals waiting in the darkness, hunched in their traps like sprinters, waiting for even the lightest brush to sound their release.

'How are you guys going to get girlfriends?' said Bart frequently, rightly concerned, 'stop buying your cloths from Kmart, hang some pictures, get a TV.' Bart wasn't the only Brit worried, finding a mate for Salmon and I was concerning the whole tribe, a wood pigeon and a scruffy seagull, nearing thirty, one pasty white, the other fat and fast balding, surrounded by birds of paradise, taken from cold water and shadowy

glades, placed into a tropical wonderland. It was no wonder
our feathers attracted little attention from the ladies of the
Gold Coast. My life hung between the mines and the surf, one
thread like spit the other like mud, the swings they wrapped
around my head. We had entered a cocoon from which there
was no escape. Salmon would cry out, 'I'm moving to Kenya
to join my brother's band.' Walt, my Cornish mate, he would
laugh so hard, Salmon wasn't going anywhere, FIFO mining
had us all bound up, all three of us, hanging from the wire. It
was a period of profound transformation, as Red from Shaw-
shank prison said, 'You can get busy living or get busy dying.'
I crawled out from that thick coat of FIFO mining four years
later a changed man.

The critic might point at the bumpy flight of a
mud-coloured moth and laugh, as if to say he has broken out
from his cocoon much the same, for his wings don't really
work, his eyes are blurred, and he knows not the difference between lamp and moon, until that is, he lands clumsily upon the
neon bulb and burns his fragile wings, only to drop upon the
floor, where upon the moth gathers his strength for another
fail. The critic might laugh at the moth's mud-coloured wings,
'Bet you thought you'd come out fluorescent blue or red, or
yellow, but brown, all that time in the cocoon for mud wings
that don't really work, what a joke!' The critic might think his
opinions correct, from his shallow stool of slander he cannot
see where and what the transformation has done for the moth.
It is in an unseen place that the caterpillar is undressed and
dressed, hidden from the world. When the moth re appears, it
will never be satisfied eating from the leaf of a rotten vineyard
again, the moth jumps because he has been reconciled to light,

his pining and craving is for a sphere outside his shallow vision, a sphere his natural senses can't fully behold. It isn't about his flight so much as it is about his heart and the objective reality of his destiny, as observed not by him or from the short-sighted lens of a dim-witted world, but instead from the eyes of light, calling him into the failures and trials of his new creation.

Paul asked me to come with him to church. I had palmed off this invitation many times, but like one of his shaking eggs, or banging drums, like the rifts he would play so casually on the strings of his beloved guitar, the question kept coming. There was no weight or agenda, Paul threw out the invite as if he had just boiled a kettle and was making a pot of tea. The churches out in Australia were dressed different to Britain, no stones or stained glass, just letters on a bill board. The pastors would hire a hall or acquire some rectangular shaped shed, there was no observational difference between a church and a secular building other than the roadside sign. The lesser the church, the greater the sign, with bold text and capital letters, trying for every timber and dull stone, to shout, 'I'm a church, I'm a church.' One could gaze across miles of flat farmland and not see a single spire rise up above the treeline. Paul didn't find his church; his church had found him. Either dejected by the prospect of another eight days underground, or perhaps having been booted out from his flatshare, maybe Salmon was love sick, maybe he was day dreaming of home or a place in his brother's band, maybe he was en route to Sydney picking up his mirror dinghy, whatever the reason, Salmon somehow tuned into a Christian radio channel, not only did he tune in but he listened to the adverts, beyond listened in fact, Salmon was crazy enough to answer the call. 'How did you find us,' said the pastor. 'Advert on the radio,' replied Salmon. He was the only person on the entire Gold Coast to answer the advert, it went out to the multitudes once and it caught hold of Salmon, hooking my red headed friend, the wiliest, the untidiest, the most erratic of my British comrades, but deceptively intelligent and unknowingly generous, was the fish on the line!

Walt and I met Dave the pastor in a coffee house accidently whilst chilling with Salmon, we'd eat breakfast together every morning when back from the mines. Putting a face to the church, that was the stained glass window Walt and I needed, that was the spire above the grass for us. Dave was filled with light! We talked and joked like friends. Walt and I decided to attend church with Paul that coming Sunday. Nothing was discussed as such at the time, but in that moment, I like to think anyway, the matter was settled.

20

Gold Rush

He was dressed in schemes, he wore his bargains about his waist, he kept away from the wild, from the woods, whose shadows stretched out beyond the reach of his control. It was a place of encounter that forever changed Jacob, an encounter that dressed Jacob in the Lord's favour, for he landed on higher ground, and he found in that place, a living God and the fertile soil of belief.

Belief is not a character trait, or a thought or an emotion, belief is not learnt by hours of study, not handed down the generations like a golden watch. There is no certificate! No one owns that patch of ground between the raging tides. Belief is a place. 'How awesome is this place,' said Jacob, 'this is none other than the house of God, this is the gate of heaven.'[24] Jacob woke from his dream, early the next morning and took the stone he had used as a pillow and set it up as a pillar, and poured oil on the top of it. He called it Bethel, though the city used to be called Luz. The rock Jacob had been sleeping on became the pillar he lived by, a place of anointing, where the mercy of God descended and where his praise and worship rose. That picture of belief and encounter, as written about in Genesis, opens wide this next short section of the journey.

Ever since the Gideons came to my primary school, I kept their little red bible close, it lived in a black plastic ding repair box in the bottom of my rucksack. I took that book to boarding school aged 13, I took it to university, I took it on dozens of surf trips all around the world, I took it to Australia, I sailed it back home aboard Coconut, but I never opened my bible to read from it. Like a seed it was carried but not planted, the season all wrong for growing. I slept upon that little red bible, I understood not the power, the majesty, the holiness, the righteousness, the sacrifice, the love, or the glory. I had experienced God though, I was tricked away, I moved off by my own ill choice, like a coward or like a thief, like a thrill seeker. I was raised in the rut, down in the stem of the olive branch, down where knot meets root, surrounded by the hard bark of a good old fashioned Catholic upbringing. Such was Dad's faith, my two brothers and me, we were educated at Worth Abbey, a Benedictine boarding school. I remember my confirmation aged thirteen, I picked the saint's name Michael after my grandfather who had recently passed away. Given my middle name was already Michael, an interesting choice. Grandma, Mum and Dad flew over for the confirmation service, busting into the monastery book shop to look for a suitable gift. 'A bit of a gap in the market here,' said Dad to the monk, 'nothing on the shelves for youngsters.'

'Not a gap in the market,' replied the monk, 'but a gap in the boy.' His reply might have seemed both abrupt and comical, but the monk was right, that gap was there, with gravity and appetite, rumbling like an empty stomach and consuming like a thirsty mouth. Popular culture, ill choice, and the recognition of fellow man, they all fell in, but so too did the gold, the prayers of believers, resting beneath the heap of trash that followed. At Worth it was all about the long game, those monks sat still like rocks in a river, their legs old, their eyes weak, dressed in black. A constant flow of boys passing, a mass of water, full of whitewash and whirlpools. 'Get them all done,' said the abbot! We washed through Worth's walls like a torrent of hill water, spat out into the valley of the shadow of death. I remember the church at Worth well, a beautiful curved building, wrapping round a grey stone altar, an altar left bare like a winter branch, save for a single flickering candle. An altar whose footing was raised just above the floor, floating like a dried-out leaf on a dark lake. The roof was a dome, raised aloft like an ocean sky. At night in the darkness that single candle sat like a mast light, dipping and swaying, suspended in space, both strength and fragility sown into the flame. I had an experience of God's spirit in that church. I had been to confession, I was alone, a feeling of profound weightlessness came upon me, a deep and bleeding joy. That which burns in happiness bled out and I was lifted into a floating state, I was up with God, drifting above the dark waters, above a world void of form, above the wasteland of my youth, that blunderbuss of drunkenness that havoc train. An existence that ran off in front of me for well over a decade. Coming back to church in Australia, I was heavy enough to stand in the tide of life and not get swept away. I could stay put on that patch of ground for long enough for something inside to take root. The time was right, the season at hand, my Gideon's bible opened and a hidden kingdom unveiled through the word, the kingdom of God on Earth.

I never pictured sailing on Coconut again, Harry was married and prepping the boat for round two with his wife, she conceived and the trip evaporated. Coconut was put on the market, she was taken from the water, placed on a trailer and wheeled up to a field. That five miles could have been 500. I picture a down cast day when thinking about that leg, a funeral procession, the wheels of the trailer popping beneath her weight, a long queue of cars running behind, honking with frustration as the boat slowly walks away from the drink, to sit beneath the trees, surrounded by a sea of Jersey potatoes. Stuck in the mud, waiting in the shadows, mast missing, boom in the barn, remnants of our year at sea rusting beneath coils of rotten warp. I did not sit and ponder, I let her go and got on with life in Australia. Thankfully Little Coconut looked like a corpse, like a dead fish, consequently no one brought her in four long years!

Providence is an amazing thing, those wasted days of youth can be lit up in a single breath, a sunken boat brought to life or a burnt-out house restored, whether bagging up the years like bundles of hay, or taking a blunt minute or a blundered prayer, and making a sharp point of it, igniting the present with purpose, through the power of Christ's sacrifice, reconciled to God, the waymaker, who can cut through ice or sustain his servants in cauldrons of fire. We think we are rich in the West, but really, we are wretched. We think we have everything, but we are pitiful and poor and blind and naked. For we live only in part upon that hillside of belief, our eyes are heavy like stones, our house is split, contaminated around the collar, and our hearts are full of wickedness.

I was out in the sticks of Queensland, the landscape was flat and hot, probably the hottest place I have ever worked. Underneath the earth is usually cooler than the surface, a break from the crippling desert sun, but life in this mine was hotter in the darkness than it was in the light. The rock one mile down was fifty degrees. Big refrigeration units on the surface had to pump down cold air. Dressed in thick mining overalls, sweat would run like a river, saturating the cloth, and pooling up in my welly boots. I struck gold down there, and found beneath the earth, in a place of thirst and loneliness, a thread of life, a silk road, a narrow way, one which led off into a new dawn.

Six years had passed, and I hadn't heard a peep from Miranda, not a phone call, a Christmas card or an email. Since finishing university, she had told me not to contact her unless it was an emergency. I had kept her wishes! Miranda would not go out with me at university, she couldn't have, because going out with me would have drawn her off the narrow way. But she loved me even then I think. Her love broke hard at times, it felt almost unconditional, not a fleeting rush, not a flash flood, but a steady stream. Over the course of those three or four years, we became good friends. I had a string of knee operations. Weak joints, and bush-league Cornish rugby, not a good combo. Three operations in total, starting in second year and rolling all the way through. What started in a flush of tries on the rugby pitch, ended in crutches. I danced around those farmers, those doormen and doll rollers, those creatures of Cornwall's underbelly. But it only lasted one year. My knees were shot, I never sprinted again. Miranda and me, we would swim together, which was the only exercise I could manage for a time. It was on those trips to the pool at Camborne leisure centre we really bonded. Talking to Miranda was the easiest thing on the planet, we laughed a lot, and talked about faith and life. I could not understand how she could take the bible so literally, so seriously, almost blindly in fact. It was me who was the Pharisee, one should add, not her, and the only sign Jesus gives to that type of pride is the story of Jonah and the whale! How I chuckled in the car to the pool about that story.

I prayed for a wife out in the mines. Was it the heat or the solitude? which drew the bow of that prayer to God, who became for that breath, a sort of celestial wingman. My prayer was answered practically the next day. Miranda messaged me through LinkedIn. I was only on that site to find a new mining contract, something more permanent. Instead of finding work I was reunited with an old flame. It was like, the God of the Heavens and the Earth was moving both again, for out in the darkness, he dropped down the brightest of moons. After speaking on the phone, I booked a flight back on my next swing off, I found myself like Jacob in Genesis, bound for home soil, off to take Miranda out for a drink. I only had a short week to make the trip there and back.

One could happily breeze over the bridge without a thought, but I want to focus for a second on the turbulence below. Miranda had been praying for me for years, she had let me go after our time together at university, it was the hardest decision of her life emotionally. She was led by that verse in Matthew 10 which goes, 'Whoever finds their life will lose it, and whoever loses their life for my sake will find it.'[25] I had no links with Miranda save for an army bible she gave me, with proverb 19v21 written on the inside. 'Many are the plans of a man's heart, but it is the Lord's purpose that prevails.'[26] I still have the bible, but at the time I didn't bother to read the proverb, which is actually rather amusing, because not paying the verse any attention at the time works to reinforce the words. I love that proverb. In a world that tries so hard to control every minute, to crown self upon a quaking pedestal, the proverb helps to blow the human back off, to gaze upon the might of God's will from the right place, from the ground.

My flight back to London looked like a car crash to some, and a few of my friends were worried when I said out of the blue, 'Jesus has just landed me a wife see you in a fortnight!' They thought I was nuts. To some it could have been said, that I steered a ship of neglect and selfishness, it could be said that I was steaming back into an angry sea of jealousy and unforgiveness. But it was no car crash, it was a gold rush! One of the most exciting moments of my life. We got taken back, and there beneath the fireplace of belief, I found an ember still ablaze, just a single ember in the ash, in the burnt-out wastes of a selfish youth. This was love like a new language, like a language I could not yet speak and could barely understand, but I knew where to find the words and I knew where to sit to gather my breath. That relationship was rebuilt. Faith in God was our mortar. A faith that took our worries off the floor, like a tender hand, a faith which washed us down and pegged up our souls, out upon the washing line, a faith that gave us time to dry off in the sun. Miranda moved out to Australia after her studies, I proposed to her under the lighthouse at Fingal

Heads. White sand, that thick sharp Australian grass, a fever of green, broken up by boulders of black volcanic rock, cut alongside a crystal blue sea, that was the setting.

My time working down in the mines was fast running out by the end. I would miss the bus on occasions with no option but to hitchhike to work up a long straight tarmac road, just the fifty miles, sometimes rocking in hours late. I was on warnings for health and safety breaches, the old guard had gone, I was back at the mine I had started out working, it was under different hands now. The manager would say things like, 'Why are we paying the crew to take a shower.' The gig had gone stale! The new boss came in like bad king John. He axed Wednesday morning barbeques; he axed the tech services minibus. The best guys all got fired or bailed. Good king Richard, he was nowhere to be seen, fighting the crusade of another damp dirty hole. 'Robinhood!' you might cry, but alas there were no trees and no maiden of the woods to lure our hero in. The bad king had it all his own way, he put a drip for a sheriff in charge of my department, even the girls from geology had all bolted. The place sucked. Miranda and I had reached a crossroads together, I was close to getting fired, I had no option, move onto Miranda's visa, she was a textiles designer, or go sailing! Either buy an apartment and settle, or spend all the cash and make for the sea again. There was an old map of the world hanging on my wall. I drew a route out across the pond, her eyes like marbles, glistening in the dim light. My kitchen table a plastic fold away, my cooker a plugin hob. I started the pencil line at Jersey and weaved a curve across to the South Pacific. Miranda was keen, probably more excited than me, the climate out on the Gold Coast definitely helped fight our cause, blue sea and golden sand, had I floated the brief on a British beach the trip might well have never started. 'Do I need to learn anything before we leave,' said Miranda.

'Course not,' I said, 'the journey will toughen you up in her own way, no training required, no thought required.' Miranda then promptly booked herself on an RYA competent crew course, she was raised in Northampton with no experience on the water whatsoever. We were to get married at the end of a British summer and head off with the fall, chasing the sun down Europe till the butter melted and the trade winds opened wide our world. I did not live with Miranda before getting married, our life as one would start aboard Little Coconut. I left Australia a few months earlier than Miranda to resurrect Coconut from the mud, our wedding set for early August. In less than one year my world had exploded, I need not add any embroidery regarding belief in a living God, the simple facts speak better than any volume of words. I was given wings, a boat, and a wife. Out of that damp dirty cocoon I bolted, with $70K (Aussy dollars) in the back pocket from 4 years mining. Having not really thought about saving, having no appetite for gadgets or possessions other than surfboards and surf trips. I never in all my days pictured a well spring like that, our bumpy journey across the world began, we had started weak, frayed cords from two different tides, but God's plan was for us to be strong, he spliced us at the break, bound with grace and mercy, united under light, joined till death do us part, for his purposes. To think the glory of God shines out in the redemption and sanctification of human souls. To think the God of our heavens, the God of eternity, delights and shares in our individual stories. To think his glory is somehow written in with our freedom, written in with our joy and peace. To think his glory manifests in mercy and compassion, in the story of salvation, in the living work of Jesus Christ. To think that the battle with the devil and death has been won for us, to think the only fight we have, in the eyes of heaven, is the good fight of faith. Then to think this faith is a gift from God, set down on a place, on a patch of ground, so that no thought, or emotion, no distortion of the mind, or deception of an evil tongue, can stop the encounter if we peg ourselves in. Jesus said 'seek and you shall find, knock and the door will be opened.'[27] That promise is mighty, a bearing to the ears that will hear, a promise that will take those whose hearts are ready, out to the starting blocks of a true and lasting journey.

Indian ocean crossing

Washing

Day out at the cricket, St Lucia

Jamie bracing for a night watch

Sea swim Nambia,
H & Dan

Harry and Hugh

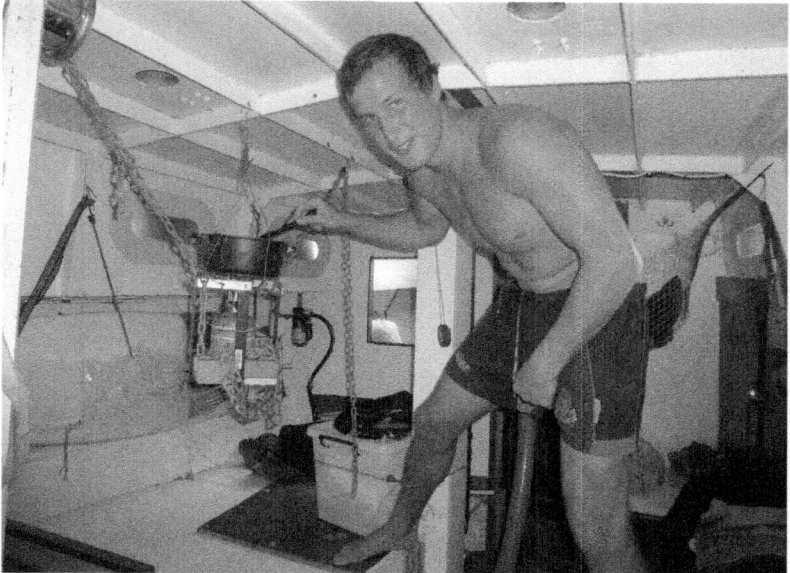

H cooking up a storm

Hugh on helm

Simon (Dad)

On passage to Samoa

View from the mast

33 at sea, Panama

Pacific side, Panama

Anchored, Hiva Oa

Leaving Cape verde-
Atlantic crossing

Anchored in the Pacific

Off for a wave, Tahiti

Out back off Teahupo

Flying fish

Mahi Mahi

21

Bay of Biscay

I've heard it compared, a marriage to a journey across the sea, and I've heard it said, that a man and his boat are like a marriage. But rarely will reality strike, rarely will a couple head straight from the altar to the drink, rarely will they wake in a steel hull, slamming and rattling across the Bay of Biscay, sickness and health, for better and worse, till death do us part, sat aboard more like passengers than promises, as the foam rips past the hull, and as the wind draws that hatchling of a house further and further away into the drift, swimming for the avalanche, heading for the oblivion that is the deep. It is written of marriage, 'A man shall leave his father and his mother, and shall cleave unto his wife, and they shall be one flesh.'[28] I'd flown out of Jersey 100 times, in ever-increasing circles, off and back like a boomerang, but until that Autum, I don't think I'd ever properly left. With Miranda aboard, and

Coconut pointing into a setting sun, the new frontier had been reached before nightfall on that first day out. My world was not beyond the horizon, as it once was, but instead below deck, snoring peacefully in her bunk, with cotton socks on her feet and two goose feather pillows beneath her head. It was a shift in the wind only marriage can bring, which changed the dynamics of this second adventure on Little Coconut, not an extension of the last, one should add, but instead, the start of the new.

The bracken was brown on the cliffs when we motored out, and everything looked tired except for the swallows, whose summer hatchlings flew in restless circles, dipping down to skim the water's edge, then shooting up like arrows, up into a September sky. Packing one's bride away into a no-nonsense cruiser is harder than it writes. Miranda looked troubled when I mentioned scrubbing her down on deck as the washing facilities. She froze when I picked up a bucket and said the word 'toilet'. She had a bag for everyday of the week, and more shoes than Little Coconut's wildest dreams. Our old kettle from Australia was put on the scrap heap, along with all the other rusty medallions that rattled around Coconut's ribs like a bag full of old bones. Pearl white, were the bed sheets she brought down into the lair, into a cabin once famed as the naval equivalent of Osama Ben Laden's cave. She turned Coconut into a place of comfort, with soft cushions and the smell of baking bread. Our galley had been transformed! Our wedding gift from H, a real oven. What a gift! Hot bread out on a hard leg, a game changer, a gift not given once, but given again and again and again, given in the rain and given in the sun. Bread, the smell of comfort, bread to fill the belly when everything else lies empty.

Leaving by sail is not the same as leaving under foot or hoof, it is not like flying out or driving off. A thread slowly unwinds, until there is nothing left for the natural senses to hold. The eyes of the cliff can't make out the sail no more, and the eyes of the boat can't quite make out the face of the cliff, so thin and grey she stands, her scrub to dust and her rock to ash, all colour and stature, lost to wind and water. Out with the swallows we went, to migrate the same old track with new wings.

My eye lids felt like concrete that first night. Miranda started to feel sick upon sun set, it was her maiden night under sail, so I sent her down to sleep and held the wheel until the blinking lights of France started to reflect off the water. 'H' I had shouted half-dazed, clutching the wheel, at about 03:00 in the morning, but alas he was not there to carry the weight and take the wheel. Four or five years had passed by in a blink, the unforgiving nature of the sea, I'd forgotten all about it, my memory had somehow sieved away the hardship. Everything came back on that first night sail, sitting on a wooden bench and hand-steering, pissing into a bailer by the wheel, taking a compass reading, then running it up into the heavens to find the closest star, turning off the torch to hold one's line across the water and fight with sleep until dawn.

I got Little Coconut in before the tide turned. We slept inside a walled harbour as the elements closed our road south. We woke to run back out with the good tide, making it all the way to Aber Wrac'h, picking up a buoy, and rowing into shore for a plate of mussels and chips, for a glass of cold beer and a walk down some sleepy French country lane. Wild flowers and pastel-coloured houses, quiet tidal bays all lost in countryside, it was blissful.

We sailed down the coast to Camaret, a pretty little port near the city of Brest where we waited for a window to cross Biscay. Little Coconut not the only boat heading south one should add, the last wave of summer cruisers had all made their dash, an unorganised mob, frantic for miles at the back end of a long season, trying to reach Spain and Portugal before the weather turned. With French croissants on the breakfast table, and a wave to surf over the hill, it was perfect. We had found in Cameret, a counter current, a warm fresh water spring. Peeling our tired bodies away from the food and the surf felt like climbing out from the warmth after a heavy lunch.

Married life aboard a small yacht, the reality slowly started breaking in. 'My friend is getting married,' said Miranda, 'I need to fly back and go to her wedding, I'm a bridesmaid.'

'Then a bridesmaid you shall be. In spirit but not in person,' I replied! In came the first argument, like two plates crashing, lava foaming from the mouth.

'She's my friend, and a very special one!'

'If she is, she'll understand, if she isn't, she won't, we got limited funds and a long hard road. If you go, I'll have to sail Biscay alone and meet you in Spain!'

Poor Miranda, she came around to my reasoning and missed the wedding. As the bride walked off down an aisle, the sailor walked off a plank and into the sea. We threw in our stocks, saw the weather window opening, and cast off for Spain. It was a split of atoms; we were cruisers now and there was no going back.

Chilling behind the wheels of the plough, with sails like horses, with a Coconut for a carriage, with furlongs rushing past and furrows ploughed through the deep, with an auto-helm steering, with a book whose pages like spokes are turning, a warm bunk, a steaming kettle, with days like minutes and a sunny face of cliff to spot at the end of the paddock, a face of cliff, rosy and full, waiting beyond one's labour like a roast dinner or a rack of barbequed ribs. That is what a Biscay crossing should be like, a rich vein of sailing, a seam of good ground in hard rock, a narrow way, a job waited for and a job taken. We found the thread, but it took us nearly three hundred miles to come by. We were paid the same as all those other sailors, who had it dialled and made, who had been pushed since France by a steady hand. But it wasn't the wages we so treasured, it was the thread, which took us away from the market square, from a place of waiting. Out of the labyrinth went our muddled miles, and into a new season of sailing in the light.

Miranda was sick as a dog to begin with, and I got so tired I lost my reason, opting to re thread the genoa mid Biscay because of a minor issue. I parked the boat up, heaving her to, ripping down the rag, then I attempted to re thread the self-fuller with 25 knots smashing into the boat, with Miranda's eyes like golf balls and her knuckles white as bone. I was out on the bow spirit, I'd lashed the wheel into wind and was trying to hoax Miranda to gather in some strength and winch up the genoa halyard from the mast, as I attempted to thread the sail back through the fuller groove out on the bow spirit. Why I didn't hoist the cutter and attempt the stunt under the steady hands of a moving boat, I'll never know. Why didn't I wait and fix the genoa properly in Spain? Instead, I made it as awkward and as hard as humanly possible!

'I don't have the strength,' said Miranda as she clung to the mast, her legs were shaking with fear.

'You're strong like a bull, go for it, dig deep and unleash the ox within.'

'I can't there is no ox!'

I crawled back from the bow spirit, took the halyard off the winch and put it into my mouth, I crawled back and wrestled the rag up her track from out on the bow, heaving and feeding, nailed by salt water, I hadn't slept in two days, I had hand-steered all night and Miranda was sick and weak like a kitten. I went into a frenzy, like a shark feeding, red mist on the rigging. Up went the sail and back down wind we ran. What a terrible soldier, not roman but barbarian, a club wielding nut. A minimum of three hours asleep in 24, that has to pull some priority, even if it is broken up into slots. A sailor must hit the bunk. I was trying to get us across Biscay in my own strength, no self-steerer working and with a sick wife. But Miranda was well enough to take the wheel, I had to start using her strength, Coconut was not set up for sailing alone and marriage is a joint partnership, not a dictatorship, not one resting and the other grafting, but a relationship, a two-way thing.

From that moment on things got better. Miranda took the wheel for longer and longer periods, my mind started to unwind and rest, I found patches of sleep, longer and longer. The weather dropped and Miranda stopped feeling sick and started cooking and laughing and talking.

I can't forget landfall in Spain, of all the landfalls that go down in a circumnavigation, this one was special. I was in the galley, cracking pepper and cutting onions, boiling water and dropping spaghetti into the pan. We had a great dinner out on deck, Miranda was on the wheel. After eating I washed with fresh water, sponging it on from a bucket, it was cool, it took away the sting of the sea, I felt new and alive. Then we got hit by the most amazing scent of eucalyptus, the wind had died away completely and a faint offshore breeze gently streamed off the land. In came a wave of heavenly scent, a rich aroma, delivered on a sea of sparkling silver from a forest of hilltop trees. As the sun set, we were paid in full, it was the same as the other yachtsman, not more and not less, the same denarius for us who had waited so long to get going. The parable of the workers in the vineyard from the gospel of Matthew had jumped off the page, 'the last first and the first last.'[29] We motored into Vivo in the dark. A fisherman was out on the pierhead, it was the dead of night by the time we eventually reached land, and I wondered what in the world he was doing, as he no doubt wondered what in the world, we were doing, entering his home in the early hours. I tied up on the first pontoon available, climbing into my sleeping bag, I fell straight into a deep peaceful sleep. It must have been the weekend, because a distant nightclub was playing brick-in-the-washing-machine music, music I hate with a passion. I didn't care, it was nothing more than a lullaby. Miranda woke me in perfect sunlight and we walked up the harbour, found a little café. I drank an ice-cold beer and ate an omelette, at ten o clock in the morning, with hard crusty Spanish bread. It was the best breakfast I have ever had to date, made not just with ingredients from the hills, but with hard miles fought at sea. We came in wiser and stronger and more able; we had been pruned, the chaff burnt up, and from that hacked stump, I felt new growth coming from the inside. We had been joined spiritually at the altar till death, but Biscay had brought us together in the waves and trials of life. Australia was a long way off, but the prospect didn't frighten us. In the dying moments of a hard crossing, we found that thread, and received the wages of a full breakfast beneath a hot Spanish sun.

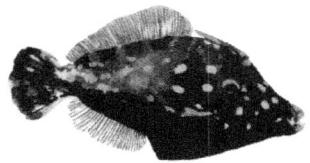

22

South with the Sun

Galicia must have once held the gaze of Europe, back when spices from the New World lit up the seas. The merchant ships ran just offshore, floating past like giant pots of honey, rolling by, white icing, stacked up like cakes on a trolley. Gunslingers and privateers lay in wait, battling Atlantic storms, risking it all for a slice of the tart, for a shot at the ice cream van, so sweet the mouthful. Any nation game enough to float flag on water entered the race, whether they liked it or not, hunter or hunted. Old relics often get washed up, copper cannons, rusty galleon anchors, broken merchant jars, remnants of a wild youth. Nations rise and fall on the water, and so do their sailors. We rocked up aboard Little Coconut a few centuries too late, we missed the mayhem, arrived in the twilight, her sapphire eyes all faded, her hair cut short and curled with a purple rinse. No prize, no golden locks, just tapas and cold beer. The cliffs were still unchanged though, rising high and falling fast, and the swell from faraway storms, beat down upon the rock.

We had a ball sailing the Rias, waiting for the wind to turn north, sailing like gentle folk, when the sun was shining, when the bath water was suitably warm and the salts smelled fresh and appetising. Every resting place was slightly different, a day at sea just long enough to bring out the colours. Moving forward came naturally, especially with the onset of autumn. In chasing down the sun, every step south was a step in the right direction. Vivero, Cederia, La Coruna, Camarinas, Muros, Bayona. Miranda and I just faces in the crowd. It felt refreshing to be on the outside looking in, watching the birds one day, the fishermen another. Busy market streets, silent hilltops, it didn't matter which.

Coconut was settled, she suited the deep Rias with their forests and sleepy towns. The only gales she had to ride out were those between Miranda and I, thunder and lightning, flashing and rumbling. We had some storms in those early days. Miranda would get down sometimes, I thought she was spoilt or soft, but that wasn't the case, I thought it was the boat or me, but that wasn't entirely true. I was used to living alone, emotionally I mean, I couldn't settle when Miranda was sad. The more I'd try and talk her out of it, the worse it got. She couldn't survive on a whim or on the hoof, reacting never planning, she needed a structure. Take eating for example: I feast then famine, I'll eat till it hurts, eat till I'm out cold staring at the ceiling, mind all numb trying to work out what just went down. 'Why Hugh?' I whisper, 'not again.' Only the hiccups can slow the pace. Whenever Miranda hears me hiccup, she knows I've taken down an entire burger before her first mouthful has been finished. She looks across in disdain. But I can walk on an empty stomach.

Miranda however, she eats like a princess, she never hiccups, never ploughs pastry down the hatch, but she cries like a princess too, when the food doesn't arrive in an orderly scheduled type of way. If I was to change our plans with the weather, and leave without notice when the sky went from grey to blue, with the instruction, 'Don't worry about lunch we can eat like dogs when we're in.' How the squalls would fall! How the blue sky and glistening sea, would become troubled and angry.

We got into a routine of sorts down Spain, eating together at set times. Naval discipline, it has a place at sea, for the common good. With no paid work, no social engagements, nothing but the weather to keep any sort of beat, we had to find and create a system to live around. Meal times were as good a place to start as any, add in some painting for Miranda in the morning and a hill climb in the afternoon, and the days would pass by happy and full. Small things matter on a boat. That thunder and lightning we sailed through down Spain, it came when two different weather systems met in a 30-foot hull, her world and mine. Pushing through and coming out as one system, it wasn't about dropping certain things and keeping others. And analysing, looking into the storm, that was fruitless for us. No, uniting is simply a case of weathering, of persevering. Rejoice in the suffering and be refined. If you want to take the ice out from the Evangelical, and the negligence out from the Catholic, throw them in the same boat and pray they don't come out lukewarm. I still eat like a caveman and her like a princess, nothing has changed, hot and cold still, but we have persevered, and in those moments of despair, found solace in Christ. Love has to grow if it is indeed love, if it belongs to God, love can't be contained by selfishness, it will break the chains of inward thought and selfish desire. Things got better. In the first anchorage for example, I persuaded Miranda to come looking for surf with me. It was a pilgrimage, I rowed the dinghy till my hands turned red raw, we walked miles in the rain and didn't get anywhere near the surf. Arriving back to the dinghy, the tide had dropped out and the swell had picked up, we got swamped, and I had to row back through the chop, face to face with a wife at boiling point. It was a proper pilgrimage in other words. By the next anchorage, I had learned from the previous. I didn't for a second contemplate not surfing, but simply nipped off to find a wave alone and tried to return at a reasonable hour. Miranda stayed put and painted. I got back and we went swimming, the sand was lined by a quiet forest and the water was clear and cool. It was an amazing time, popping in on the tender to go buy lunch, coming back and hanging out on the boat, rowing ashore for a sundown beer. The good life had come, by the time we left Spain, things had become a lot smoother between Miranda and I. We were learning to live together on a small boat, and part of that was accepting who we were and not trying to change the other. More trips get sunk from couples breaking up or giving up on the dream, than from boats sunk by rocks or trashed in storms.

***

Portugal came in slow, like a drunken march, legs all heavy from the pace of the road. We reeled in those harbour lights for hours, chasing plumes of smoke rising from refinery towers. It was exhausting, she rose out from the mud like a Mississippi cat fish, eyes all cloudy from the dark, teeth rounded flat from the river bed stone.

It was late when we eventually tied Little Coconut up, the dockside was peppered snow white with gull droppings, it smelt of rotting fish and burnt oil, a far cry from the fresh scent of those Spanish hills. We missed the tide for Porto river and entered the only harbour available to us. Passage planning aboard Little Coconut more vibe than precision, rolling with the punches part of the art. Attempting a river entrance on the ebbing flow was beyond me at that time in the evening, we settled in for the night a stone's throw from the refinery, a Goliath-sized slab of industry, grinding away in the backdrop. Our new home was a creaking pontoon, a place Porto's bird population descends upon for their morning dump. Despite this we were happy to be in, Miranda over the moon in fact, her eyes on the showers from twenty miles out.

A wise couple would have batten down the hatches, excepted their fate and waited for the morning sun! Not us, 'Just one cold one,' I said, 'We'll have a hoot, be back in no time.' That was step one. Step two was when we stumbled, straight into the frying pan, smoked dry like a couple of kippers. We somehow got caught in an episode of Gordon Ramsay's kitchen nightmares. I was even aware of our predicament at the time, the waiter had contracted a hot flush of bird flu, coughing between orders, spluttering rasps of breath out into the damp stale air. The fish came out from the kitchen crying, bone dry, the potatoes reheated, the salad flopping gloomily around the plate perimeter, lifeless like a burnt-out prison guard, limp like the ears of a caged rabbit, hopeless, beyond rescue beyond repair. After the stumble, when reality struck, when we realised Cinderella had left the ball and we were alone in the clutches of her ugly sisters, then came the fall, in spectacular fashion. It hit in waves, sharp pulses, running wild and frantic through poor Miranda's stomach. It didn't seem to affect me, I have my Grandma's cooking to thank for that, but poor Miranda was laid low. She puked in the marina when we eventually landed at Porto, she puked down the pontoons, she ran laps from Little Coconut to the dockside toilets, three days straight, running like a wild washer woman, like a tortured distance runner, hair all tangled, face pale white.

That was dawn breaking for us in Portugal. After three days Miranda was up and about, wary of the local cuisine she approached dishes like a fat man walking on an iced up river, tiptoeing around the sides, careful not to wade in gun hoe. There was a bonus ball in it for me, whenever we ate locally great forkfuls of Miranda's dish were generously handed over, also chains Miranda previously turned her nose up at were now considered safe havens, places like Pizza Hut became fair game. Every saga has its silver lining, and this was mine, no more pretentious joints full of finger food and stick thin vegetarians, none of that in Pizza Hut, I was stoked.

We left Porto on the wings of a dying breeze, four knots soon dropped down below three. Little Coconut felt heavy, her arms out of time with her body, sails flapping violently in the rolling sea. With the flick of a switch our struggling sail boat was turned into a chugging train, and with gib rolled up and main clamped in we ran off into the night. I never feel totally at ease under engine, too many parts chattering away down there, too many loose teeth. I suppose my expertise in that realm only goes so far, like the delegated workplace first aider, one or two plasters and a good rub, that is my lot, changing the filters, checking the coolant, hoping she keeps the beat. Our plan was to sail for Cascais, a good spot for the boat, a town close to Lisbon with some waves over the hill. By sun set on the second day it was time to rethink, fog rose up thick and fast, great billows jumping out from the water. Coconut was stuck in pea soup, senses cut off by the curtain. We were left wide-eyed, staring away into the mist, into that cruel face of uncertainty. The visibility soon dropped down to one or two boat lengths, it was time for the foghorn. Out of the packet she came, twenty quid or so, brought at the start of the season for games like this. I'm not sure where the chandlery got that foghorn from, a Chinese trick shop maybe? or two for one out the back of Del Boy's yellow three-wheeler perhaps? The horn didn't blast it croaked, like a wet and tired cane toad, mill pond whispers, useless like tits on a bull. We burst out laughing, 'What was that? Who stepped on the goose?' I shook the can again, 'Maybe she just needs to warm up a bit, get some air in the lungs,' I tried it again, and again it softly croaked, we laughed some more. I threw it back below and we turned the wheel, heading for the closest harbour available, a fishing town called Penchie. It is a weird feeling, watching the GPS with one eye, gazing out into the fog with the other, left flank lost in a computer game, right flank caught up in a ghost story. Ten feet away there it was, creeping out from the shadows like a drunken beggar, back bent, head down, unmistakably the outline of a harbour wall. We were in. Miranda didn't feel tense in the slightest, she didn't bat an eyelid. You can sit and watch some budget Hollywood movie with her and she'll jump at every gunshot and scream at every twist, put her in a setting where she is in legitimate danger, not a peep, she sat at the wheel like a roadside kangaroo. We found the small boat pontoon and rafted up next to a young French couple, it was late when we eventually turned in. As we fell into a deep sleep, those old oak doors started to creak close, our window down to Lisbon was shut, there was no way we would be leaving with the morning sun. A big low was flying in from the Atlantic, we had the legs to beat it, but not the will. Safely in port our plans changed, we took a road trip to a pretty hill top town for Miranda's birthday and waited for the low to sweep through, continuing our road south when the weather turned.

***

C ascais sat on the hill like Papa's favourite child, all polished and pruned, bathed in shade, skin shinning, hair brushed twice. We arrived as the sun fell, spending our first night rolling around on anchor, watching from the water as the roadside cleared, as darkness descended and as the town slowly fell into a peaceful sleep. Little Coconut was creaking and rattling all night in a low swell, loose wires inside the mast were the main culprit, ticking away relentlessly, out of time and out of reach. We woke early and cranked the engine, making our way into the peacock's nest, a grand marina where boats of plastic were stacked up like dominos, all floating sickly sweet, baked off white in the sun. Surrounding the nest were streams of flash lit cafés, they jumped out from the black tarmac road, giant pots of honey, tempting us cruisers to indulge, to empty out pockets and quench the thirst. Cold beers, hamburgers, fresh coffee, it was all on our doorbell, less than a stone's throw from the boat.

It is hard work at the best of times, keeping wallet away from wife, in Cascais it was impossible. Lisbon waited in the shadows, nets baited and traps set. The promise of a day in the city was looming, art galleries, tile shops, gardens and wine bars, there was no escaping it, we stepped too close to the quick sand, sailed too close to the bright lights. Miranda was running wild, caught up with the neon glow. She wanted the lot, the smart motionless shops, the tinsel wrapped confectionary, the lush green garden walkways.

Our first stop a modern art gallery. My curses are no doubt still echoing around those hollow walls. For me art is about escaping confusion not creating it. There has to be some glimpse of truth in there, something behind it all worth preserving, some light, some hope. Why bottle poison for the drinking? why frame a turd fit for flushing? it is crazy business. That work fell like hard rain, it blew in cold through the window, numbing the mind, stunting the brush. There was gothic metal wire bent into twisted shapes, piles of dead wood thrown on the floor in no particular order, there were badly drawn faces all cracked and shouting, broken cups, charcoal scribbles, off coloured shapes and mud sodden colours. The public seemed to enjoy it, all shackled together in huddles, cackling waves of discussion into the frames of confusion. It took me awhile to recover, we had lunch outside, I looked up into a beautiful canvas of green sun filled leaves, my head stopped spinning, my legs found their feet, and we bolted, out into the quiet shaded streets.

Lisbon was a maze of cobbled corridors, a patched quilt of pastel colours, it was alive, every garden, every walkway, every turn in the road, every step we took, alive with the buzz of people. It was a tiring day, we walked for miles, stopping for a drink, resting up in a cafe, we went to another exhibition then drank beer in a boutique bar overlooking the docks, returning to the boat after dark, time for a quick hamburger then straight to the bunk, out cold, done and dusted.

As the weeks pass certain things happen when cruising, when confined to a small boat. One thing for certain is two people slowly merge, they start dressing the same, buying the same rucksack, the same-coloured caps, two for one T-shirt deals become a reality, it just makes sense. It isn't that one adopts the others style, not at all, both evolve to fit the practicality of a boat, fashion falls by the wayside. In Cascais it was bikes, luminous green on black foldaway bikes. There was no way around it, only foldaway bikes fit on a 30-footer, with two options available only one had gears, 'Two of them please.' That was it, we cycled off looking like a right couple of lemons.

We spent about a week in Cascais, Miranda found a place she could relax and paint, Little Coconut was turned into her makeshift studio. I ran errands, reworked our self-steering, moving the blocks beneath the seats, buying new rope, greasing it all up, praying she would come good. It was a final attempt, one last crack at it. We hand-steered all the way from Jersey to Lisbon, we did it with a perfectly functional stainless steel wind vane resting idle. Miranda had to watch

German boats come in drinking cold beer, grinning ear to ear like they had been passengers on a cruise ship. We would come in exhausted, all energy and laughter consumed by the wheel. With 500 miles of blue water ahead of us it was time to get our eggs in order, get things sorted. We got the boat ship-shape, went to church Sunday morning, then left, back out into the wilderness. The worship music in church, it came out with us, a full congregation singing with all their souls to the almighty, I felt light and alive, refreshed and ready, no doubt Miranda felt the same.

23

Offshore At Last

We came in like starving dogs, bumping blind into a sleeping bunk house of travelling boats, our bellies empty and throats dry. Porto Santo rose up proud, jumping high above the roadside, great hills stood tall like bearskin guards beneath the silver clouds. It was a leg of seasons, of changing colours, of highs and lows, a leg that reflected our life at sea aboard Little Coconut. We had slipped out from the coast of Portugal unnoticed and unnamed, just a mast out there lost against the white horses. I remember expecting twenty knots, sitting at the wheel blowing my harmonica, thinking the first night out would be a breeze. Great spades of angry wind came in on darkness, we were running wild, rollin and tumblin, fed giddy like a drunk pig. I folded away the gib and threw up our cutter sail. By morning it was even stronger, the horizon full of squalls, grey patches of hot wind running unpredictable lines across the water. Miranda by this time had turned sheet white, she puked all over the cabin, looked like a pickled rock pool fish, all lazy eyes and horizontal, clutching her sleeping bag with both arms, suffering away the endless procession of minutes, damp and cold. For me it got tough too, she wasn't fit enough for watch, even when I lashed her down up on the wheel, I still couldn't settle below, every time the boat luffed, I was up, every crack and hiss I was listening. I didn't sleep for the first two nights, my mind stuck in overdrive, all tied up in knots.

After two days the wind dropped down, it moved onto our beam, Miranda started smiling and I got some rest. Spring was upon us, the clouds all drifted away. I remember sitting beneath the mast in perfect peace, watching the blossom unfold, watching Little Coconut dance through waves of silver lace, fluorescence blinking beneath our feet, running out in streams of wake, it was awesome. Things started slowly changing across the way, the weather got warmer, the water turned a deep blue, our self-steerer started working and we caught our first fish, it landed on Coconut's deck, the first flying fish of the trip. We kept three hours on, three off watches across darkness, then whatever suited in daylight, our evening meal being the main event. Having the wind vane working at last changed everything, it is indescribable how vital that piece of kit is when travelling with two, it opens up your world at sea, things become possible, you can spend a watch reading in the cabin, sitting up at the mast, you can make tea, tidy up, go to the toilet, it all becomes enjoyable, you start to live instead of just exist, watching your world skip across the drink, like a floating island.

It took us five days to reach the island of Porto Santo, by the time we made landfall our appetite for blue water sailing, had for the time being, all but disappeared. We walked the soft coral sands, climbed a hill, got the bikes out and cycled, had a cold drink, swam, brought ice cream, ate meat and played cards. There were probably twenty boats heading south, it was a social place to berth. After four days the egg timer was up, Miranda's parents had flown in to see us, they were hauled up in Funchal, we squared everything away and got ready to make tracks, a short hop across to Madeira.

Our departure from Porto Santo was one to remember, comedy for the bystander, panic for the boat owner, every head on the harbour wall turned to watch the spectacle unfold. Wind and keel teamed up for an eclipse of epic magnitude, holding our rudder ransom, making me look like a right tit. 'Poor Michael,' Miranda reflected quietly when the shock had worn off. Michael was the 70-year-old English dude dropped to his knees; he was dragged down the pontoon trying to hold our bow line. 'He nearly drowned' she added.

'He didn't nearly drown babe; Mike is a solo sailor they're practically unsinkable... a rare breed of wanderer... he was fine, enjoying the challenge if anything.'

'He was not fine; he nearly fell off the pontoon.' There was a short pause, Miranda was reliving her account of the tale, running it back through.

'That Swiss woman was going mental,' she added, 'shouting... solar panels over and over again!'

'We nearly cleared them up M, of course she was going mental!'

'I counted,' Miranda continued, the ball now rolling, 'there were 10 people helping.'

'You counted?' I replied trying to work out what goes through Miranda's mind in a moment of crisis, instead of helping herself she finds the time to count others helping, classic. In the end we managed to spin the boat using the trusty combination of warps and man power. There were cruisers running in with fenders, cats pushing one end, cats pulling ropes on the other, there were people shouting orders, people watching and laughing, people open mouthed and wondering, 'Who on earth is in charge of that vessel? what an amateur!' Eventually it all worked out, we left to a standing ovation, every boat on the pontoon cheered us off.

A new challenge was fast coming, one of a very different nature, it wasn't the breaking waves crashing right outside my living room, or the hot angry squalls simmering right above my kitchen, it wasn't losing my bedroom from my anchor slipping, or catching a rail and tripping, it wasn't warps in my garden snagging the prop, or gib sails jamming in unbreakable knots, it wasn't rain or sun, wind or hail, lightening flashing or the smack of a gale. No, this new challenge was a real one, two weeks in a resort, with in-laws included. I'd never set foot in a resort before, my family had always holidayed on the hill, in the rain, eating soggy sandwiches and catching wild brown trout. Getting pampered pool side, sipping champagne, the prospect was daunting. I was worried, like a wild chicken who cautiously enters the cage, one full of fresh straw and dry grain, channelled into a battery farm for Brits, where people get turned into livestock, cattle tagged and sent off for some organised fun, Hawaiian night or beach volleyball. Miranda had spent very little time with her parents, I'd whisked her off to Australia, then married her in the summer and now she was on a boat sailing. It was time to butt out and enjoy the ride. Coconut was docked in a soulless marina on the east of Madeira and we caught a bus into town.

We found the hotel and walked through the doors; it must have been around 13:00. I looked out over a grand hallway, people were walking around the reception area dressed in white robes, all sun reddened and soft bellied, they were holding iPads! A rolled-up newspaper tucked under the arm would have looked natural, but white robes and iPads! It felt like we had walked into a *Star Wars* movie, a universe full of strange and bewildered characters had descended upon us, Madeira had given them exactly what they wanted, tailored a suit to fit, butter cup smiles and cold Carling with your fish and chips.

Funchal is a fun town, houses are piled up on the hillside like stacked plates, roads run down the valleys like long twisting washing lines all pegged up with colourful shops, everything rolls downstream, ending up in the old part of town, where bars and restaurants chatter away like draws full of wet crockery. Norman and Linda, Miranda's parents, hired a car and we all bundled in one day and drove up to the hills. The road ran straight as an arrow, it had the trajectory of a flight path, climbing steeply into the clouds. We drove till our wheels hit the snow, we opened the car doors in a different country, our hire car could have been an airplane, there was thick forest, sheer drops, then these rugged snow-capped peaks. What a place for a walk, it was refreshing landscape, the type of trail that turns back the clock and makes you feel like a kid again.

The date was coming for us to leave, attempting to make the Canaries on the backend of a northerly blow, we only had three days in the locker before a southerly was due to spin, enough time, but only by a nose. Friday night was our farewell dinner, the steaks came out thick and juicy, the wine rich and full. Over the course of that meal, we forgot all about the leg ahead, it didn't even enter our minds. I turned over at 07:00 and Miranda was sick as a dog. Not felled this time by the sea but by the drink. Leaving was not an option, getting sick on passage one thing, starting a passage sick another, I canned our departure and spent the day moving Little Coconut over to Funchal, Miranda spent the day in bed. Madeira had managed to suck us in for another week. That southerly grew teeth and gave us a real flogging, we were sandwiched between a big cat and the harbour wall, the water turned thick like soup, hundreds of fallen branches littered the pontoons, it was like rafting up in a river. Maybe it was the Lord's provision, had we left that southerly might have given us a real shoeing. Norman and Linda departed earlier that week, the next window out was ours, in the mean time we moved back on Coconut, she had been left in the shadows for two weeks and needed some attention. It felt good to be back on the boat, back to the trail ahead, softened by the hotel beds and hot showers, softened but not lost.

***

We weren't long in the Canaries before that ocean crossing came knocking, it swept in fast, bounding up the lane, tapping on the doors, whistling through the window pane. By the time we reached the Canaries Miranda had become a seasoned adventurer, I started to sleep better on passage, trusting her to read the elements, she knew when Coconut was running wild, or when Coconut was wallowing, she could feel when the boat drifted off course just by the changing sounds, by the swinging pitch, or by the flapping sails. She could tweak the wind vane or hand-steer a line for three hours straight, I'd sometimes hear her singing on the wheel, or whispering to the wind, it felt like perhaps this trip was starting to spread its wings.

Madeira had been left behind our stern, back down and belly up, snoring beneath the stars, her steep hillside walls wake-side, faintly glowing and slowly burning, blinking and glistening in the dark. We ran out into a frantic sea, taking crashing white horses on the beam, spray leaping over the rails. I furled up our genoa, plugging in Little Coconut's trusty cutter sail, we marched off into the night, into the last gasps of a dying breeze. The front which had kept us at bay for a week, whose heavy paws had wrapped up the whole island, it was moving off, our window down to the Canaries appeared. In reality it was more of a trap door, one to climb through slowly, one to squeeze out of gently, out through that unchanging corridor of hours, three on three off all the way to Tenerife.

The island seemed almost fragile at first, a delicate sill on the horizon peering up in silent grey shadows like it had been placed there by hand or blown in with the clouds. It floated on the water, weightlessly, slowly gaining stature with our approach. As we got close it was as if the rock suddenly dropped roots, sending heavy anchors crashing straight to the seabed, rearing up all rugged and full of teeth. Peaks of volcanic stone rose high, touching the clouds. We sailed in like a piece of drift wood, somehow finding our way back onto the beach, all salt covered and tattered from life afloat.

It was mid-December, Little Coconut was parked up at Santa Cruz, sitting snugly in a marina full of travelling boats. Miranda had just come back from the market, bags full of freshly baked bread, salad, cheese and salami. 'Lunch,' she said smiling, looking up at me from the long swaying finger pontoon. I was crouching over the rails, paint brush in hand, touching up patches of surface rust. We ate outside by the wheel all huddled close, breaking off great strips of bread, we ate with no idea what day of the week it was, our working lives dropped on the floor somewhere far away, shed, like reels of old snake skin, it was perfect. There was plenty to keep us busy, we were slowly sharpening the axe, getting ready for an ocean crossing. A vague plan had been laid down, it was centred around our new recruit, brought in especially for the Atlantic. He was a wise old hand, not the prettiest crew member you've ever seen, not the steadiest on his feet, but the best none the less. The old man was coming back, Coconut's very own boomerang, back for another run, back across another ocean. Dad's idea of a good holiday is getting rolled around a floating can for three weeks, catching fish and surfing two thousand miles of desert road. Three weeks of watches, three weeks of pasta rice pasta rice pasta rice, three weeks of water chiming on steel, of changing sails, three weeks of ebbs and flows, bucket and chuck it, stops and starts, broken sleeps and salty sheets. I was so happy to have Dad with us for another crossing, with Dad comes many things, one thing for certain, fish! We hadn't caught one all trip, we needed him for this alone, our luck would change with Dad, the fish would come in. How would Miranda cope with two mad hatters on the boat? she struggles at times with one. Dad's ticket was booked up for early January, he was flying into the Cape Verde Islands, 900 miles south, right down in the heartland of the trades. If Columbus thought it best to leave from Cape Verde that was good enough for me and with this in mind Miranda and I got ready for our first Christmas together at sea.

Shopping for big stints out deep is an imprecise art aboard Little Coconut, full of rough on the spot calculations and optimistic predictions. Just like that *jungle book* song we start proceedings with the bare necessities, peppered crackers, canned tomatoes and bottled water. This combination won't fail, it is tried and tested, if gas bottles get taken by ravenous waves, or if Coconut's thirty-quid car-boot-sale cooker stops working you can still eat and drink. Be prepared for some cold stares whilst standing in the checkout queue at the supermarket! 'Nutter alert!' they'll whisper. 'Look, he's got three trolleys full of bottled water and one full of canned food. What's the game? when's the hard rain a comin'?' Fear not, these ingredients are the bones of your supplies, 100 quid tops, enough sustenance for a good run across the pond. From the bones you work out, grabbing toilet roll and baby wipes, pasta and rice, a couple of spare tooth brushes for the sins, and maybe some shower gel if you're feeling fancy. Then you hit the fresh section, cabbages and onions last the longest. A cabbage will go a good 40 days no worries, best pick a mean looking one, one which carries some weight, rough on the hands, ugly on the eyes. After this bag some fresh tomatoes, greener the better, throw in a load of oranges and lemons then wander over and load up with eggs. A cat once told me you turn over an egg every 24 hours and it will last six months and ain't nothing better than eggs for breakfast. Near the egg section you'll probably spot some bread, this will then jog the mind and a few bags of flour and some yeast will be added to the shop. Last thing, rock over to the spices and load up with different jars, Moroccan seasoning for the hot pot, Italian herbs for your spaghetti, Mexican burrito mix. Go mental, throw in bottles of soy sauce and cooking oil, salt and pepper, dried chillies, lemon juice, whatever stands out. When you feel enough is enough roll down to the checkout grabbing some corned beef and canned fish en route, making one last minute dash for powdered milk, corn flakes, oats, tea and coffee, that's your lot, done and dusted in half an hour top, hand over the credit card praying you manage to snag some fresh tuna. Miranda somehow managed to sneak in a bag of treats, not really in the spirit of a pilgrimage but what can you do, her longing blue eyes too much, chocolate, biscuits, wine, Christmas stockings, honey, all the good stuff, that came with us too, we were bagged up and got ready for the off. My last-minute checks on Little Coconut all stemmed from the big three, floatation, direction and momentum, follow these down the wire and you'll end up tinkering with a load of stuff. We paid up at the marina and left lunch time, sailing down the coast on a cloudy downcast afternoon. It had been sunny for two weeks straight, on the day we left, in come the clouds, rolling thick and walking heavy, pushing us south.

A nasty gale came up on the second day out, we were caught napping, heads in the sky, eyes already looking to Cape

Verde. Every dog has its day and every section of water can bare its teeth and make life uncomfortable for a while. We hung on for three days straight, hand-steering because the wind vane wouldn't hold. The swell was confused, coming in undersized and angry like the little red-face drunk man in your village boozer. It was half-stunted, half-crippled, sucking off the land, running wild from shots of Saharan heat. Clouds of red sand filled the air, painting everything in rust coloured dust, our visibility dropped down to a squint, we sat at the wheel peering out at white capped horses crashing, coughing and spluttering in the smog.

Christmas Eve morning was spent heaved to, there was too much weather on the beam, it was either run out wide or sit tight and chill. After a few days at the wheel, I opted for the latter, drawing the boat up close, dropping the cutter and throwing a third reef in the main. Coconut was parked up, a beautiful slip running out from her full keel, she was rising and falling slowly, dancing with the gale. Miranda was down in the saloon, horizontal in the bunk, she was wrapped up snug. 'I hope this drops down before Christmas' she said as I got in to join her, we had pictured blue water and fair winds, sipping down our gin and tonics, watching the day unfold. The gale raging outside our door felt like coal in your stocking, like Santa had forgotten all about Little Coconut. Rudolf the red nose Reindeer had just flown overhead en route to the big city lights, his present for us a mid-flight dump, we were stuck in the hiss and blur, getting soaked and flushed, holding on inside the chattering chest of a floating Coconut, copping it all right on the nut.

Our worries, as so often the case, were misplaced, the weather died down that afternoon, and bit by bit Miranda and I started hoisting up all the rags we had dropped, bagging up the cutter, spilling out more and more genoa, rebooting the main sail. Soon we were free, the boat was steering herself, the destination wasn't our only refuge anymore, we could enjoy the present and live for the journey.

For the last few years I had been working through Christmas, out in the middle of nowhere, lost down the bottom of some dark faceless mine. Christmas would roll around too quick, it had become a day of reflection, Christmas reflecting! All joy had been lost in the cloudy twists of my mind; my inward thinking self-seeking carcass was standing tall but walking empty. My last sailing trip was buried in the gutter, sunk beneath the falling drives and reeling stopes, wrapped up in rock fall and paste fill. I was living only to fill my own boots, walking around the centre peg both blinkered and all the time on the move, ploughing the same tread week in week out. What was I doing? Where was I going? As Solomon mentioned in the book of Ecclesiastes, it felt like I was chasing the wind and chasing it alone, my labour beneath the earth had become meaningless. This Christmas I couldn't have pictured in my wildest dreams, sailing again, out on the ocean with my beautiful wife. The horizon ran wide full of colour, our future lay with it, an unknown expanse of sparkling blue water. Praise God for the break and for the heart to take it. We opened our stockings, put a Christmas pudding in the oven and celebrated, it had been a long time since I shared a joyful Christmas. For the next four days we skipped all the way down to Cape Verde, arriving in daylight for once.

Cape Verde awoke beneath our very nose, rubbing sleep from its eyes, brushing away the thirsty night, unwrapping its hot body from sheets of desert sand. Dry brown hills encircled the bay, which lay protected from the trade winds on the north west of the island. A fan of faded shades fell like beads of sweat from the half-baked hillside stone, dropping all the way to the water's edge, old and new bound together, arm in arm, broken walls next to sliding doors. We had reached Mindelo, a good spot to rest and prepare for the Atlantic. Outside the marina gates sat a group of beggars, their clothes tattered and teeth missing, their eyes wide and intense, drawing you close like glistening marbles in the dark, their handshake catching you by surprise, netting you quick, roaring in like an Atlantic gale. 'Where you from, brother? 'The UK,' I replied.

'England, I love England! Chelsea, you like Chelsea, they are the best, no?!' I was easy pickings, walking through the gates smiling, kicking my heels, stoked to arrive in the outer reaches of Africa. That was where I first met Dom, he had a once-orange trucker cap, only heroes don trucker caps, blues nuts, captains or ball players, period. He had a worn-out pair of crocs. I had a worn-out pair of crocs. He wore a ripped faded T-shirt and some shorts held up with washing line, I wore a ripped and faded T shirt held up with boat rope. He walked with a swagger, his limp didn't hold him back, his smile a swinging crescent of yellow and black, tooth, missing tooth, tooth, missing tooth. I liked Dom from the outset, he found cabs for me that were already waiting, he walked me to shops a stone's throw from the dock, shops I could have found my way to with a blind fold on, he helped me back to the boat with water, him walking me carrying the water. We spent a fair bit of time together, Dom and I, he spoke the type of broken English you only pick up from the street. We made trips to the gas station, filling Coconut's bottles up for the Atlantic. He showed me to the market, told me what a good price for fruit and veg was. I'd see him coming 100 metres away, grey and white curls poking out from his cap, his fast-paced limp overtaking the tourists, a beaming smile on his face, he must have somehow bugged me with a GPS beacon, probably a dam site craftier than I gave him credit for. As we left, Dom hugged Dad and I, a big bear hug for both of us. 'Jesus Christ,' he said pointing to the sky, 'Jesus protect you.' He said that to me, with us sailing a mini battleship, him struggling to survive in a poor dusty windblown corner of the world, a place unin-habited until the West Indian trade routes started, an island so dry it could suck the sap from a cactus, bake the wings off a cricket, flake the scales off a snake. When Dom said that it was a blessing for us make no mistake, the pope himself could not have called down such favour. We left Dom by the bins, he dropped back into the shadow, back into the timeless tide, into the stillness of his town, that faded orange cap drifting slowly off down the road, floating away behind our stern like a tin can in the drink. The Cape Verde islands had just waved us goodbye, that was our parting moment, for me anyway, at day break we would be off, out into the bones of an ocean, 2,000 miles of water all the way to Barbados.

Sao Vicente and Santo Antao were the only islands we had time to visit in the Cape Verdes, both cut from the same cloth, both forged deep beneath the seabed from the same womb of molten rock, distinct in their appearance, but different in so many ways. Antao holds his mother's looks, green eyes and soft skin, lush gorges and high ridges. Vicente is a pricklier version of the old man, practically built with heavy paws and strong arms. The siblings work hand in hand, they prop each other up, fending wolf from door and lifting head from dust, one offering fertile soil for growing fruit and veg, the other a perfect natural harbour, an enclave in the desert, offering much needed shelter to many passing boats.

We spent most of our time in Sao Vicente, Dad flew straight there from Lisbon, white as a sheet from the English winter. He was rearing to go, coiled up like a spring and ready to rumble. I had to slam the brakes on just like H and I did in Cocos Keeling all those years ago, get the old boy acclimatised, let his skin redden up a tad before we hit the open water. With no wind forecasted for a few days it gave us all time to kick back and enjoy the islands. Miranda and Dad bonded pretty quick, I got lost in Santo Antoa, they waited for me and missed the last ferry back, their only option bedding down for the night in a nearby village, Miranda bunked up snug with her father-in-law, witnessing first hand his husky snore, its unpredictable rise and fall, its ability to stop the night, to drop the clock dead, vibrating anything in the room not made of bricks and mortar.

I got lost way out west on the other side of the island, or rather we did. The landscape of Santo Antao comes alive when you leave the sanctuary of its cobbled roads, the hills gain weight, the miles don't tick they crawl, you feel the environment for what it is, man's voice just a whisper on the breeze, his strength outside the glass like that of a child. We got disoriented in the heat, we lost track of time in the water, the desert trail took our legs, the walls of whitewash took our arms, we eventually found our way to a quiet village on sun set, three shadows walking across a black sand beach. It must have been a strange site for the villagers, one tall ginger Irishman, one blond Viking cut Swede, and me, a balding Channel Islander, all soaked in sweat, stomachs rumbling, mouths dry and skin burning. It felt amazing, sitting down in the shade of that village, detached from its comings and goings but still submersed. What luxury, just to sit and watch a peaceful pocket of the world unfold around you. Children played on the beach, fishing boats lay idle in the water, locals sat in small circles, hidden beneath the trees, their houses quiet, their doorways left ajar, their windows all open. They lived between two frontiers, the mountain on one side, the ocean on the other, nourished by a small trickling stream which fell slowly from the clouds. They looked out over the setting sun every evening and awoke to the sound of cockerels crowing above the pounding swell. We had surely stumbled upon a unique spot. It was an epic day of adventure, we sat that evening as thick as thieves, drinking cold beer and eating like kings. Owain and Oscar had been strangers on the dock a few days ago, crewing on different boats, crossing the Atlantic at the same time, we bunked down that night as old buddies, I could have been on a trip with some cats from home.

A knock at the door woke us up well before sunrise, the village was already on the move, land cruisers rested on idle, getting loaded with people and goods, all tangled together half asleep, bound for the port away to the east of the island, up and over the hills. We managed to snag a lift, shoulder to shoulder like a tin full of sardines, boxes of fish between my legs, windows wide open. Owain's boat was meant to leave at 10 am, his crew had been left waiting, his skipper smoking from the ears no doubt. We weren't late though, it was meant to be, we got gobbled up by a big fish is all, hitting the sanctuary of a village, waking before the sun to make our trail back east. We spotted Miranda and Dad at the docks, two white faces walking down the roadside. I was worried about them and relieved to spot them in the crowd. A round of coffees and a few back rubs later they were both grinning ear to ear, we packed up and got ready for the off, a well-oiled team, rested and ready to rock and roll.

***

I t all feels like no sweat now, as so often the case when you return safely to land. That twenty days at sea simmers right down, all the juices and flavours which once floated way above your head, governed by the heavens, whose volume seemed mountainous, whose spices hit in angry squalls, whose days rolled by slowly, all spinning in a thousand leagues, they fall away when you climb out of the cooking pot. You look back down on it all in a different light, adding a dash of salt here and there, your work complete, burned at the edges maybe but cooked up none the less. The journey takes you from inside out, crop growing to pot cooking to chef watching to fat cat eating, you see it from all sides when you cross an ocean on a small boat. Certain flavours get preserved, soaked in honey and set apart, whipped into a cream coat or poured over the top in a chocolate glaze, others lie lost to the mix, hidden beneath a thick run of crispy skin.

We dined out on our trip across the pond for a good few days, Dad, Miranda and I, right up till we waved the old man off. That was when our chapter across the Atlantic closed. It wasn't when we dropped hook in Carlisle Bay, diving down into the perfect milky blue water, it wasn't our first cold beer which I dispatched in great thirsty gulps, drinking it down so quick the bubbles burned the back of my throat, it wasn't walking across the beautiful white sand beaches either, feet firmly on dry land at last, the chapter closed when our party went their separate ways. The ocean crossing had crowned those precious minutes ashore, slow-cooked for three weeks, seasoned by 2,000 miles of road. Our last nightcap a sad one, the pipers played slow as Dad's red sunburnt legs walked through the departure gates, he turned around for one last wave but missed us in the crowd, his month aboard Little Coconut over in the blink of an eye. We can reminisce on that leg together in years to come but never again will we taste the fruit first hand. Arriving is all about the journey, getting to the gates and making it through. It is the journey that makes that finish line stand tall, it is surely the journey that gives the whole thing light. There is no way I could cruise around the world if it was holiday after holiday, if it was easy, if the waves didn't shake me and if those endless hours at sea didn't rise up like great mountains.

Our entrance into Barbados had been like jumping the last fence in the Grand National, we were tired, our legs heavy, our eyes wide shut. It was the dead of night when that squall hit, the genoa was poled out full and Miranda was on the wheel. I awoke to her cries for help, 'Hugh,' she yelled, 'quick, come quick!' The sail was full of wind, bursting at the seams,

Miranda's voice full of panic. I swore blindly whilst trying to turn Coconut's nose up into the drift, working hard to shake the wind away, pulling with all my might to furl those rolls of fat in. After I bagged up the gib, I dropped the cutter halyard, it swung off into the night, running up the mast out of reach. I was dancing around the foredeck bare arsed, torch in my gob, spitting expletives out from beneath a mouthful of clenched teeth. The skipper's hand book had been ripped up and tossed to the raging wind, with pages all torn and flying, untethered notes of calm thinking and calculated action, they dropped cold, falling to the waterline as the red mist fell. 'You're not going up there,' Dad said as I got ready to climb the mast and retrieve my halyard without a safety rope. He wasn't alone, 'Yeah Hugh,' added Miranda 'you're not going.' They had joined forces, the good doctor and my missus, they had formed a front, it was mutiny on the bounty all over again, the black night and whistling wind my witnesses. It must have been quite a sight, me naked on the deck, torch still in mouth, spitting out the words 'I'mmmm the... sssssskipper.' My voice didn't resonate, the words numb inaudible sounds falling short, dropping dead, tired and lifeless. 'I'm your father,' Dad added as Miranda nodded, 'you're not going up there.' What was I going to do, flog my dad and wife? Maybe I should have? Francis Drake wouldn't have held back, Lord Nelson no doubt would have bog-flushed the pair of them. I looked up at the black sky and saw sense, we were 20 miles out, Dad 64 at the time, could still swing wild, there was no point fighting the tide. Climbing naked up the mast untethered in a squall was a miscalculation, they were right. For once I listened, we unfolded a handkerchief of genoa and sailed for a faint glow which rose up from behind an island of thick black cloud, Barbados lay asleep just beyond our very nose. We were checked in and anchored by 12:00, laughing about our hectic night in, Dad doing impressions of me saying, 'I'm the skipper,' with a torch stuck in my mouth. We were sitting on the beach, the ocean behind us, cold drinks in hand, our crossing still very much alive, smoking beneath the ash, embers a glow, fire still burning. It was my third Atlantic crossing, Coconut sitting proud in Carlisle Bay, just a mast on the skyline to the bystander, to us the Grand National winner, the boat that brought us in.

24

To Be or Not to Be

'To be or not to be!' We were in that place, anchored on the white sand of a Caribbean chain, whose unspoilt corners still clung with life, to the windy reaches, to the rocky shores and to the hilltop forests, locked up by sheer cliffs and trade wind gusts, left alone, like a misunderstood stranger, nothing to give and nothing to take. Mac cheese and Mahi-mahi, my plate of choice out in the Caribbean, seasoned with hot chilli and set down on a white sand beach.

Things were getting tough out on the water though, we were two thirds into the trip, and like any marathon, a wall rose up from the seabed. Our emotions had somehow found their way out from the oars into the wheelhouse, whispers of mutiny, foaming up from the stomach, fuelled not by spirit but by flesh, by living dust. Miranda was starting to find life hard on the boat, no working toilet and no shower, no taps, no luxury, she was breaking up a bit. No fans and no fridge. It was tempting to give up at that stage, to sail north through the Caribbean chain, into the Bahamas and then finish up in America. Break the tape at Fort Lauderdale Florida where Little Coconut's journey began, a circumnavigation for the boat, a clean end, an easy end, an end where the work had already been done. We kicked on and sailed south, hoisting the genoa and making for the Dutch islands en route to Colombia and Panama. Once the decision had been made, it was liberating, we might have not felt like sailing that day, perhaps the Pacific still seemed too much, but as we pushed on despite it all, there was a sense of peace. What a rush, to be that leaf, cut loose and on the breeze again, flying with the wind.

We took off and pulled into Bonaire, an island en route to Panama. We snuck in at midnight, creeping around Bonaire's south east lighthouse, tiptoeing down the stairs to the anchorage, all to indulge in the sanctuary of landfall, that coolbox of rest, where you can sleep for more than three hours straight, where your feet feel the tread of solid ground, where that rolling motion is stopped and stillness returns to your walls. It was all too tempting to resist, our passage to San Blas was put on hold, we picked up a mooring buoy in the early hours and turned in, falling into a deep sleep at last, our heads resting heavy on salt-covered pillows.

The island was an oasis for us, with amazing wildlife and crystal-clear water, the bluest Miranda and I had witnessed together. The shoreline at Bonaire holds every type of fish imaginable, some dance softly in fast moving shoals, others roll solo, armed with heavy beaks they bite into the coral, spilling off clouds of sand as they feed with erratic twists. The landscape is flat, the trees stand like tin soldiers, dry to the bone and filled to the brim with thorny branches and lizards. The flamingos were Miranda's favourite, feeding in shallow runs of brackish water, stooping down to sieve through the mud with their spade like beaks. I managed to dig out our bikes from the hold, we spent a few days cycling around, flippers sticking out of our backpacks, we'd cycle for an hour or so, go for a snorkel, hit some lunch, sleep it off, then find some flamingos in the evening, body and mind satisfied, what a fantastic existence. One evening I remember the falling sun, pockets of liquid gold spilt across the waterline, running out in reels of colour. We sat by the shallows watching the Flamingos, their elegant sills moving slowly across the shoreline. It was a picture of peace. In the stillness of the banks we embraced the silence, forgetting about Miranda's punctured bicycle completely, with twenty miles of road sitting between us and boat, we luckily managed to snag a lift back with a local just before it turned dark, piling the bikes into the back of his Ute with relieved smiles.

Wildlife was top of our list, supermarkets a close second. Miranda reckoned she hadn't been to a proper supermarket since the Canary Islands way back in December. 'Define proper supermarket,' I'd say.

'You know,' she'd answer, 'Nice things, cold things, fresh things, brands, air conditioning.' The Dutch supply chain had it wired, the shops were full of reasonably priced produce, everything you get back home and more, after months of sparse shelves gloomily selling five buck cans of mixed veg it was novel just to walk and look. How we took it all for granted, how we'll take it all for granted again, but in those moments ashore at Bonaire we didn't, we saw everything as clearly as the waters that surrounded us. Beneath that newfound banner of appreciation, we sat joyfully and recharged the batteries in full.

***

If Bonaire was the first hop en route to Panama, then Colombia was the skip, a fast four-day sail. We ran down those miles at sea effortlessly, not having to touch the wheel or change the sails for the duration of our trip. Our landing was dramatic, it was 01:00 am, the night was black, no moon and no stars, we'd spun into the shipping channel, turning little Coconut hard up into a stiff breeze. I was standing on the engine box when the incident happened, that hot release of high pressure, the whoosh, the fizz, the pop. My heart skipped a beat. I hastily opened up the box, fluid was spilling out everywhere, pulsing onto an overheated engine, clouds of steam rose up, clutching my face with burning talons. I reached down and shut the engine off. 'What's the matter?' wailed Miranda, a thin frightened voice faintly made its way down the companionway hatch to my ears. I popped my head up, shining a head torch straight into her eyes, they bulged out, wide like saucers, white like shark's teeth. 'I think the head gasket has blown,' I replied, a total misdiagnosis, tilting my head down so as not to blind Miranda. 'Could be in for some trouble, steam everywhere!' With no engine and with the wind right on our nose we suddenly found ourselves in a spot of bother. The channel was far too thin to attempt beating, not that Coconut would partake in such an arduous activity anyway. A pair of scissors had just risen up from the sea bed and cut us loose, we were drifting around the channel hopelessly like a dead leaf in the river, still ten miles from the anchorage, meanwhile Colombia slept peacefully on a bed of flickering white lights. She suddenly seemed a long way off. My first thought was to sail on, roll out the gib and head for Panama. Would anyone hear us on the hand held? Would they understand us? How much would they charge for a ten-mile tow? When the steam subsided, I inspected the damage. The engine heat dial was strangely working, tuned up to the max, 115 degrees. Despite this my negative thoughts were soon cast aside; a hose had blown off from the radiator that was all. 'We'll be alright to limp in,' I found myself whispering, plugging it back on and screwing it tight. At the time I had no idea our thermostat was frozen; the blockage meant our fresh water wasn't cooling the engine. I had no idea what a thermostat was. Beneath that engine box slept a temperamental and misunderstood creature, whose tentacles dropped down confusingly in a tangled array of hoses and wires, whose calls for attention were let loose at the most inconvenient times, filling the air with belches and groans. In short, my heart only rests steady when under sail. After re filling the coolant Miranda cranked her up, she started with an angry jump, hot fumes and steam continued to leak out as we slowly pressed on, eager to drop the hook and wake up in Cartagena.

Our engine troubles were completely forgotten as soon as the anchor dropped, it fell fast, drawing great lines of chain with it, sinking down into the dark still waters. We awoke to an armada of local motor boats which whizzed by at great speed, smiling and waving as they left their walls of wake. The city surrounded us on all sides, we were immersed in it, sitting like ducks in a castle pond. Us cruisers, we weren't a collection of faraway boats, a party of strangers unto themselves glistening away in peaceful seclusion, we were part of it all, lying right in the hustle and bustle, feeling the echoes and the waves. Miranda got the shower stuff ready and packed our boat papers and passports whilst I hastily pumped up the tender.

Five days in Colombia weren't nearly enough, we barely had time to get our bearings. From what I can tell, the old city sits like a protected jewel, polished and groomed for the coachloads of tourists that wander around her pretty stone walls. The best view of it all is from the Catholic monastery, a hilltop retreat overlooking the whole show. You can see the high-rise peninsular running down the spit, wrapping up the anchorage in its protective arms, at the base of this peninsular lies the old city which slowly unravels itself onto a flat plan of residential blocks, they fall away like rows of card houses. The streets come alive when the sun drops, the city buzzes with life, flamboyant and full of colour, food and dancing, huddles of locals sitting on the pavement, doors open, children up late playing in the parks and squares. The culture is polar opposite to western suburbia, not even the beggars seem lonely in Colombia.

The jump came with a sorrowful goodbye, I hauled up 100 feet of chain till my palms where red-raw, till my muscles shivered with fatigue, heaving and heaving till eventually the anchor surfaced from the muddy waters. It was too early to go but we had no choice, Panama Canal lay waiting, a bottleneck for cruisers heading into the Pacific. The wind blew gently the whole way to San Blas, the sails slept peacefully as we marched through the milky nights, just three days or so, short enough to stay lively, long enough to change the scene. San Blas awoke with the rising sun. As day dawned landfall broke, faint pockets of palm trees crouched just above the emerald green water, floating weightlessly like lilies on a still pond, Miranda was excited, the picture postcard cruising destination waited outside our walls, slowly becoming more and more visible as the wind drew us close.

***

Our adventures in San Blas were very nearly cut short, it would have been a sad sail down to Colon having missed out on the jewel of Panama's Caribbean coast. It was our engine again. After ten minutes on idle she'd start to boil up. We stayed put on our first night, anchored just off the Customs island at Porvieir. A thick black electrical storm rolled off the mountains, it shut out the north east wind and we got hit by westerly squalls. The second night we managed to limp across to an easy anchorage but our mood was low. 'We might have to sail on,' I said to Miranda, 'something is just not right with that engine, we can't stay here without it, we'll end up on a reef.' Miranda could see my pain, I'd been talking about San Blas for months, and there we were all the way from Jersey, held up by hot fumes, faces flat like two battery chickens.

In the anchorage beside us sat a sleek swan 36 with a massive American flag blowing proudly off its tail, Apollo moon landings massive! It was then something clicked. 'Americans!' I said to Miranda with a relieved look.

'What about them?' she replied perplexed.

'They're all engine nuts, they spend entire childhoods beneath the bonnet, hours every evening in the garden shed making things tick, I'm yet to meet one that doesn't know their way around an engine.' It was a eureka moment, or as close as you get aboard Little Coconut. In that neighbouring boat sat a soul who had the answer, I was sure if it, and hastily boarded our tender to find out.

Mark was sitting in his centre cockpit drinking a cold beer, long hair, an old sea dog type, looked like he had blown around the world a few times. We exchanged pleasantries then I waded in, telling him our troubles. 'Sure, I'll come over and have a look,' he said, 'my buddies are leaving today, I'll see them off and come over around lunch.'

'Great,' I replied, 'thanks a bunch, we'll get something cooked up for the occasion.' With that, as far as I was concerned a mechanic was booked, I told Miranda we were in, then snuck off for a quick snorkel.

Sure enough, Mark was a dap hand at engines, flicking through my Kubota manual like it was a Sunday newspaper. 'I'll be betting it's your thermostat,' he said 'thinking out loud. 'Saltwater pumping out, no leaking coolant, you've checked the heat exchange, no water in the oil so it can't be the head gasket, burst hose by the radiator... got to be the thermostat, frozen up most likely.' He looked up and eyed my blank expressionless face. 'Thermostat, they're heat regulators, they release when your engine gets to a good temperature for combustion, about 80 degrees or so, your one could well be frozen so it will stay closed blocking the freshwater side of your cooling system.' He waited for a second then carried on, 'Good news! we are in the tropics! so you don't need one!

They are designed for colder climates, just unscrew these,' he said pointing in the manual to the spot on the engine near where the hose blew off, 'And pop it out, I'd be betting it is the thermostat alright,' he repeated. Engine diagnosis complete we moved on, chatting about San Blas where Mark first sailed back in the 1980's. We slurped down Miranda's tasty soup then all boarded Mark's tender and moved onto his swan for an afternoon of cold beers and cocktails. It was a breakthrough moment and cause for celebration, Miranda even got to wash her hair in a shower.

That evening, I took out our thermostat and we cranked the engine, watching and waiting, using our bare hands to check the temperature. 'I think it's working,' Miranda observed with a concentrated look on her face, 'it isn't getting as hot!' We ran it for thirty minutes or so and it definitely seemed good, it sounded healthy and didn't burn like hot rocks upon a quick touch. 'Praise the Lord for Mark,' Miranda concluded, and with that our short passage through the islands began.

As time passes those memories of San Blas start to surface, slowly rising up through a thick mix of windswept nights and long sun-beaten days. It is a special place because it is unique and unspoilt. All the clutter surrounding our modern world somehow hasn't found its way through the door sill, the Indians have managed to shut it out and go their own way, living in small communities, travelling in dugout canoes, hardy characters in a strangely fragile place. Maybe that is the key to its charm, sleeping head just above the waterline, ocean surrounding all four walls, pounding away through the night, only palm leaves between you and the stars, only tree trunks for protection, maybe that is how they've stayed grounded after so many centuries. I made good friends with an Indian, we couldn't speak a comprehensible word to one another but talked none the less, looking to Miranda strangely for translation, of which she offered none. I used hand signals and drew in the sand if things got really bad. He was one of the good guys, living in a wooden hut and cooking on fire, no electricity, no radio, no gadgets, basic tools and a canoe was all that family needed, and the surrounding Indian community of course. He had a wife, a baby daughter and two puppies, he couldn't have been older than twenty-five, short, tough looking, white teeth and brown eyes.

We spent our last anchorage camped out in his backyard. Before raiding the larder, I asked if it was alright to dive for lobsters, not that I was doing much damage, three mornings diving, one lobster in the pot, still I thought it best to ask. After five minutes of stickman sketches in the sand and much laughter he caught my drift and gave me the thumbs up walking off to his hut. Minutes later, to my surprise, he was back with a mask and snorkel of his own and a twin pronged spear. We dived together, following the reef round the bay, swimming through gutters and tunnels in crystal clear water, above coral so alive it jumped up in great plumes and fans. It felt pretty amazing to get that type of hospitality from the Indians, and it is rare in this world to find. He came to our boat one afternoon and sat down below, nailing Miranda's flap jacks. Before we left, he gave us a polished shell, it was a sad goodbye, we would be off to Panama in the morning. It was the simple living in San Blas, that is what I loved. Their jewels the nature that surrounds them, sparking bright in the mid-day sun, emerald green off the shallow mangrove banks, sapphire blue behind the reef where the seabed falls away in vertical cliffs of coral. Necklaces of golden sand line the palmed islands, turning white and silver in the moonlight. It is a magical place, that boarder line between land and sea, a fragile ecosystem, threatened in so many ways, tourism, sea level rises, industry, modernisation, mining, pollution, to name but a few, threatened but still standing. We felt very privileged to have sailed our little floating home through those islands as so many cruisers have done over the years.

25

The Panama Canal
and Ecuador

The tankers lay tethered to the seabed, herds of them huddled close, sitting quiet like livestock in the rain, bellies on the grass, chins down, eyes rolling tired. Half of the herd were anchored outside Colon's breakwater the other half inside, all cattle tagged and waiting for their departure date through the canal. Out in the distance plumes of smoke rose, the port was in full swing, a hot bed of industry bubbling away, a sprawled out dirty old town just like that Pogue's tune. If Panama City is the country's show-horse with her glitzy bars and swanky American styled hotels, then Colon is surely the working mule, cranes on the skyline and smoke in the air. Little Coconut was a fly on the wall, nothing more, nearly swatted away as we entered unannounced, coming head-to-head with a massive container ship mid channel. I promptly cranked the engine and gave her some governor, moving square across to the red buoys. We snuck in through the pier heads and turned off to the small craft marina at Shelter Bay, a place where yachts get measured up and sort out paperwork for their transit through.

I was worried about officials and red tape, Little Coconut isn't exactly street legal, to get a transit number your vessel has to be measured and checked by the authorities, it has to fulfil certain criteria to pass the inspection. The problem lies in interpretation and translation, aka who holds the red tape? Are they friend or foe? Is the official that milk monitor from your schoolboy days, the class rat. Does he eyeball the letters of his job description like they've been written in stone and taken down the mountain by Moses himself? Does he uphold this newfound scrutiny with the twisted precision of those Pharisees of a bygone age? Well thankfully for us in Panama the red tape fell into good hands, in Panama my worries were cast aside. The dude rocked up with his shirt untucked, it looked like he had just rolled out of KFC, taken down the family meal with the bargain bucket, given it was only 10:00am quite a feat. After about ten seconds in the belly of Little Coconut, a steel box sweating under the Equatorial sun, he wisely said, 'Right best do this outside in the shade, somewhere half-sensible.'

'We're in,' I whispered to myself, like a trespassing teenager.

'Can your boat do seven knots?'

I looked at him, he'd just seen the boat.

He half smiled back, adding kindly, 'It is a rough number.'

'Coconut can move,' I replied grinning, 'when she has to.'

'Do you have these dials and do they work?' He handed me a list.

I nodded or winked and he just ticked, we got the magic number, we were on the list of boats waiting for transit.

Our agent Erik emailed me a date, it read the 6th May, 'That's 31 days away,' Miranda said.

'31 days!' I replied, 'what a screw up! We could make it halfway across the Pacific by then.' It was a big let-down, especially given our schedule, all the way to Australia in one season, our trip was threatening to turn into a delivery, two or three day stops where you need two or three weeks. The South Pacific is vast, arrive too late and you'll get pushed through paradise like a blinkered donkey, cracked by the whip of that fast-approaching cyclone season. What could we do? We were powerless, we had arrived in good time and couldn't have gone any faster if we tried, there was no use worrying about it, I booked a mechanic whose earliest date was a week away, it seems everything takes a long time in Panama. Shelter Bay was a good spot, especially for nature lovers, we were surrounded by pristine rainforest. I paid up for 12 days, this reduced our per day cost and we settled in amongst a wave of other cruisers also waiting to cross.

Waiting on a boat is not like an airport, there is no over-weight American sweating buckets in your grill, no queue jumping Arabs redefining European definitions of public etiquette in quite brilliant displays of disorder, as fun as those displays are to watch sometimes, to see us pompous Brits get effectively backhanded by travelling families from the Middle East, who arrive like a wandering tribe with countless bags and numerous wives, whose culture refuses, whether rightly

or wrongly, to comprehend the very notion of waiting sub-
missively in strange statue like poses, in those long lines of
boredom we call queues. Waiting on your boat is very different
to an airport. There are two worlds on a boat, a life at sea
and a life ashore. Life ashore becomes the holiday, luxuries
like sleep, electricity, washing facilities, cold beer, restaurants,
walks, social interaction, these are all luxuries of the waiting
room. A week or so in the marina, despite our demanding
schedule, wasn't the end of the world, we embraced the home
comforts at Shelter Bay and found our rhythm. Before long the
days melted away.

The rainforest was beautiful, it truly was another world in
there, it felt like stepping through those *Lion and witch and in
the wardrobe* doors every time I went for a walk. Miranda had
rolled her ankle so I had to walk alone most days, following
faint tracks till they doubled back, or faded out, sometimes I'd
get lucky and the track would run for miles ended up on the
shoreline, where the green trees would meet the ocean in coral
flats. I saw hundreds of amazingly coloured butterflies and
dragonflies, some of the butterflies were electric blue, the size
of a man's fist. Armies of ants used the tracks carrying sliced
leaves, guarded by bigger fierce looking brothers. I saw families
of howler monkeys moving slowly through the canopy, carrying their babies, resting for long intervals at a time. There were
other monkeys to, slender and more agile, lighter coloured,
their faces looked frighteningly human, watching me close
from way up above my head. The trees rose high competing
for sunlight, green with heavy waxed leaves, the air felt thick
and hot in the forest. It was a great place to sit and watch, to
get away from the boat and the worries of our trip. I wished

Miranda hadn't rolled her ankle and came up with a cunning plan for her to experience the forest. Three clicks down the road ran a small creek. One that weaved off into the thick jungle. 'We could get our tender down that,' I thought aloud, picturing the perfect day trip, Miranda shooting photos as I paddled her up the waterway deep into uncharted jungle, sloths and monkeys around every corner, it would be epic I was sure of it.

By the following morning Miranda was keen, I had succeeded in persuading her to come, commandeering one of the marina trollies as our buggy. Our kit list included, one deflated tender, a foot pump, two backpacks, water bottles, oars tied to the side, and Miranda on top, the injured cherry, sitting pretty as I wheeled her kilometres down the road. I chatted to the park rangers and left the trolley with them, carrying our heavy tender down to the water's edge, I was soaked through with sweat before we even started. 'Will I get bitten by mosquitoes?' Miranda asked, that was her first question, faced with the rainforest, having been carried like a beauty queen for miles.

'We're in the jungle,' I replied sharply, 'mosquitoes are the least of your worries, trust me.' The rangers had been joking about crocodiles.

'I'm worried,' said Miranda.

'About what?' I replied.

'Are there crocodiles?' she carried on.

'Probably nearer the shore,' I said, 'look how thin the water is, more likely to see a newt than a croc, now let's get going it'll be a hoot.' We paddled for about two minutes until a massive tree blocked the stream, there was a small gap underneath some branches, we squeezed through unwilling to turn back so soon.

'Aww,' cried my flustered princess, she'd been grazed by a twig. 'I'm not enjoying this,' she said, 'how did you talk me into coming.'

'You're kidding!' I replied, 'this is untouched wilderness, you'll not experience rainforest like this unless we comeback one day... some twat will have probably chopped it down by then! This is historical,' I added angrily.

Miranda wasn't buying it, we paddled on in silence until another tree blocked the road, this time we had to climb out of the tender. I pulled it up and over whilst Miranda balanced on her one good foot. She looked distressed, the heat was getting to her, the insects bugging her, the paddling irritating her. We pressed on, crossing more branches. After half an hour we had only moved 500 metres, our mood was rock bottom, not so much as a monkey in the trees, my day trip had turned sour, the creek was getting shallower by the paddle, the forest eating into our real estate, engulfing the stream with thick branches. 'Let's go back,' Miranda pleaded.' I looked around, and slowly my reality disappeared and her reality started growing in the back of my mind. I thought back to adventures with H. He would have followed that stream till it ran dry, I'd have been the one pleading to go back after camping out with the insects all night having ditched the tender and carried on by foot. This was role reversal, the scale was different, the endurance levels involved polar opposite, but I had been in Miranda's shoes many times. 'Okay babe,' I said, 'this was a bad idea, sorry I shouldn't have dragged you out here, I had no idea the creek would disappear so quick.' We made up on the way back and spotted a tribe of monkeys in the trees. We sat and watched taking photos. You don't have to beach yourself in a sticky swamp to experience wildlife in action. Our trip back along the road was topped with a massive eagle, it flew great circles above the tarmac, dipping out of view then rising up again. We arrived to the boat at 11:00 am, that four hours felt like a full day. 'Fancy a swim,' Miranda said, we were in the pool by lunch, she was smiling again, no love lost, lesson learned, 'no cripples allowed in the forest.'

After a week or so in Shelter Bay we left aboard a Norwegian boat as line-handlers, to give Marinus a hand and also to get a vibe for the canal, test the water if you will. Marinus had a mint boat, it was luxury, life afloat with a fridge, with proper beds, with storage space not hand crafted by my brother H. A boat designed by a boat designer, it was like a holiday for us and we had a good crack anchored in the lake having crossed the Colon locks. The next day we completed the trip, making it into the Pacific just before nightfall. You could see the relief in Marinus's face. After a month of waiting, he was free. The vast expanse of the Pacific opened out wide, Marinus was through the bottleneck, I was almost more excited aboard Bora Bora than when we crossed in Coconut. The relief of getting through, all that money and time worth it, freedom at last. Marinus was going to try for Australia in one hop, 74 days alone. He was an ex-sea captain, a good drinker, a hard nut from the old school, an all-round good egg, part gentlemen part brawler.

We got back to Shelter Bay, an easy trip, just one hour or so on the bus. The diesel engineer came and checked our engine, we cleaned the boat and had just booked a few nights in a hotel

Panama City side when the phone rang. It was our agent Erik. Miranda took the call, she ran up to me with an excited if not slightly frightened look on her face. 'It's Erik,' she said,' He wants to know if we can go tomorrow.' She paused whilst I took in the news. 'He needs to know now, someone has just cancelled.' We had no line-handlers ready, nothing prepared, we had just booked nights in a hotel, it was completely out of the blue, we weren't scheduled to leave for two weeks.

'We got to take it,' I said to Miranda, 'we have no option.' It was a weird feeling, needing a date so bad then suddenly landing it right on the kerb beneath your feet. Before you have the time to even play the fish there it is, flapping on the boardwalk, staring you straight in the eyes, you kind of freeze for a second, the shock numbs your senses. If you're hungry you dream of hamburgers, but you don't want one rammed down your throat by the chef's club hands. One minute we were just about to leave on a mini-break to Panama City, the next we were manically trying to sort out line-handlers, buy two days food for our three extra crew plus pilot, do engine checks, pay up at the marina, wash clothes, get the boat ready to sleep three guests, all that afternoon, we were due to leave at 12:00 the next day. We managed to track down Louise, a really sound Swedish girl who had been looking for a boat to cross the canal with. Her boat had got to Panama City before she arrived. It was perfect timing and we felt blessed to have her onboard.

Getting through the canal is to leave one road and start another. That passage is a cocoon, a hanging chrysalis, a canyon, a sender stretch of water all boats must take to reach the next chapter. Arriving out the other end is to, if but for a passing moment, become that electric blue butterfly. Opening one's eyes to find great wings at your side. The days of crawling around on your belly in day trips to Linton Island over, the weeks penned in at Shelter Bay like a pack of fat caterpillars finished, you lose that sluggish skin, that mossy undercarriage, when those Pacific locks open the transformation is complete. It is a moment of great arrival, of reeling off the old and starting the new, of breaking out, a sensation of utter freedom, whether it be a none stop passage to that big yellow crescent swinging in the heavens, or bang! straight into the double glazing! A new chapter begins when you set those wings and prepare for flight.

***

My expectations upon departure soon evaporated away, reality had indeed unveiled itself in a heart stopping manner, stomping down the aisle with heavy uncoordinated strides, hooves for feet, a toothless bride of no escaping, pre-arranged it seemed, coming straight out of left field, a salty sea bass to the face, a burnt-out stake on the dinner plate. Had I over fed Little Coconut before we left? was 50 days' worth of water, four months of food and five days of fuel too much? Was it the windless beginning, with diesels fumes that leaked out from our 1980's tractor engine, baking our brains as we motored for two days straight? Was it the electrical gauges which all gave up the ghost or the oven we sat in which cooked us to toast, was it Coconut's slow over loaded tread or the lightening which flashed above our heads, was it the southerly set of a nowhere breeze which blocked the road and upset the seas. Whatever the list of reasons, our candle had burned out by day four, we were over it, beating into the sway, pointing fifty or sixty degrees off, stumbling, Colombia down one drunken barrel, northwest to oblivion down the other. The start of the 'milk run' as sailors say, had turned out sour, curdled thick in the circling corridors of the doldrums. We sat heaved-to beneath a roaring squall, with lightening filling the air. I wondered what it was all about, this sailing lark, why do we put ourselves through it? How does the sea manage to keep calling us back? The boat was soaked through, the skies dull and grey, patched black with ink-stained squalls. We needed the front hatches open when motoring to vent the fumes, my makeshift tarp attempting to offset the tropical rain proved ineffective. Miranda had been getting headaches, upon further inspection smoke was pulsing out of a hose which ran from the oil bay, it looked like some sort of overflow device, the hose dropped down into the bilge, it wasn't connected up to anything and looked like it never had been. My bookmark is still stuck on page one of the diesel mechanic handbook for dummies, a crazy predicament considering all the time I've spent afloat. I found some spare tube, taped the hose leaking smoke to it and fed it out the boat, a quick fix solution, good enough to keep the show on the road.

We soon hit a current heading north, the south westerly had pushed us too far over, when the wind dropped below ten knots, we were motor sailing on the starboard tack at about 1.8 to 2 knots, it was soul destroying. Our engine appeared to be drinking juice at a rate of 2 litres an hour. How is that possible I thought to myself? (Something to do with the fumes no doubt) having predicted 1.4 to 1.5 litres per hour.

It soon became apparent getting south of Galapagos would take weeks, we would be out of fuel within two days with 600 miles still to cross before the trade wind sets in, 200 litres of diesel had vanished in thin air, slurped up like a slush puppy, all our fresh food would be eaten before the ocean crossing even started, before those 3,500 miles unveiled their blue eyes. Plans would have to change, we decided to hit Ecuador, take fuel and fresh food on there and hop down to the trades that way, Coconut was just too heavy to move in the light fluky winds. It was however touch and go if we would even make Ecuador under engine, she sat back across the railway track, like a frozen friend, arms outstretched on the platform pavement, we slowly etched away, bound up in ocean carriages all heading north, lost the wrong side of the wire, swimming upstream like a bloated jellyfish.

After two days of beating into black skies, we were given a break, the clouds disappeared and the sun returned, wet covers and cushions were dried out and a degree of order was brought back. With the wind gently resting on our port side we managed to motor sail at a civilised pace, 3.5 to 4 knots, it was a well needed respite. By day seven, after hearing my dad's latest weather forecast, there was just one option left on the table, the only port we had enough diesel to reach was Esmerelda. The name jumped off the page, it sounded enchanting, Esmerelda, the mermaid on the rocks, she softly sang us in.

The river was running fast when we hit the bank, Miranda shouted up with a panicked hiss, 'the depth is two.' Twenty-five feet to two in a heartbeat, Coconut ran up on that thing like a beached whale. The current quickly grew teeth, spinning Coconut beam on. Our full keel then bedded square into the mud, the weight of flow rose up, pushing over our starboard flank, driving it down hard. Coconut was healed over so far, our seacock for the engine was lifted completely dry, I had to shut her off. Three local fishing boats motored in to help, they buzzed around us like hungry wasps, shouting Spanish limericks that I couldn't understand. A tug steamed in next, waiting out in the deep water, unwilling to get too close due to the depth. The tug was promptly followed by a boat load of marines, they stood out on the touchline like a crowd of silent rugby spectators.

The fisherman were legends, they didn't hold back, risking their engines to steam us off, motors churned and groaned, warps were thrown and tied, re thrown and retied, the boats bumped into each other and into us, struggling in the strong current. We somehow spun Little Coconut around so our nose ran flush with the flow, this released our starboard gunnel from the clutches of moving water, our boat levelled enough for Miranda to turn on the engine, the downward pressure driving us into the mud was reduced when our keel ran straight, we were then free to slide off, which after some heavy revs and in a thick black cloud of smoke, we did. Free at last, what a fiasco, the buoy system was still American, my GPS was out, all the classic mistakes they teach you about in the RYA classroom, the type of rookie errors you chuckle about with a group of aspiring sailors. 'Who would be stupid enough to rely on their GPS in a river?' 'Who would sail into a new country without checking the buoy system?' Well, guilty as charged, that tit was me. After a full Esmeralda escort to the anchorage, which included all three fishing boats and the marines, I was escorted off to explain myself to the navy. Miranda, God bless her, was left guarding Coconut in our new Ecuadorian home, a commercial fishing port on the Equator. In the mayhem Miranda had managed to dish out some bottles of rum to the fishermen as a thankyou, they seemed over the moon and smiled at us with great beaming grins. What a rush, the third grounding I've had in Coconut and definitely the most hair raising. If Little Coconut had been designed with a cockpit setup instead of a flush deck, in all likelihood we would have sunk there and then, trip over, boat lost to a muddy river in Ecuador. I suppose we have Mr John Hanna to thank, his boat designed to weather the gales, the reefs and the river.

Esmeralda was our home for just 24 hours, a mud-coloured grey lined harbour packed to the brim with every type of industrial boat imaginable. Flat-bottomed fishing boats lined up on broken-down pontoons, chattering away in waves of heavy wake. There were tugs and trawlers sitting side by side, there were long liners and navy boats, tankers sleeping out deep and dugout canoes in the shallows, pulled high and dry, basking like pop bellied lizards on walls of black rock. It seemed every man and his dog had some sort of amphibious craft. Strangely Little Coconut fitted in there, despite being seen as an inconvenience by the authorities, her purpose-built lines and rust stained flanks were the natural order, the stripes of Esmeralda's uniform. The navy officers were good eggs, I think they liked practising their English and asked questions about the boat, where we'd come from and where we were going, 'Dangerous out there on a small boat,' they said, 'plenty of bad guys off Colombia.' Sailing vessels are only allowed to berth under emergency by all accounts, no wind and low fuel was good enough, given our tragic entrance, we were told to wait for an agent, he would stamp out passports and sort out clearance papers. It all happened late that evening, by the morning after ironing out some errors in translation, aka it cost me 300 bucks and they didn't give receipts, we were ready to hit the road, watching the buoys closely we ran out of there, back into the still windless waters from where we came.

Three nights later we arrived at Port Lucia, a supposedly sailing or cruising friendly harbour. Not all harbours along a coastline claim to have services for travelling boats. If the river nearly sunk us at Esmerelda, the prices threaten to do the same at Lucia, fifty bucks a night, that is robbery in cruising terms. We were learning many lessons in Ecuador, this was one of supply and demand, with electrical repairs needed we sucked it up and paid for four nights, happy to be on dry land.

The marina at Port Lucia was something of an infirmary for boats. A place where one's sailing dream gets better or dies. I felt the heat rise up off the land just motoring in. There was a heaviness, a staleness to the dock. 'So this is where they end up,' I thought, 'those that don't cut the mustard out at sea.' Our first night in, a band of Ecuadorian marines came out of the water and busted the last boat on the dock. The drug smuggling cruisers, were there one minute and gone the next. Their neighbour, one boat down, was a massive towering Russian dude, an ogre, a great beast of a man, apparently mid-way through his delivery. He had as a chaperone, one very small and thin Ecuadorian minder, who stood like a child at his side. The chaperone held aloft a crate of beer, from dawn to dusk, and the great Russian giant drank from the crate, one can after another, from morning till night. The sheer size of the man was something to behold, his great straight back, his skull of rock, his arms like oak branches. The authorities were worried and rightly. If the beer was to run dry everyone was in trouble. They grabbed him one day and took him off the boat, somehow bundling the giant on a plane back to the motherland. Ejected out from the sea with the push of a button. Our next neighbour was a lone Australian chap on a smart catamaran. His motors had failed out from Panama. He'd made it along the Colombian Pacific coast. The Wild West. It was quite a feat, to have landed in a safe haven without suffering a major robbery. He was hauled up waiting for parts. In that dockside infirmary, out of four boats, two were well and truly out of the race.

Other than the marina prices I loved Ecuador. With light pockets we floated around the markets, the dusty corners and grey sand beaches. The taxi drivers smiled and spoke with rusty Spanish tongues, driving fast and skipping red lights like it was part of the road etiquette, honking their horns as regularly as they changed gears. I even managed to squeeze a surf in, paddling out into the grey water, unfit and out of practise, letting loose and getting the blood pumping again, it felt so good. We stocked back up with fruit and vegetables. Re filled the fuel and water, took a breath, went to church on Sunday, sang a hymn, said a prayer, then sailed out for round two across the sea. We had to make the trades this time, we just had to.

26

Marquesas Crossing

It was a mistake to look back at the shoreline, my eyes lingered for too long, resting on the grey sand beaches as we chugged out again. The transition had been quick, our time in Ecuador brief. One minute we were walking around the busy market streets, surrounded by people, next we found ourselves back in the drink. The world that so delighted us had been shed. Our new reality sprang out bold, a toothless scurvy ridden jack-in-the box. Little Coconut felt smaller than a grain of sand, my pulse a fickle tick, head all knotted and bones hollow, like the hermit crab's last hovel, I knew there was no going back. I tore my eyes away from the shoreline and looked out beyond Coconut's bow, the sea appeared hungover and full of heat, it was sprawled out neglectfully like a damp towel on the bathroom floor, head down and eyes shut, buckled up by a thick run of grey cloud, dusted sour by a weak shower of white horses. 'Here we go again,' Miranda said, her lips moving slow, her body warm and soft sitting next to me at the wheel. 'We'll be alright M,' I replied. It was the dawn of our Pacific crossing, attempt number two, having failed miserably to make ground from Panama. Another chapter across the ocean had begun, not with horns blowing or drums beating, but to a soft mouth dry whisper, the same inner voice that brings every Tom, Dick and Harry around to meet another day, with a splash of cold water across the face and a boot out of the front door we were off.

The last of the southern westerlies hit us like the dregs, a bitter mouthful, stagnant and indifferent. When the wind hits your nose with 3,500 miles to sail, it does so with a smile, you become children again, the wind your war hardened Grandparent, rough at the edges, brought up on rationed corn beef and Churchill's radio broadcasts. Finally we did it, we swallowed the last crumbs, we beat past the grey skies and the south westerlies. They had hounded us, haunted us, stalked us, and provoked us ever since leaving Panama, but Coconut prevailed, the tortoise won the race again, the wind backed around, the grey sky broke into a thousand soft pieces, until the cloud, which like reels of cut sheeps' wool, blew away, revealing that skin of heavenly blue we had so been dreaming of.

Stepping out across the Pacific was an act of faith for Miranda and I, not a mature faith, not the type that sleeps in the face of death, unshakable to the very bones, but faith in infancy, the type that steps out wide-eyed and doubtful, worried and fearful, apprehensive but captivated, feet stumbling, eyes fixed on that light burning up above the road ahead. For if courage can be measured in our footsteps, then faith is the ground we walk on, the weight that lies beneath, often unseen and unheard, a great sunken island, an iceberg in the deep. Jesus laid out life afloat pretty simply when the disciples woke him in a storm saying, 'Lord save us we are going to drown.'

'Ye of little faith,' he replied, 'why are you so afraid?'[30]

Well, it turns out not much has changed, fear and sea still go hand in hand unfortunately, for the sea is a place where props get washed away, where the truth rises up from the seabed. The type of faith I need out there is the one I have little of, hence the fear, that cut of beef which sleeps through the storm, unshakable to the last shackle, that run which falls straight from the house that saves, that beat the grave, that holds light and love beneath its roof top. I draw in to God, his strength made perfect in my weakness!

Once all doubts had fallen by the wayside we hit a good rhythm, Fridays and Sundays were days to look forward to. Friday, contrary to seafaring superstition, was the day we left, Sunday the day of rest. Miranda would throw an extra spoonful of sugar, at not in, my bowl of powdered milk cornflakes, she might bake some flat jacks or make a gin and tonic for sundown. Celebrating our progression across the ocean, it helped those miles tick. The trade winds were perfect for us, 15 to 20 knots around the clock, a constant kick up the arse. We had reached the highway, that old channel of latitude that takes you places, that changes the realms of possibility.

We read a lot, Miranda and I, we sat and chatted, drank coffee together in the mornings, watched the sun melt away in the evening, the magic of it all lies in those moments that wake the senses, a pod of whales rolling in, or a shooting star ripping across the night's sky. A day of hot squalls brings out a day of fair wind. Everything spins around the weather, it sets your mood, sets the pace of things. Given the fact that the weather will always come good if you wait long enough, out at sea is as good a place as any to be. Coconut was in her backyard, a Tahitian cutter let loose across the ocean, she slowly marched those miles down, 100 a day, one day at a time. Miranda would ration the cabbages, peeling off a fresh leaf and cutting it into our dinner pot, which alternated between a coconut curry or canned tomato pasta. Fish was the one thing that opened wide our menu, bringing a touch of class into the galley. The Pacific was very different to the Atlantic. It was lonesome at times, there was no trace of human life, not the faint whisper of airplane smoke way up in the sky or the slow-moving shadow of a tanker passing, no cracking voice on the radio or coke cans floating by, nothing, we didn't see a ship until four days out from the Marquesas. My Dad on the sat phone was our only link with the world, and I must confess it was a luxury, as soft as it makes a sailor, that thread running from phone to home. The old man's weather updates were one of the few comforts on the table and I looked forward to them.

34 days later and there it was, landfall, a shadow rising out from the dark, a face of coal blacker than the night's sky. Morning changed everything, by sun rise we were just ten miles out, that face which had been veiled through the hours of darkness, it turned grey at the edges then broke into a golden green blossom. Valleys and mountain peaks were bathed in morning sun, rising straight out of the blue ocean in giant cliffs. Many different species of bird circled Little Coconut as we sailed around Fita Hiva's southern tip, open mouthed

and pinching each other, over a month at sea and we had hit land. Our anchorage was called the Bay of Virgins, it sat like a giant goalmouth, great posts of vertical rock marked the spot, hillsides surrounded us, packed to capacity with a thousand shades of the forest, rafters higher than the clouds, shelves of woven green, it was spectacular. There was just one other boat in the anchorage, Jolly Roger. Our crossing was capped off sitting in their spacious cockpit, drinking cold beers and exchanging stories about our trips across. We were in, Little Coconut had made it safely to the Marquesas.

27

Blossom in the Blue

There isn't anything better than an island chain to break the captivity of endless miles adrift. A raft of molten rock, thrown forth like a spear, landing in front of one's weary bow, let loose from the dungeon of the deep, delivered back into the land of the living, like a shard of light, hitting and exploding with embers that turn rock to earth, with notes of life and revival, that cut through a barren room or a cold cell, breaking into pieces those spells of darkness.

Fresh water fell down from the high hills, dropping in mighty falls, birds and fish in abundance, thick forest groves with insects and butterflies, fruit hanging from the branches. The biggest grapefruit I have ever seen one should add, green peel and pink flesh, sweet and refreshing. Make no mistake, there was no better cruising destination in my circumnavigation than the Marquesas. The contrast, the colour, the blazing wilderness, still untouched, still without trail, peaks like spires rising high into the clouds. With villages only connected by the water, with tight knit family communities, who cultivate patches of land down where sheer cliffs fall upon beds of still water. It was already late June early July, but I didn't think about the road ahead. The rush to reach Australia had not broken through yet. Most of the other cruising boats had already left for the Society Islands, all the anchorages had space in abundance, the weather was beautiful, the sea warm, with a gentle breeze running through open hatches. I remember arriving at the village in the Bay of Virgins. We traded some stocks from Panama for local fruit. There was a little child by her father, who took a living crab out from a bucket as we talked and traded, she ripped a leg off, like it was a sweet wrapper, and sucked the juice straight out from an uncooked crab, like it was a slush puppy. Bare footed with a shell necklace, tough like her dad, who was built to brawl, who had a soft smile and a broken nose, big shovel hands to anchor down his calm, shy manner.

The locals were used to travelling boats dropping hook in their backyard. We were part of a yearly migration, a fleet passing through. April to August is the cruising season at that end of the Pacific, for by October a boat should be out of the cyclone belt, a giant waistline of sea that runs from New Caledonia right through to Tahiti. For boats attempting the ocean in one season, there is a point in time, when the old jaws start closing on the croc, and to stay in the waters of the South Pacific, is to risk a death roll, a surging spinning tropical storm. I think the villagers like to see us come and like to see us go. Picture an eccentric relative taking up a decent portion of one's front room, chicken legged and white skinned, with wet bag and camera swinging from the hip, thin lips and an energetic handshake. To break in and separate from the fleet, would take proper commitment, an encounter of magnitude perhaps, or a long time investing and sharing in the community. I asked if there were any tracks up in the high hills, and they smiled kindly. 'No one walks up there,' they said. The landscape was striking and giant, the heartland of the Marquesas, unreachable perhaps, for us travellers. The mystery of the hills and the heart of the people, both seemed impenetrable, closed behind heavy cliff doors. But the shelter remained, and we were kindly looked after like swallows in a warm barn, kept out from the house kitchen perhaps, but allowed to rest in the yard, enjoyed and encouraged, allowed to dip in and fly off.

A trip around the world doesn't break out in flower all the time, there are seasons of hard yards, moments of utter panic, the trail can grow old, the shoot turns brown and stands lifeless in the wind, but the sap is always there beneath the ground, waiting for the right time to bring forth new buds. Little Coconut had sailed us into the blossom alright, and we picked tracks through the sparking sea, watching the petals fall, ending up in Ua Pou, with great sharp peaks in front of the bow and the mighty Pacific running off flat and wide behind our stern. We didn't want to leave but knew deep down it was time to go!

From that moment on, the sand in our hourglass fell fast and time was squeezed out with hard hands, from soft segments of our journey, like juice down a thirsty hatch. We nearly wrecked the boat in the Tuamotus. I got rolled surfing the reef breaks of Tahiti. We were drenched by a heavy squash of wind and rain in Bora Bora. Rushing through Samoa and Fiji like a midnight train. We struggled to catch our breath in New Caledonia, making it in for the 9th of November already a month into Cyclone season. I suppose looking back, underpinning Coconut's 2017 dash, was a weight of worry, and much of that was not due to anything else but me. I didn't trust our engine, she was leaking fumes and looked by that stage in proceedings, like the hand of death was fast upon her. I ran with the wind and took every opportunity to make ground. Gear cables snapped, electrical things started flickering and dying. Despite it all, armed with duct tape and cable ties, we pressed on relentlessly, our rudder and rigging and steel hull could not be dropped, all obstacles in the road were flattened beneath the wake and tread of Coconut, a prop forward, a weight carrying reef busting nut, mad for the line, in her element, a Tahitian Cutter train, past her prime, sailing out for its namesake and beyond.

We dropped the ball in Tuamotus, big time. The try line was right there, the hard yards already run. Right on the white line we dropped the pass, we missed the try, after running erratic lines across half the South Pacific, after all the hard work, we dropped that dam egg. It was not the incident I don't think, for that was but a scare and we were used to scares. And I can't for one second blame it on Miranda either, for it was I, that had neglected to weigh up our stocks properly in Panama. By the Tuamotus we were out of food, it was too expensive to stock up in the Marquesas. We had enough to survive, like a few bags of rice, some pasta, a dozen or so cans of tomatoes. There must have been oats and maybe some crackers, a teabag or two hanging in the shadows, some tuna perhaps, but Miranda, like a kettle slowly boiling beneath the heat of circumstance, was starting to steam and squeak. 'I just need some fruit!' she said.

'Technically, this is a fruit of sorts,' I replied. 'Look, it even says the word "plum" on the can.'

'Plum tomatoes are not fruit!' she snapped, 'I'm serious, Hugh!'

I had filled up our water bottles from a spring in the Marquesas, a bubbling creek that fell from high hills. The water didn't turn green I might add, but there were green things in it. Handing Miranda, a bowl of stale cornflakes swimming in powdered milk and Marquesas spring water, a degree maybe, above the sweating cabin, held aloft by an aroma of pond algae, which rose like wet steam from her cheap plastic bowl. It perhaps didn't set the day's tone on the right foot! Not even the beautiful reef fish could bring Miranda round. We met an Italian skipper who told us not to leave for Tahiti under any account before visiting more atolls. He had a heart of gold that chap, running charters on a cat out of Tahiti, sailing the Tuamotus for a living. I went snorkelling with him, we swam out of a false channel and gazed down in electric blue waters upon vertical walls of coral, they dropped into the deep, it was stunning, rays and sharks and turtles.

In a night of heavy wind, we came off the mooring, our host family had wrapped thick chain around a coral head. The coral broke under the weight of boat and gusts. Miranda was awake miraculously; she saved us from grounding hard onto the reef. I managed to release the loose chain, she cranked the engine and untied the wheel, and we just escaped running aground, unbelievably close. In the morning, I ran over the scene with snorkel and flippers and couldn't figure out how we didn't hit the shelf, it was a miracle. Maybe that was the straw that broke the camel's back, I can't remember exactly, but not long after we left for Tahiti. Right on the try line of exploration, we got pulled away, but I shall not regret a moment, maybe one day, God willing, we will return. The delights of the Tuamotus were tasted none the less, in an amazing dinner gifted by a local family. Reef fish caught in a trap, cut fine and left to marinate in a lime sauce before cooking. There were lobsters too, and cans of drink that had seen the light of a refrigerator, what a luxury. I went out to help catch the fish from the local trap in the reef, but instead of getting involved, I just watched in amazement, as my host sorted fish from shark like a farmer might weeds from his crop. The traps were stocked to the brim. It was supermarket shopping Tuamotus style, with enough fish to feed the atoll for months. Everyone in the anchorage enjoyed an amazing spread, the next day Miranda and I sailed off for the Society Islands.

We sailed into the heart of the Pacific, but also into the heart of a community, a group of sailors untethered from their old skins, born again it would seem, from a life of work, into a life of adventure. We felt like citizens of another realm, passing through, bound for a shared run of coast, a place of bright light and sheltered water just beyond the horizon. Of the solitude of miles in the ocean, of the hardship we endured in dark squally nights, never was there a time without hope, never did I feel totally alone. The anchorages of the Pacific were meeting places. Iron sharpens iron, we were encouraged, having endured the passage, we could now all share in the fun. Our fleet was somehow united, across flags, across cultural divides and ages, each boat unique in some way. Families with young children, lone sea dogs who drank like fish and howled at the moon. There were couples, some looked twenty, some looked north of seventy, it didn't matter. For any depth of relationship, for a bond to develop naturally, there has to be a sacrifice and there has to be a reward, and both these realities were felt in each step, in the blue water of trial and in the anchorage of rest, and in that, for every passage undertaken, the grip tightened, our dockside embrace was not one between strangers but between friends. We ate out on so many different boats, I can't remember them all. I was helped in some way, in perhaps every anchorage, whether it was old Frank who wiped off his salt crusted specs and reworked our broken outboard until it hummed again, or Paul and Jenny letting Miranda continually shower in their cat. Surely it was the people, who brought in the splendour of the time, who brought home the magic of the reef.

H and I as young teenagers, had watched videos of a wave called Teauphoo busting onto a shallow shelf, spitting buckets, a roaring, erupting keg, a beautiful blue barrel, with a foam ball chasing the rider down like an angry bull, with a deep channel cut into the drift where spectators could watch the race unfold from an armchair of deep water. My mission, one not voiced comprehensively to Miranda at the time, was to sail Coconut in close, anchor up and try my hand at dropping in. Like a magnet the wave was calling me out from the cruising circles and into the fire. Now certain factors were not in my favour, firstly Miranda, she would have to leave her cruising buddies. She would have to head off into the wild again, alone with me. Second slight hitch in the cunning plan, my surfing abilities, all gravel, no melody, not a slick blond-haired Australian, but a balding oaf, raised in a shallow sea, born in Reading, a rock pollack adrift, out in the tide, taken with the wind, away from the safety of the slipway, away from the reach of my home breakwater. I love to surf more than anything else. I'll surf in the bitter cold, in raging onshore winds, I'll paddle out at maxing beach breaks or distant reefs. The number of hours in the water, against time actually spent on a wave, is so out of balance, no mathematician under the sun could make the figures work. 'Give up immediately,' the statistical response. 'How long has he been surfing for? Two decades, close the account, get that man out of the water!'

'Screw the stats,' would be my reply. As a youngster I was hooked on surfing at a time when my friends back in Jersey were all getting involved with drugs. I hated the drugs. The image of God, desecrated in the heart of creation, not a Tibetan Mountain range but a human soul. Black smoke, where the surface of the sea should run wide, thick stale walls where waves should be crashing on sand, violent music hammering, right where the sound of birds and the rush of wind should resonate. That shot of adrenaline one feels from time to time in the wilderness, replaced with numbness, with a cheap neat liquor substitute, poured out from a wretched bottle of lies. The grip of evil makes large what should be small, takes captive that which should be free, complexity where there should be simplicity and rebellion where there should be light. Evil then dresses its prey in a filthy garment of lies, the knowledge of God blocked out, the image of God locked in. Evil then condemns the prey using the sum of its works, using that same run of rancid cloth. Fed down into a dry and parched land, into a bitter and thirsty mouth, onto a dark and lonely hill, a spoon full of vinegar. Into the hand, so lost and so trembling, a stone or a snake, a spade or a rope! Into those ears so governed by darkness, the word, 'dig,' or 'throw,' or 'bite,' or 'noose.' All eyes turn to the rafter, a branch, a pit, or a bottle of demon laughter, an exit, an end to the suffering, a knot of blight, to torture a life lived without light, with a black hole that remains, to continue the shame, as the garments of that hopeless grave, dress those broken hearts that remain, in the same lies, to live and to die, without promise, without purpose without hope.

My little mission down to Teauphoo was a pilgrimage really, I had been delivered out, into a creation of awesome splendour, of majesty, where the fire in the human spirit finds a place of wholesome expression, one that unleashes potential instead of exploits, to breathe life and share in the glory of creation. We were anchored but less than 2km off the wave, one of the heaviest on Planet Earth. Old Frank on Jolly Roger had even resurrected my outboard, so I motored away from Coconut's anchorage. We were in a perfect position, a sand-bottomed enclave, protected by shelves of coral, in crystal-clear waters, with these lush peaks in the background. I'd like to say I caught a massive set and rode the waves I'd watched as a teenager, but that wasn't the case. The world tour was just about to start, so the best surfers on the planet were all in town, warming up just before their competition kicked off. It was an intense line-up, they might have flown in on a sponsored purse, with big dreams, but I'd sailed all the way from the bailiwick 'me old cocker,' and I wasn't going to leave without sending my chicken legs over the falls or attempting some form of head dip rooster dance. I paddled out a few times in smallish conditions for the Pacific, and got half a bag of average drops, a few scrapings and a big shaker from the travelling professionals when they fanged passed me in a flat-bottomed speed boat. I was alone in Coconut's four-foot rubber duck, engine out already, rowing back to Coconut in the dark, no lights. Miranda was probably worried stiff in the belly of Coconut, cooking pasta beneath the thunder of wave on reef. It was fitting really, us pilgrims are called to walk the mountain stairs, not light up the altar. It was enough to just sail in and cop an amateur's flogging, I was stoked to just be a fly on the wall, a sparrow sharing an eagle's roost. We buddied back up with the cruisers and continued our journey through the islands. My ride through French Polynesia was a shared one, the beauty of a boat is the teamwork and the people, we ended up in Bora Bora, spat out into a deep lagoon of blue water, sheltering from a heavy squash of rain, drenched, soaked through, but so happy not to have been hit by the squash out at sea. It was our last stop in the Society Islands. I was helped again by my cruising buddies upon leaving. The anchorage was so deep I couldn't lift up the 70 feet of chain suspended in the dark water. I had to get Andras to haul the load with me, his son even got involved, it was a team effort to get us off.

28

Treasure Island

Desolate but magnificent was the water, pooling up in a frenzy of life. His eyes were sharp as sickles, he found his portion on the borders, dressed and fed out in the fringes, with a cloak of coral sea wrapped about his weak and frail body. With buttons of green hills and long tails of ocean passages, trailing behind his stern. He drank through a cup of clasped hands, upon a bended knee and brought forth from the glean a river of words that ran true and clean. Back down the valley of his walking, beneath the fog of his suffering, back into the seams of his past, through its furrows of sorrow and fissures of darkness. Up came the water, through rock and bone, in a harvest of tales, the bubbling burn returns to the glen, the deer drinks, and the hunter finds his way home.

Robert Louis Stevenson came to rest just beneath the brow of a hill, his grave sat upon an altar of white stone, up high in the trade winds, overlooking the sea, wrapped up in a nest of tropical trees. Miranda and I had arrived in Samoa, Navigator Island as it was once known. We found there, in a spot of land purchased with a price, in the testimony of a prolific writer, in the sight of burial and in the verses written in bronze inscription upon his tomb, a haul of treasure not of this world.

The locals named the narrow track up to Robert's grave the Road of Loving Hearts. A sharp climb cut in by 200 mourning Samoans, who carried their friend's body up high, and buried Robert in death, upon the altar where he had laid himself down in life. The verse of scripture placed on his tomb is taken from the book of Ruth, it reads, 'Where you go, I will go, and where you stay, I will stay. Your people will be my people and your God my God. Where you die, I will die, and there I will be buried.' [31]

This verse was first spoken out beneath a grey dawn, before the rising sun came to be, into a blinding gale, when every part of the sailor would want to give up and seek fortune for oneself. It is a verse spoken into the jaws of defeat, into a hail of hard rain. A verse spoken into crazy odds, by Ruth the widow and daughter in law, to Naomi the widow and mother-in-law, who had lost both her sons under the same moon, whose God seemed, at that point in time, more distant than the stars. A verse which says in simple terms: 'I will lay myself down for you no matter the cost to me. I will look after you if it means life or if it means death.' A bearing of righteousness that does not waver to circumstance or emotion, or ambition, that accepts hardship, a verse that sets forth a new line of travel, into a bleak and uncertain future, with daily sacrifice. A bearing through the drink, that preserves the blemished, the weak, the lost, in splendid and righteous robes, in sanctifying grace. A line that leads to life and peace. Robert Louis Stevenson did something special in Samoa, he laid himself down and found there, a new way, after years of searching, and it resonated in the hearts of the people he lived alongside, the people he served, who crowned his grave with jewels of scripture.

'Under the wide and starry sky, dig the grave and let me lie, glad did I live and gladly die, and I laid me down with will. This be the verse you grave for me, here he lies where he longed to be, home is the sailor, home from sea, and the hunter home from the hill.'[32]

Miranda and I heard this poem, penned by Robert himself, and placed upon his grave, sung out into the air, in beautiful Samoan. God had prepared Robert for death in Samoa. As splendid as any he ever wrote was the story he lived, a story that points to the rest he would find, in the kingdom of his saviour Jesus. The churches were full of worshippers. Miranda and I got invited along, they translated the entire service into English just for us. I can't remember one word of the sermon, I can't remember one scripture that was read out, but I remember the sight of heavy set men weeping beneath the spirit of God's holiness, a spirit that calls all who belong to God, down upon that narrow hard road, to pick up their cross and follow, to deny the biggest obstacle of them all, oneself! Jesus summed it up with this instruction, 'Whoever finds their life will lose it, and whoever loses their life for my sake will find it.'[33]

Samoa was a welcome break, a much-needed rest. Out from French Polynesia, we sailed right up to Surrarrow atoll in the Northern Cook Islands, passing it by in the middle of the night. Brother H said the long-term weather forecast was looking patchy and muddled, I picked the wind instead of the atoll, it was a hard decision, for I had wanted beyond anything else, to enter that reef. I was worried about having to use Coconut's engine for a sustained period, so we sailed right by a pristine ecosystem, full of sharks and fish and birdlife. We landed in Samoa after a good ten days on the hoof, lifting our luminous yellow foldaway bikes out of the hold. Instead of reef corridors, full of tropical fish, swimming from sharks, we took to the cracked tarmac roads, beneath a burning sun, and peddled in hot gusts, like frightened cats, from the stray street dogs of Apia, that barked and snapped at our heels, as we whizzed into town from the marina. It was a rush. Instead of eating lobsters from the reef, I brought deep fried pies, for less than a dollar, and ate them straight out of paper bags, sitting on hot brick walls. No one else seemed to have a bicycle on the whole island, the children and the dogs were greatly impressed. The island of Samoa is poor but also free, there is hardship, but also hope, I felt very much at home in Samoa. I loved the island, the Christian values it upholds, the beautiful hills and the blue sea. We missed the reef of Surrarrow, but found in the everyday, a lot of the adventure we were looking for in the wilderness of an unreachable atoll. There was a dinner hall in town, where the poor could come to eat. The punters left with a full belly and ate for pennies what others would sell for a pound. It was a cruiser's paradise of sorts, a rock pool, a place of rest, nourished by cheap food, wrapped up by lush hills.

Miranda and I often laugh when recounting our trip through Samoa. We met some tourists from New Zealand. They didn't find the dinner hall, no room in the hold for their bikes, they flew in, not looking for shelter as such, city folk after a cheap holiday. 'We don't like it,' said the husband to the wife.

She looked across at us nodding like a duck, 'yeah, we don't like it much, we don't even have a swimming pool. Not what we were expecting, yet another dud island.' That phrase 'yet another dud island,' it really got us laughing, it implied the kingdom of Samoa was not alone, there were other dud islands out there, lots of dud islands perhaps, littered across the sea. The phrase almost uncorked itself from a thin neck and fragile glass face, to sit perplexed, on the river of booze that had been flowing. I dare say, not even a storm glass of gin, could drown the sobriety of her disappointment. Samoa, the 'treasure island' of Robert Louis Stevenson's childhood dreams, had just been called a dud, the Kingdom of Samoa given the same reviews as Bognor Regis in West Sussex, after a fortnight of summer rain. Miranda and I still chuckle at this episode, we unwrapped the phrase many times over in the hard legs still to come.

After a long week, it was time to set sail again, for the hurricane season was starting, one could feel it in the heat, the sky was so hot it felt like it might crack beneath the weight. I had one more deep-fried pie from the market. A rat must have fallen into the pot, for I was sick as a dog, Miranda took the weight for those opening days of our passage to Fiji. The sea got wild, heavy clouds rolled in, and it started to rain hard. We entered Fiji from the north, dancing in the heavy wind, with breakers hitting shelves of coral as we sailed in. The water was dark and deep, the sky black and ominous. Landfall was just beyond the brow, hoped for, within reach, but not yet a reality, and as such we were not complacent, we kept a watch through sheets of heavy rain, all the way in.

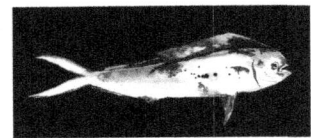

29

A New Dawn

Like ancient drums were those waves that beat down upon the reef, pierced by the shrill cries of diving birds, that fell like stones from the sky and hit like daggers, those balls of bait swimming in a thrashing sea. Fiji was a cannibal kingdom right up until the missionaries arrived in 1830. An island chain adrift. Such was the peril, William Bligh in 1789 limped past without putting to shore, half-starving in an open-topped launch boat, having been ousted from his perch on the Bounty. He saw through the lines of coconut trees waving softly in the wind, right into the heart of the cannibal. Those rumours of savagery had spread! Fiji was a kingdom to be bypassed at all costs, better to wait offshore for a squall of passing rain than to row in through the reef and collect fresh water from the clear cool streams of Fiji.

The islands were first put on the map by a man named Abel Tasman in the year 1643. A fitting name one should add, to reach out and find, in the oblivion of the South Pacific, that spirit of barbarism and rebellion that laid his namesake in the dust, right back at the birthplace of humanity's fall, when sin grew legs and started to crawl, and the mouth of Cain stood upon a blood-stained patch of grass, and cried out to God in that mocking line, 'Am I my brother's keeper?'[34]

Now this book is fast running out of pages, to undertake a history of Fiji this late in the game could sink the whole endeavour. All I will say, is what was once isolated, once bound, once living in darkness and fear, reached out and received the light. 'The hope of the ends of the earth,' as the psalmist wrote, 'and of the farthest seas,'[35] it landed in through the reef.

I sailed through Fiji, those summer islands, like a winter Grinch. I was impatient and irritable. I was fearful and I hate fear, I was reckless in the wrong ways, grappling with white knuckles when everything in the water was drawing us in. I fought where I should have rested and rested where I should have fought, swimming frantically in a current flowing so gently and so perfectly towards its destination. It was a lesson in how not! Rushing head down for much of the time, through a creation wonderland, a ring of perfect reef, studded without measure, by diamonds of the deep, lavished with mother of pearl, a land spoken into existence, where the coral sand sits white and warm and the water sparkles in magnificent blue. One could play the victim card, 'We had no money!' Or, 'The sand was out from our hourglass, and we were burning in the sun.' Or, 'The cyclone season was upon us and we had to move fast.' But that would be gutless. All trust in God's providence fell through my fingers like water, I carried an empty clenched fist and took the weight of it all upon my own shoulders. The motor would break, the wind would stop, thunder and lightning would fill the sky. My fears got intercepted by the prince of the air, they rested on earth instead of up in heaven, dispersed widely, instead of placed safely in the hands of one mighty creator.

The rain had dropped its buckets in full, the clouds were empty, we were wet as soaking dogs, but the sky above our heads started to turn blue. We entered Fiji in the north, and arced around the coast of Vanua Levu, with its armour of reefs, tying up on a dock in the port of entry at Savu Savu.

We had to wait for a cruising permit before starting our journey through Fiji. It was already October; the cyclone season right there on the horizon. We had planned for a trip of about two weeks, sailing through the Bligh Waters to the Yasawa Group, before checking out at Lautoka. Yes, a boat could spend two years sailing around Fiji, we had two weeks. The port of Savu Savu was a hub of sorts, there were many different ethnic groups living in the town. The Indians made up a fair-sized portion, they had arrived in Fiji before the split between India and Pakistan in 1947, very interesting, because some were Hindu and others Muslim. Both groups had a head for business and served with equal distinction in various flavours of the same convenience store, or in a battery of phone shops that bordered a loose coil of shaggy street. The water flowing from the harbour tap was brown. An old sailor said he'd been drinking it for weeks and it was fine. I took him at his word and filled up our containers with brown tap water. We got a bus around the island, found some good snorkelling spots, filled up the boat's larder with fresh produce from the market, picked up some Kava roots and got ready for our little cruise. In Fiji, if you're sailing through the islands, there is etiquette to follow. Upon anchoring, the first port of call is to find the island chief. You give him some Kava roots and he welcomes you into his protection as a guest. We bagged up the roots with great anticipation and headed off into a flat and protected Koro Sea.

Our first anchor spot was an island called Makogai, famed for giant clams, also the sight of an old leper colony. An island which gets some decent rainfall due to its close proximity to the high hills of Vitu Levu, clad in thick forest and protected by shallow reef. We rowed in not knowing what to expect. There was no village, but we found a care taker who accepted some Kava roots with thanks, he welcomed us to the anchorage, pointing out the best place to snorkel and look upon the giant clams. He also showed us where the old leper houses stood. The anchorage felt isolated, pinned up close to the trees, boxed in with tight reef channels, shielded by thick forest, a pocket of shelter surrounded by natural walls. No wonder it was sighted as a suitable spot for lepers, who came from all over the Pacific during a brief period of colonial rule. An effective cure for leprosy wasn't discovered until the 1940's. The job of overseeing the colony and looking after the sick was entrusted to Catholic nuns. All nuns need a strong mother, a queen hen, with soft feathers and a hard sharp bill. An old bird to protect the chicks and keep the nest in good order. A hen that fears God above death, and puts the call of whole hearted sacrifice above the fear of catching disease. The Lord in his wisdom sent Mother Mary Agnes, who for the next 34 years, devoted her life to caring for the sick and dying. The colony grew from 40 lepers in 1916 to 700 by 1950. Just as the medical world started rolling out their cure, Mary's time was up, her work done. She stepped down but stayed at Makogai. For Mary that pocket of reef was not a prison. Her dying wish was to be buried in the patient's cemetery, after 34 years nursing the sick. The giants of Makogai are hidden both beneath the water and beneath the earth.

We rushed through Fiji that is true, we missed one thousand things, but there at Makogai we found the X on the map. Beneath the vines lay souls who surrendered their lives, who found a treasure not of this world and who became in that exchange, a jewel on the crown of the highest, a treasure in the hands of a saviour who bore his thorns on earth, to gain his pearls in heaven. That X on the map is a ladder up, a place to climb not to dig. To drop everything of this world. A way out from the law, from the precepts of righteousness that hit like a hurricane, that break like a raging war inside a pilgrim mind. A mind whose pathways and patterns are all tuned by a perishable fork, a mind every bit as sick as a leprous limb. A mind whose liberty is bound, whose body is strung up like a puppet, dancing in the highs and crying in lows, fearful of the shadows beyond the garden wall, masters of nothing but money and dust. That X on the map is a route out from the canopy, deliverance found in Jesus.

'Since the children have flesh and blood, he too shared in their humanity so that by his death he might break the power of him who holds the power of death—that is, the devil, and free those who all their lives were held in slavery by their fear of death.'[36]

Our next stop was the Yasawa Group. We pitched up at the top of the chain, the northernmost island, sailing a beautiful night through the Bligh waters. We didn't have time to sail back east and cruise the remote reefs windward, instead we went with the elements in true Coconut style, and took a trip down a shallower patch of coast. It was raw and beautiful. Anchored off a peaceful little village on the island of Wayasewa, right at the end of our cruise, we rowed ashore and gave our roots to the chief who invited us for dinner. Miranda and I had a few hours to kill so went for a little walk. As we passed the Fijian equivalent of a village green, a rough and ready rugby pitch, a little bell rang out. It was late afternoon, all the men slowly congregated for a game of touch just before sunset. I couldn't resist, and joined the boys as Miranda went to feed some pigs with a friendly local. The lads ran like the wind, and I struggled with my chicken legs to keep the line. After the game Miranda and I went and found the chief, we ate with him and his family on the deck of his hut, sitting on the floor. We gave them some batteries and other small gifts from Coconut's hold. Right by the sea was a large open wooden platform where the locals all sat beneath the stars, shooting the breeze together as darkness fell. Miranda and I felt very much at peace in that warm village by the sea.

There was no money left by this stage in the game, Mum and Dad had wired over some emergency funds and I had borrowed a thick wad of bills from good old Paul Salmon. Also, it was now the end of October, and Australia was still roughly 1,600 nm away, 16 days non-stop wind dependant, 100 nm being Coconut's max. Bear in mind we would more than likely have to lay over in New Caledonia to sort out visas for Australia. I was getting fired up, as it could easily be early December by the time we hit the Gold Coast, tropical storm season. The Grinch came out, I forced Miranda into exiting on the next window, the day before her birthday. Our temperamental self-steerer had given up the ghost. As a result, Miranda and I were glued to the wheel, making blue water passages hard work. The hob was burning red hot, the lid was just about to blow off. We sailed out on the 20th of October in the afternoon. The wind had set in hard from the south-east, gusting a good 25 knots. We entered the outer reef channel with our genoa bursting at the seams, laden with wind. Miranda broke out crying in uncontrollable sobs. We were somewhere off the southwestern tip of Fiji, a small sail running out as darkness set in. I swung Coconut around in the reef pass, and ate hard gusts as big swells erupted either side of us in the fading light. I turned on the engine and battled like a dog to get Coconut back inside the reef. We found a quiet anchorage there in the dark and I hugged Miranda with both arms as she cried from the pits of her being. Why did I rush? A few days would not have changed anything. We had other cruising friends around and could have celebrated Miranda's birthday all together, anchored off a white sand beach, sipping a gin and tonic. I got it badly wrong. Those rushed decisions, they took the celebration out from our sails. Those precious moments weren't lived in the Christian spirit, without worry, trusting in a higher power, with thanks, with kindness, with patience, with gentleness, with self-control. I was restless and cold, and pushed Miranda too far. A shameful episode really.

We left at dawn the next day after a good night's sleep and worked a hard leg of three hours on three hours off, glued to the wheel. Seven days it took, a quick week, and New Caledonia came into the fold. We rested up for a few days to get prepared for our last leg. Entering Australia is not what one might think! No beach bum on the boarder, sizzling prawns on the barbie, with beers on ice! You get a frenzy and a stutter, a reel of red tape, a black clip board and a cold glare. We booked in our Australian arrival, ate a couple of French croissants beneath the sun, then got ready to rumble. It was a pit stop nothing more, we didn't see any of New Caledonia. About five boats left on that window of wind we took. I say 'window', but it slammed shut halfway through. A big bomb low flew up the coast and ragdolled the faster boats. I mean, properly throttled them. The wind was on the beam, Coconut was sailing hard, a third reef in the main, our cutter set like a slab of stone up front. We walked right through the back edge of the low finishing the race strong. Some boats hove too in the blow, and waited it out. But Coconut was sailing like a dream, running hard and straight, we dug in and soldiered on without skipping a beat. 'God won't sink us this close to the end,' said Miranda. The day we landed, the wind dropped back off, the sandbar at Stradbroke Island stopped breaking. I shook out the reefs in the main and we headed right for a white beach. The high-rise buildings of Surfers Paradise caught the early sun, they were standing like flaming sticks of light, the water was emerald green as the ocean depths gave way to the shallows. The beautiful Gold Coast of Australia held her hands out wide. I opened up a red flare as we sailed into the spit, a thick deep brown creek, a river of brackish water. I could hear my mate Andy Sawden wailing from the land as a roar of emotion and thanks welled up in our eyes.

The landing was a strange affair, not the incoming one would imagine after sailing around the world. Like thick cream poured out from a paper carton, once we hit those docks of officialdom, for a brief moment anyway, everything curdled in the sun. 'You can't just run off like that,' said the Customs officer, 'health hasn't even arrived yet!'

I had walked out from the dock to find our friends. Once checked in the women at the yacht club looked at me like an alien when I said we had no insurance. Her face screwed up like she had just swallowed a winter berry. Miranda was told she could not have a shower! After sitting in the salt for a good week, after crossing the South Pacific from Ecuador to Australia on a 32-footer. 'Bum's Bay is around the corner please leave our pontoon immediately!'

We promptly sailed off, dropping hook up the road, grabbing a weekend bag and leaving Coconut sitting with her brethren in the bay of bums, to join our friends on the beach. We got in Andy's car and headed off for Tugun at the south end of the Gold Coast.

What was I expecting? A kind word from the yacht club? A free night on the pontoon? One cold shower perhaps? Coconut was built for the deep, built to carry bums around the world, built for the thirsty sailor, built to cross oceans. It was an epic landing, the thorny reception we got, it crowned our trip in true glory, and opened wide the gates to finish this book, not with us, but with him, him who bore those thorns, him who wore that crown, who bridged the great divide, who crossed the chasm and delivered us out from the depths of a troubled sea.

The sailor's thirst gets quenched, the sailor finds the sun and is reconciled out beyond the horizon, delivered, from death unto life, out from the grasp of Satan, into the hands of victory in Christ. For to be, is to be found in the deep, to be found by Jesus, King of kings and Lord of lords.

The Bear Tune, written by brother H

Deep in the woods where the birds don't sing,
lies a snoring bear who will wake in spring.
He'll rise real slow this grizzly king,
while all around a sound will ring,
the sound of melting snow.
Who knows where this hungry bear might go?

Just a little glimpse of a story told,
a single grain of sand out in this endless desert of gold.

And down in the deep where the blue whale dives,
there's a world that waits for human eyes.
A shower of shades of blue and green,
filtered to black in a thousand leagues.
Much more we do not know,
it's a place no man can go.

Just another tone in this tune that hums,
a single wing beat amidst this mighty host of drums.

And in the southern sea there's a monsoon shower,
as two ships pass in the midnight hour.
On a heap of trash there's a blooming flower,
and a coral reef bares the power,
the power of water crashing.
Like the bright things that's lightning flashing.

Just a single blowing shower in this broken dawn,

for every drop that swirls,
another sweeping torrent of storms.

There's spell bound dust in a still nights sky,
spinning around those that rush by.
Dancing in the light of the moon,
to the rhythm beat of this silent tune,
this hymn that's roaming slow.
Like a river of light, it does flow.

And in this misty morning that's moving through,
just a single blade of grass in this shining coat of dew.

From the regal thunder that rolls on through,
to the tiny squeak of a pygmy shrew.
The cool sea breeze late afternoon,
the heaving hum of a didgeridoo,
his spinning mind is swimming to,
her ocean eyes of the deepest blue.

Just a single flicking flame in this fire that burns,
in this steaming train just a single wheel that turns.
In this coat of many colours a single thread,
a lone cobble stone in this turning trail we tread.

1. Information regarding the Tahitian Ketch drawn up from John Stephen Doherty's book, A Ketch Called Tahiti. No direct quotes but a great source of information.

2. Bible passage, NIV version, Jonah's prayer: Jonah 2 v 2-9.

3. Bible passage NIV Psalm 23 v2-3

4. Quote taken from: A new voyage to the East-Indies by Francis Leguat and his companions. Containing their adventures in two desart islands, ... Adorn'd with maps and figures. Written by Francois Le Guat. Published 1708.

5. Quote taken from: A new voyage to the East-Indies by Francis Leguat and his companions. Containing their adventures in two desart islands, ... Adorn'd with maps and figures. Written by Francois Le Guat. Published 1708.

6. Quote taken from: A new voyage to the East-Indies by Francis Leguat and his companions. Containing their adventures in two desart islands, ... Adorn'd with maps and figures. Written by Francois Le Guat. Published 1708.

7. Quote taken from: A new voyage to the East-Indies by Francis Leguat and his companions. Containing their adventures in two desert islands, ... Adorn'd with maps and Wgures. Gritten by Francois Le 7uat. Published 1085.

8. Bear Tune, written by brother H

9. Bible passage, version King James Bible, Psalm 103, v 15-16

10. Bible passage, version NIV, Mark 10v31.

11. Bible passage: version NLT, Matthew 25v45

12. Trouble Will Soon Be Over, song title recorded by Blind Willie Johnson in 1929

13. Bible passage, NIV, Psalm 92v12-14. (slight embellishment of the last phrase, NIV, 'they will stay fresh and green,' my words, 'they are ever full of sap, they are ever full of green.')

14. Bible passages, NIV version, Luke 16v25-31.

15. Bible passage, NIV version, Luke 16v31.

16. Song lyrics from *Amazing Grace* written by John Newton in 1772.

17. Bible passage, NIV version, Matthew 5v3.

18. Bible passage, King James version, John 12 part of verse 26.

19. Bible passage, NIV version, Revelation 21v4.

20. Bible passage, NIV version, Revelation 21v4.

21. Bible passage, NIV version, Romans 8v38.

22. Bible passage, NIV version, Matthew27v46.

23. Bible verse: NIV, Matthew 6:11.

24. Bible passage, NIV version, Genesis 28v17.

25. Bible verse: NIV, Matthew 10:39.

26. Bible verse: NIV, Proverbs 19:21.

27. Part of a bible verse: NIV, Matthew 7:7.

28. Part of a bible verse: NIV, Genesis 2:24

29. Part of bible verse: NIV, Matthew 20:16.

30. Bible verses: NIV, Matthew, 8:25-26.

31. Bible verses: NIV, quote stops half way through the last verse. Ruth 1:16-17

32. Poem composed by Robert Louis Stevenson in 1880.

33. Bible verse: NIV, Matthew 10:39.

34. Part of bible verse: NIV, Genesis 4:9.

35. Lines taken from Psalm 65, a classic and a beauty.

36. Bible verse: NIV: Hebrews 2 V 14-15.

Printed in Great Britain
by Amazon